SUMMER OF '49

SUMMER OF '49

David Halberstam

William Morrow and Company, Inc.
New York

Grateful acknowledgment is made for permission to use the following: "Bloody
Mary" by Richard Rodgers and Oscar Hammerstein II. Copyright © 1949 by
Richard Rodgers and Oscar Hammerstein II, renewed by Williamson Music Co.,
owner of publication and allied rights. Used by permission. All rights reserved.

"Mrs. Robinson" by Paul Simon. Copyright © 1968 by Paul Simon.

Library of Congress Cataloging-in-Publication Data

Halberstam, David.
    Summer of '49 / David Halberstam.
      p.   cm.
    ISBN 0-688-06678-X
    1. Boston Red Sox (Baseball team)—History. 2. New York Yankees
(Baseball team)—History. 3. Cleveland Indians (Baseball team)—
History. I. Title. II. Title: Summer of forty-nine.
GV875.B62H35 1989
796.357'64'0974461—dc19   89-2886
                                                                    CIP

Printed in the United States of America

First Edition

      4   5   6   7   8   9   10

BOOK DESIGN BY NICOLA MAZZELLA

For David Fine

A hero ventures forth from the world of common day into a region of supernatural wonder: fabulous forces are there encountered and a decisive victory is won: the hero comes back from this mysterious adventure with the power to bestow boons on his fellow man.

—JOSEPH CAMPBELL,
The Hero with a Thousand Faces

THE NEW YORK YANKEES OF 1949
Casey Stengel—Manager

PLAYERS	G BY POS	B	AGE	G	AB	R	H	2B	3B	HR	RBI	BB	SO	SB	BA
TOTALS			28	155	5,196	829	1,396	215	60	115	759	731	539	58	.269
Tommy Henrich	OF61, 1B52	L	36	115	411	90	118	20	3	24	85	86	34	2	.287
Jerry Coleman	2B122, SS4	R	24	128	447	54	123	21	5	2	42	63	44	8	.275
Phil Rizzuto	SS152	R	31	153	614	110	169	22	7	5	65	72	34	18	.275
Bobby Brown	3B86, OF3	L	24	104	343	61	97	14	4	6	61	38	18	4	.283
Hank Bauer	OF95	R	26	103	301	56	82	6	6	10	45	37	42	2	.272
Cliff Mapes	OF108	L	27	111	304	56	75	13	3	7	38	58	50	6	.247
Gene Woodling	OF98	L	26	112	296	60	80	13	7	5	44	52	21	2	.270
Yogi Berra	C109	L	24	116	415	59	115	20	2	20	91	22	25	2	.277
Billy Johnson	3B81, 1B21, 2B1	R	30	113	329	48	82	11	3	8	56	48	44	1	.249
Johnny Lindell	OF65	R	32	78	211	33	51	10	0	6	27	35	27	3	.242
Joe DiMaggio	OF76	R	34	76	272	58	94	14	6	14	67	55	18	0	.346
George Stirnweiss	2B51, 3B4	R	30	70	157	29	41	8	2	0	11	29	20	3	.261
Charlie Keller	OF31	L	32	60	116	17	29	4	1	3	16	25	15	2	.250
Charlie Silvera	C51	R	24	58	130	8	41	2	0	0	13	18	5	2	.315
Dick Kryhoski	1B51	L	24	54	177	18	52	10	3	1	27	9	17	2	.294
Jack Phillips	1B38	R	27	45	91	16	28	4	1	1	10	12	9	1	.308
Gus Niarhos	C30	R	28	32	43	7	12	2	1	0	6	13	8	0	.279
Johnny Mize	1B6	L	36	13	23	4	6	1	0	1	2	4	2	0	.261
Fenton Mole	1B8	L	24	10	27	2	5	2	1	0	2	3	5	0	.185
Jim Delsing	OF5	L	23	9	20	5	7	1	0	1	3	1	2	0	.350
Joe Collins	1B5	L	26	7	10	2	1	0	0	0	4	6	2	0	.100
Ralph Houk	C5	R	29	10	7	0	4	0	0	0	1	0	1	0	.571
Mickey Witek		R	33	1	1	0	1	0	0	0	0	0	0	0	1.000

PITCHERS		T	AGE	W	L	SV	G	GS	CG	IP	H	BB	SO	ShO	ERA
TOTALS			30	97	57	36	155	155	59	1,371	1,231	812	671	12	3.70
Vic Raschi		R	30	21	10	0	38	37	21	275	247	138	124	3	3.34
Allie Reynolds		R	34	17	6	1	35	31	4	214	200	123	105	2	4.00
Tommy Byrne		L	29	15	7	0	32	30	12	196	125	179	129	3	3.72
Ed Lopat		L	31	15	10	1	31	30	14	215	222	69	70	4	3.27
Joe Page		L	31	13	8	27	60	0	0	135	103	75	99	0	2.60
Fred Sanford		R	29	7	3	0	29	11	3	95	100	57	51	0	3.88
Clarence Marshall		R	24	3	0	3	21	2	0	49	48	48	13	0	5.14
Duane Pillette		R	26	2	4	0	12	3	2	37	43	19	9	0	4.38
Bob Porterfield		R	25	2	5	0	12	8	3	58	53	29	25	0	4.03
Hugh Casey		R	35	1	0	0	4	0	0	8	11	8	5	0	7.88
Frank Shea		R	28	1	1	1	20	3	0	52	48	43	22	0	5.37
Ralph Buxton		R	38	0	1	2	14	0	0	27	22	16	14	0	4.00
Frank Hiller		R	28	0	2	1	4	0	0	8	9	7	3	0	5.63
Wally Hood		R	23	0	0	0	2	0	0	2	0	1	2	0	0.00

THE BOSTON RED SOX OF 1949
Joe McCarthy—Manager

PLAYERS	G BY POS	B	AGE	G	AB	R	H	2B	3B	HR	RBI	BB	SO	SB	BA
TOTALS			30	155	5,320	896	1,500	272	36	131	835	835	510	43	.282
Billy Goodman	1B117	L	23	122	443	54	132	23	3	0	56	58	21	2	.298
Bobby Doerr	2B139	R	31	139	541	91	167	30	9	18	109	75	33	2	.309
Vern Stephens	SS155	R	28	155	610	113	177	31	2	39	159	101	73	2	.290
Johnny Pesky	3B148	L	29	148	604	111	185	27	7	2	69	100	19	8	.306
Al Zarilla	OF122	L	30	124	474	68	133	32	4	9	71	48	51	4	.281
Dom DiMaggio	OF144	R	32	145	605	126	186	34	5	8	60	96	55	9	.307
Ted Williams	OF154	L	30	155	566	150	194	39	3	43	159	162	48	1	.343
Birdie Tebbetts	C118	R	39	122	403	42	109	14	0	5	48	62	22	8	.270
Matt Batts	C50	R	27	60	157	23	38	9	1	3	31	25	22	1	.242
Billy Hitchcock	1B29, 2B8	R	32	55	147	22	30	6	1	0	9	17	11	2	.204
Tommy O'Brien	OF32	R	30	49	125	24	28	5	0	3	10	21	12	1	.224
Lou Stringer	2B9	R	32	35	41	10	11	4	0	1	6	5	10	0	.268
Sam Mele	OF11	R	26	18	46	1	9	1	1	0	7	7	14	2	.196
Merrill Combs	3B9, SS1	L	29	14	24	5	5	1	0	0	1	9	0	0	.208
Walt Dropo	1B11	R	26	11	41	3	6	2	0	0	1	3	7	0	.146
Stan Spence	OF5	L	34	7	20	3	3	1	0	0	1	6	1	0	.150
Tom Wright		L	25	5	4	1	1	1	0	0	1	2	1	0	.250
Babe Martin	C1	R	29	2	2	0	0	0	0	0	0	0	0	0	.000

PITCHERS		T	AGE	W	L	SV	G	GS	CG	IP	H	BB	SO	ShO	ERA
TOTALS			29	96	58	16	155	155	84	1,377	1,375	661	598	16	3.97
Mel Parnell		L	27	25	7	2	39	33	27	295	258	134	122	4	2.78
Ellis Kinder		R	34	23	6	4	43	30	19	252	251	99	138	6	3.36
Joe Dobson		R	32	14	12	2	33	27	12	213	219	97	87	2	3.85
Chuck Stobbs		L	19	11	6	0	26	19	10	152	145	75	70	0	4.03
Jack Kramer		R	31	6	8	1	21	18	7	112	126	49	24	2	5.14
Mickey McDermott		L	20	5	4	0	12	12	6	80	63	52	50	2	4.05
Tex Hughson		R	33	4	2	3	29	2	0	78	82	41	35	0	5.31
Walt Masterson		R	29	3	4	4	18	5	1	55	58	35	19	0	4.25
Earl Johnson		L	30	3	6	0	19	3	0	49	65	29	20	0	7.53
Mickey Harris		L	32	2	3	0	7	6	2	38	53	20	14	0	4.97
Frank Quinn		R	21	0	0	0	8	0	0	22	18	9	4	0	2.86
Harry Dorish		R	27	0	0	0	5	0	0	8	7	1	5	0	2.25
Windy McCall		L	23	0	0	0	5	0	0	9	13	10	8	0	12.00
Boo Ferriss		R	27	0	0	0	4	0	0	7	7	4	1	0	3.88
Jack Robinson		R	28	0	0	0	3	0	0	4	4	1	1	0	2.25
Denny Galehouse		R	37	0	0	0	2	0	0	2	4	3	0	0	13.50
Johnnie Wittig		R	35	0	0	0	1	0	0	2	2	2	0	0	9.00

PROLOGUE

In Boston the excitement over the last two games of the 1948 season was unprecedented, even taking into account that city's usual baseball madness. The fever was in the streets. On Saturday morning the crowd gathered early, not only inside Fenway Park to watch the Red Sox and the Yankees in their early workouts but also outside the nearby Kenmore Hotel where the Yankees were staying—the better to get a close look at these mighty and arrogant gladiators who had done so much damage to the local heroes in the past. Such veteran Yankee players as Tommy Henrich and Joe DiMaggio loved big, high-pressure games like these. Henrich particularly enjoyed playing against the Brooklyn Dodgers and the Red Sox because the parks were so small that you could really see and hear the fans. Such intimacy was missing in the cathedrallike Yankee Stadium. It did not matter, Henrich thought, that the fans were rooting against you. What mattered was their passion, which was contagious to both teams. For some of the younger players, it was a bit unsettling. When Charlie Silvera, a young catcher just brought up from the minor leagues, saw the streets outside the hotel jammed with excited Boston fans, he felt like a Christian on his way to the Coliseum. Along with his

buddies, Hank Bauer and Yogi Berra, he left the hotel ready
to run this relatively good-natured gauntlet. The fans
crowded around to tell them that the Sox were going to get
them, that Ted (Ted Williams, of course, but in conversations
this intimate, he was merely Ted) was going to eat Tommy
Byrne alive. It was, thought Silvera, as if nothing else in the
world matters except this game.

What a glorious pennant race it was in 1948, with three
teams battling almost to the last day. The Red Sox, the beloved Sox, had started slowly. They were eleven and a half
games out on the last day of May. But the Boston fans did not
lose faith, even if it was mixed in almost equal parts with cyn-
icism. The Sox came back, took first place in late August, and
stayed there for almost a month. Then the Cleveland Indians,
with their marvelous pitching staff—including Bob Feller, the
fastest pitcher in either league; Bob Lemon, judged by many
hitters to be Feller's equal; and a young rookie named Gene
Bearden—made their challenge. The possibility of winning
the pennant so electrified the Indians that near the end of the
season Lou Boudreau, the young playing manager, had to ask
the sportswriters not to come into the locker room. The players were so emotional, he said, that he feared a writer might
overhear something said in anger, write it up, and an incident
would be created. The writers, reflecting something about the
journalistic mores of the time, all agreed.
    While Boston and Cleveland battled for first, the Yankees
stayed just within striking distance. All three teams set attendance records, drawing among them more than 6.5 million
fans (the Indians drew 2.6 million, the Yankees 2.37, and the
Red Sox, in their much smaller ball park, 1.55 million). Newspapers throughout the country headlined the pennant race
every day, and in countless offices everywhere men and
women brought portable radios to work—for the games were
still played in the afternoon then.
    The best player on each of the three teams was having a
remarkable year: Joe DiMaggio of the Yankees, although hob-
bled by painful leg and foot injuries, was in his last great statistical year, and was in the process of driving in 155 runs; Ted
Williams of Boston ended up hitting .369 with 127 runs batted

in; and Lou Boudreau of the Indians led Williams for part of the summer and ended up hitting .355, 60 points above his career average. Williams, the greatest hitter of his era, hated to be behind anyone in a batting race. While Boudreau was slightly ahead of him, the Red Sox played a doubleheader with Chicago late in the season. That day Birdie Tebbetts, the Boston catcher, needled Williams: "Looks like the Frenchman's got you beat this year, Ted," he said. "The hell he has," Williams answered. He went seven for eight, with three hits to the opposite field. The last time up, with six hits already under his belt and his average having edged above Boudreau's, he yelled to Tebbetts, "This one's for Ted," and hit it out.

With one week, or, more important, seven games, left in the season, the three teams were tied with identical records of 91-56. "They wanted a close race. Well, they've got it," said Bucky Harris, the Yankee manager, speaking to reporters as the Yankees prepared to meet the Red Sox for a brief series in New York. "It couldn't be any closer. But somebody has to drop tomorrow. Maybe two of us will be off the roof. But I'm not dropping my switch."

Then the Indians moved ahead; they continued to win while the Red Sox and Yankees faltered. On Thursday the *New York Times* headline observed: INDIANS NEAR PENNANT AS FELLER WINS. The Indians had a two-game lead, with only three games left.

As the Yankees prepared to take on Boston at Fenway, the Indians played their last three against fifth-place Detroit. On Friday Cleveland took a 3–2 lead into the ninth inning behind Bob Lemon. But Lemon tired, and Detroit rallied to win 5–3. So the door had opened just slightly for either Boston or New York.

Fenway was one of the smallest parks in the majors and every one of its 35,000 seats was taken on Saturday. The Boston management noted sadly that if they had had 100,000 seats they could have sold them all that day. In the first game at Fenway, the Red Sox beat the Yankees when Williams hit a long home run off Tommy Byrne. Run-down by a cold he seemed unable to shake—despite his use of penicillin, then still a miracle drug—Williams had clinched the batting title.

There had been a special pleasure for Williams in getting the crucial home run off Byrne because Byrne normally tormented Williams every time he came up: "Hey, Ted, how's the Boston press these days? Still screwing you. That's a shame. . . . I think you deserve better from them. . . . By the way, what are you hitting? . . . . You don't know? Goddamn, Ted, the last time I looked it up, it was three-sixty or something. Not bad for someone your age. . . ." Williams, in desperation, would turn to Yogi Berra, the Yankee catcher, and say, "Yogi, can you get that crazy left-handed son of a bitch to shut up and throw the ball?"

With the victory over the Yankees, the Red Sox still were a game out of first; to win a share of the pennant they needed to beat the Yankees in the final game. That night, the DiMaggio brothers—Joe, the center fielder of the Yankees, and Dominic, the center fielder of the Red Sox—drove together to Dominic's house in suburban Wellesley. There was to be a family dinner that night for Dominic, who was scheduled to be married on October 7. Their parents had left San Francisco for a rare trip east to attend the wedding and to see the final games of the season as well. If the Red Sox made the World Series, then the wedding would be postponed to October 17.

For a long time it was quiet in the car—Joe could be reserved even with his family and closest friends and even in the best of times. "If he said hello to you," his contemporary Hank Greenberg once said, "that was a long conversation." This day, when his team had been eliminated from the pennant race, was not the best of times. Finally he turned to his younger brother and said, "You knocked us out today, but we'll get back at you tomorrow—we'll knock you out. I'll take care of it personally." Dominic pondered that for a moment. The role of being Joe DiMaggio's younger brother had never been easy. Dominic chose his words carefully.

"You're forgetting I may have something to do with that tomorrow," he said. "I'll be there too."

They continued the rest of the way in silence. The next day Joe tore the park apart; he got four hits including two doubles. One ball hit the short fence so hard that Dominic thought for a moment it would go right through. In the stands their mother turned to their father and said, "What's our Joe trying to do? Beat our Dominic out of the World Series?" The Red Sox took an early 5–0 lead, but the Yankees, with DiMaggio leading the way, chipped away, and in the sixth inning, when Dominic led off, it was 5–4. Dominic caught hold of a fastball and hit it into the screen for a home run. Before the inning was over the Red Sox had increased their lead to 9–4.

In the bottom of the eighth inning, with the Red Sox ahead by five runs, Bucky Harris, the Yankee manager, waited until DiMaggio took his position in center field. Then he sent in a replacement. As DiMaggio limped off the field, something very rare happened, particularly for a ball park where the fans were as partisan as those at Fenway. The crowd of 35,000 rose as one to give the star outfielder of the hated Yankees a standing ovation. The cheering thundered on and on. Joe DiMaggio, a man who worked hard to conceal his emotions, was so touched by the ovation that he later referred to it as the single greatest thrill of his career. In the dugout, Dominic watched the scene with quiet pride. The Red Sox went on to win the game 10–5.

In Cleveland the gods were kind to the Red Sox. The mighty Newhouser of Detroit beat the mighty Feller 7–1. So the long season, 154 games, was over, but the outcome was not decided. The Red Sox would meet the Indians in a special one-game playoff.

Many of the Red Sox players assumed that Mel Parnell, the talented young rookie pitcher, would start for them in the playoff game. Parnell had had three days of rest; he was young, only twenty-six that summer; and he had enjoyed a wonderful rookie year, winning 15 and losing 8. Fifteen games for a rookie left-hander in Boston was remarkable enough, but the truth was, he might easily have won twenty. Parnell had been beaten so often in close games in which he had pitched well that the wives of some of the Boston players had given him some stockings with runs in them—the idea being that he needed those runs.

In the spring of 1948, Red Sox manager Joe McCarthy, who was wary of rookies, had planned to send Parnell back to the minors. But near the end of spring he asked Birdie Tebbetts to catch Parnell in an exhibition game against the Yankees. Tebbetts called for a fastball, and Parnell threw a pitch that surprised him. Not only did it have speed but also exceptional action: Just as it reached the plate it seemed to slide sharply away from the right-handed hitter. Tebbetts called for the same pitch again, and again it seemed to jump away at the last moment. Parnell got through the inning easily, and the next two innings as well. Later, when the Red Sox were up, Tebbetts turned to McCarthy: "Joe, you said you were sending the kid down," Tebbetts began. "Shouldn't we?" McCarthy asked. "No," said Tebbetts, "he's ready now." "Okay," McCarthy said. So 1948 became Mel Parnell's rookie year, and a wildly successful one at that.

Despite the fact that Fenway, with its short left-field fence, was considered something of a coffin for left-handers, Parnell quickly proved he could pitch well and fearlessly in his home ball park. He had a 2.29 earned-run average in Fenway, compared to 4.13 on the road. Three of his victories had come against the Indians, a team loaded with right-handed power hitters—a sure sign that his ball was harder on right-handers. He might well have had four victories against the Indians, if not for a dubious umpire's call on June 8 in a game in which Parnell had been matched up with Gene Bearden—a brilliant pitching duel in Fenway. With one man on, Lou Boudreau hit a sharp line drive toward the right-field line. In the eyes of almost everyone there the ball hooked foul and into the stands long before it reached the foul pole. A fan who was obviously sitting in foul territory caught the ball and held it up. But in Fenway the stands along the base line jut out, and Charlie Berry, the umpire covering the play, ran out and somehow called it fair, a two-run home run.

There was no instant replay in those days, but this was one of those truly terrible moments when the entire ball park *knew* that an umpire had blown a crucial call. The fan who was waving the ball, and the fans around him, all in foul territory, started waving handkerchiefs. Parnell raced over to Berry. "Charlie," he said, "it can't be a home run—it didn't even go past the foul pole." "I made my call and it's a home run and that's that," Berry yelled at him. Parnell then raced over to Ed Hurley, the home-plate umpire, and yelled, "Ed, you saw it—

it's obviously a foul ball." Hurley answered with the words that crush a player: "It's not my call." Berry must have lost the ball as he ran to right field, Parnell decided. He tried one more protest to Berry. "Get out of here and pitch," the umpire said. Those were the game's only runs, and Cleveland won 2–0. Since the two teams would end the season with identical records, the memory of that call lasted a long time, with Parnell, his teammates, and their fans.

Parnell himself fully expected to start in the playoff game. His family came up from New Orleans and went out to dinner with him. Afterward Patrick Parnell told his son to get a good night's sleep because he was about to pitch the biggest game of his life. Mel Parnell went to bed before nine and got to the ball park early the next day. Much to his surprise, he found out he was *not* pitching against the Indians. Joe McCarthy, a very conservative manager, took him aside and said, "Mel, I've changed my mind. The wind is blowing out, and I'm going to go with a right-hander." Even more astonishing to Parnell was his choice: a veteran right-hander named Denny Galehouse, who had been used mostly in relief all season. McCarthy's reasoning was simple: Galehouse was a veteran, Parnell was a rookie; Galehouse was a right-hander, Parnell a lefty. In addition, earlier in the season in a game against the Indians, Parnell had started and gotten only one man out. Galehouse came in and gave up only two hits in the remaining eight and two-thirds innings. Since then, in two other appearances, the Indians had cuffed Galehouse around, but McCarthy's mind was made up. Parnell was wounded. He knew he was young, but he was confident of his abilities.

Among the other players there was a low rumbling of first disbelief and then discontent when the news made its way through the dugout. Among those who were very surprised was Matt Batts, a young backup catcher who had been in the bullpen the previous day. Not only did Batts think Parnell a better pitcher, but during the difficult 10–5 final victory over the Yankees, Galehouse had been warming up constantly—the equivalent of a six-inning game, Batts thought. Galehouse, he thought, was plain worn-out.

Lou Boudreau, the Cleveland manager, thought that McCarthy was up to some elaborate trick, that perhaps

Galehouse would start, throw to one batter, and then Parnell would come in. He suspected that Parnell was warming up in some dark, secret place. But it was not a trick, and Galehouse, who had not had a very good year (forty years later Mel Parnell knew exactly what Denny Galehouse's record was that year: 8 and 8), did not pitch particularly well. The Indians won, 8–3, behind the brilliant pitching of young Gene Bearden.

Bearden threw a particularly bewildering knuckle ball that seemed to dance in every direction. The playoff victory was Bearden's twentieth of the year, and it made him Rookie of the Year, just ahead of Parnell. The next year the Red Sox batters, like others in the American League, learned how to deal with Bearden's knuckler. They moved up to the very front of the batter's box and swung before it began to dance. Gene Bearden never again won more than eight games.

Denny Galehouse never started another game, and he pitched only two more innings in the majors. That playoff game remained a sore point with Red Sox fans. They had always thought that McCarthy, who was a former Yankee manager after all, had never fit in very well in Boston. One sportswriter, Jack Conway of the *Boston Evening American,* reported that he had received five thousand letters criticizing McCarthy and suggesting that Galehouse be traded. To many Red Sox fans it seemed part of a long, dark history, and years later mention of the 1948 season brought back not memories of Ted Williams's heroics against the Yankees, but of McCarthy choosing Galehouse over Parnell ("the immortal Denny Galehouse" in the words of Martin Nolan, eight years old at the time and today the editor of the editorial page of the *Boston Globe*).

Boston's final two victories over the Yankees had ended, for the moment, one of the most intense rivalries in professional baseball. It would have to be continued in the summer of 1949. The Red Sox were a young team. Their fans were disappointed but not heartbroken, and they looked forward with considerable optimism to the coming year. There was no doubt that Cleveland had been lucky and that it would be hard for so many of its players to repeat such exceptional performances. As for the Yankees, they appeared to be aging. The great DiMaggio's legs were clearly giving out. So, perhaps, 1949 would belong to Boston.

CHAPTER 1

In the years immediately following World War II, professional baseball mesmerized the American people as it never had before and never would again. Baseball, more than almost anything else, seemed to symbolize normalcy and a return to life in America as it had been before Pearl Harbor. The nation clearly hungered for that. When Bob Feller returned from the navy to pitch in late August 1945, a Cleveland paper headlined the event: THIS IS WHAT WE'VE BEEN WAITING FOR.

All the prewar stars were returning to action—DiMaggio, Williams, Feller, and Stan Musial—and their very names seemed to indicate that America could pick up right where it had left off. They were replacing wartime players of lesser quality. Indeed, a player named George (Cat) Metkovich spoke for many of the wartime players when he told his Boston teammates at the end of the 1945 season, "Well, boys, better take a good look around you, because most of us won't be here next year."

The crowds were extraordinary—large, enthusiastic, and, compared with those that were soon to follow, well behaved. In the prewar years the Yankees, whose teams had included Ruth, Gehrig, and DiMaggio, claimed that they drew 1 million fans at home each season. In fact, they had not drawn that well. The real home attendance was more likely to have been around 800,000. After the war the crowds literally doubled. In 1941, the last year of prewar baseball, the National League drew 4.7 million fans; by 1947 the figure had grown to 10.4 million. In the postwar years the Yankees alone drew more than 2 million fans per season at home.

Nor was it just numbers. There was a special intensity to the crowds in those days. When the Red Sox played the Yankees in the Stadium, they traveled to New York by train, passing through Massachusetts, Rhode Island, and Connecticut. Everyone seemed to know the schedule of their train, and as it passed through endless small towns along the route, there would be large crowds gathered at the stations to cheer the players, many of the people holding up signs exhorting their heroes to destroy the hated Yankees. The conductor would deliberately slow the train down and many of the players, on their way to do battle with the sworn enemy, would come out on the observation decks to wave to the crowds.

Near the end of the 1946 season, a young Red Sox pitcher named Dave Ferriss went into Yankee Stadium to pitch and was stunned by the size of the crowd: 63,000 people, according to the newspapers, even though at the time the Red Sox held a sizable lead over the Yankees. Ferriss had only recently left a tiny town in the Mississippi Delta. That day he was so awed by the noise and tumult that in the middle of the game he decided to commit the scene to memory and take it with him for the rest of his life. He stepped off the mound, turned slowly to the stands, and inhaled the crowd. Ferriss thought to himself: How magnificent it all is. This is the Red Sox and this is the Yankees. I am twenty-four, and I am pitching in Yankee Stadium, and every seat is taken.

With the exception of the rare heavyweight fight or college football game that attracted national attention, baseball dominated American sports entertainment. Professional football, soon to become a major sport because its faster action so well suited the television camera, was still a minor-league ticket; golf and tennis were for the few who played those sports.

Rich businessmen, thinking about becoming owners of sports teams, did not yet talk about the entertainment dollar, for America was a Calvinistic nation, not much given to entertaining itself. In the world of baseball, the sport itself was vastly more important than such ancillary commercial sources of revenue as broadcasting, endorsements, concessions, and parking.

There were only sixteen teams in the big leagues, and in an America defined by the railroad instead of the airplane, St. Louis was a far-west team and Washington a Southern one. California might as well have been in another country. The pace of life in America had not yet accelerated as it was soon to do from the combination of endless technological break-throughs and undreamed-of affluence in ordinary homes. The use of drugs seemed very distant. The prevailing addiction of more than a few players (and managers, coaches, sportswriters, and indeed owners) was alcohol, apparently a more acceptable and less jarring form of self-destruction. It was, thought Curt Gowdy, a young sportscaster who had just joined the Yankees, the last moment of innocence in American life.

Baseball was rooted not just in the past but in the culture of the country; it was celebrated in the nation's literature and songs. When a poor American boy dreamed of escaping his grim life, his fantasy probably involved becoming a professional baseball player. It was not so much the national sport as the binding national myth.

It was also the embodiment of the melting-pot theory, or at least the white melting pot theory, of America. One of its pre-eminent players, Joe DiMaggio, was the son of a humble immigrant fisherman, and the fact that three of the fisherman's sons had made the major leagues proved to many the openness and fairness of American society. America cheered the DiMaggio family, and by so doing, proudly cheered itself. When DiMaggio played in his first World Series, his mother traveled by train to watch him play. She was a modest woman, but open and candid, and she became something of a celebrity herself by telling reporters (in Italian) that the trip was hard for her because there was so little to do in New York—she wished there was some cleaning, or at least some dishes to wash and dry.

The great waves of immigration from Europe had taken place in the latter part of the nineteenth and first part of the twentieth centuries. Few of the children of those immigrants had yet succeeded in politics, business, or academe. It was baseball that first offered them a chance for fame and glory.

That this chance came in—of all places—a sport did not always thrill their parents.

Giuseppe DiMaggio at first frowned on baseball as too frivolous. Only as Joe became a major star did his opinion change, and he came to enjoy his son's success. Because he could not read English he would wake his youngest son, Dominic, at four o'clock in the morning when the newspaper arrived so that Dominic could read and interpret the box score for him.

Phil Rizzuto's parents came from Calabria. In America his father was first a laborer and then a conductor on the BMT subway. He also thought baseball was a foolish choice for a career and argued vehemently against it. Finally his wife softened his opposition—she observed that if it didn't work out, then their son could take a real job. Still, Fiore Rizzuto was suspicious of this new world, outside New York City, that his son was entering—it might be like the old country, filled with people from the Black Hand. As Phil set off on his first train ride to a town in Virginia, his father pinned twenty dollars (Phil's only money) into his undershirt so that robbers would not be able to find it. He warned his son not to fall asleep on the train, no matter how tired he was.

Johnny Pesky of the Red Sox was born in Portland, Oregon, to Croatian immigrants named Paveskovich. Pesky picked up his abbreviated surname first as a schoolyard nickname, then it became a means of simplifying box scores, and finally he took it as his legal surname. That bothered his parents—did this mean their son was ashamed of his real name? They worried as well that by choosing sports as a vocation Johnny was becoming a bum.

Tommy Henrich, grandson of German immigrants, knew how hard it was for the members of his family who had come from the old country to understand his career. On the occasion of his first contract, his father told his grandfather, "Tommy is going to play professional baseball." "Oh, is that so," the grandfather replied. "What is he, anyway—the striker?"

Baseball, then, came to symbolize the idea of America as a land of opportunity and justice for all. And in 1947, finally, with the coming of Jackie Robinson, the sport was going to open up not just for the sons of recent immigrants but to native sons of color as well. The coming of Robinson did not take place without some rumbling, most notably from players who were from the South, or whose talents were so marginal that the coming of blacks represented the most basic kind of a job threat. In spring training, 1947, Leo Durocher, heading off an early protest by some of his white players, warned, "He's just the first. Just the first. They're all going to come, and they're going to be hungry, damned hungry, and if you don't put out, they'll take your jobs."

He was right: That very sense of continuity, the belief that life would once again be the same, was erroneous. The country was already changing, the pace of life accelerating, due in no small part to the coming of a powerful new communications empire, of which baseball itself would be a prime beneficiary. In 1947, the World Series was telecast to a few Eastern cities. In 1948, there was a crude attempt to televise the Series to the East Coast from so distant a city as Cleveland by having a plane fly above the ball park in a kind of horse-and-buggy version of a satellite. That year there were so few television sets (by one count, 325,000 in all of America, half of them in the New York City area) that the Gillette Company, which was sponsoring the games, placed 100 new sets on the Boston Common so that ordinary fans might gather there and watch.

It was immediately obvious that there was a natural affinity between sports and television, and by the spring of 1949, advertisements in *The New York Times* pushed baseball as the reason for buying a set: "Batter Up! Imperial offers you a Box Set. RCA Victor Television. $375. Installation and home owner policy $55. 52 square inch screen." That was in contrast to a GE set: "So Bright! So Clear! So Easy on the Eyes! $725."

Television's vast impact on sports was still to come. For the moment, though, radio had greatly increased the size of audiences and put fans in daily contact with their favorite teams. In 1946, a radio broadcaster named Mel Allen traveled with the Yankees to every game and did the first live broadcasts of away games. Previously, those games had been done by local sports announcers using the Western Union ticker and re-creating as best they could the sounds and sights of the ball park.

Radio made the games and the players seem vastly more important, mythic even. It also pioneered in another area: the use of sports as an advertising vehicle. Until the coming of radio, commercial exploitation was limited; a local semipro baseball team might bear the name of a neighborhood car dealer on the back of its uniforms, and at a local ball park there might be signs lining the outfield fences to advertise various products. But when advertising executives discovered that sports and athletes could be used to sell products, a new, high-powered marriage was soon arranged. Radio formed the first national commercial network. If a rose was a rose was a rose, then an athlete was a hero was a salesman, although baseball players received, of course, a disproportionate amount of the new endorsement opportunities. In the spring of 1950, an ad for Camel cigarettes portrayed two major-league pitchers—Johnny Vander Meer, a veteran pitcher, and Gene Bearden, Rookie of the Year in the American League—exhorting ordinary Americans to share in the pleasures of Camels. Vander Meer said, "I've smoked Camels for ten years, Gene! They're mild and they sure taste great." Bearden answered, "Right, Van! It's Camels for me too—ever since I made the thirty-day mildness test!"

Soon the athletes would become the beneficiaries of the new commercial affluence. In 1988, the players on the starting lineup for the Yankees earned an average salary of $694,000; in 1948 that was more than the entire payroll of even the best teams, which averaged about $450,000. Even accounting for inflation, the figures reflected the coming of the entertainment society and the passing of power from owner to player.

The rivalry of the Red Sox and the Yankees was an important part of the myth of baseball. In 1920 the Red Sox's principal owner, a Broadway producer named Harry Frazee, was desperate for funds, so he sold a twenty-four-year-old pitcher named Babe Ruth to the Yankees for the unheard-of sum of $125,000. Boston fans never recovered. Ruth was an outstanding young pitcher, but he had won only nine games the year before. What made the sale so bitter for Boston fans was the fact that Ruth had hit 29 home runs that season, an amazing number for the time, 19 more than the runner-up.

Five years later Frazee opened a show called *No, No, Nanette* which became his greatest hit. However, the show's success, considerable though it was, brought little consolation to New England, since in the previous season Ruth, already well established as the premier power hitter in the game, batted .378, with 46 home runs (16 more than the entire Boston team) and 121 runs batted in.

The Yankees, with Ruth, went on to dominate the American League in the twenties and thirties, although in the years just before World War II the Red Sox were an ascending team. A wealthy young man named Tom Yawkey bought them in 1933, and proved to be the most loving of owners. In fact, some thought him *too* loving and referred to the team as a country club. Be that as it may, he dramatically upgraded the Red Sox and improved their scouting system as well. They finished second in 1938, 1939, 1941, and 1942, always, of course, to the Yankees. On the eve of World War II, Boston finally appeared ready to challenge the Yankees.

In 1949 the Red Sox were, to all intents and purposes, a mighty team. There was Ted Williams, only twenty-six years old at the time of V-J. To many the best hitter in baseball, he was nicknamed "God" by Johnny Pesky, the shortstop (who, in turn, because of his rather large nose, was called either "Needle" or "Needlenose" by Williams). There was Dominic DiMaggio, the third of the DiMaggio brothers to play in the major leagues, an all-star in his own right. According to his teammates, Dom had the hardest job in baseball since he led off for Boston. That meant he underwent a fierce interrogation by Williams about the opposing pitcher every time he came back to the dugout: What was he throwing, Dommy, was he fast, was he tricky, was he getting the corners? Come on, Dommy, you saw him. In addition there was Bobby Doerr at second base. Smooth and steady, a future Hall of Fame player, he was extremely popular with his teammates.

The basic lineup of the Red Sox seemed set. It was filled with hitters, and, especially in Fenway, pitchers hated to go against them. The feel of the team was good. It had the right mix of veterans and young players, the right balance between country boys and city boys—as exemplified by the baiting of Boo Ferriss, the quintessential country boy, whose harshest expletive was "Shuck-uns," by Mickey Harris, who was from New York City. Harris's mouth, even in this profession of unexpurgated language, was considered uniquely foul. He devoted

great energy to trying to get Boo Ferriss to say a dirty word.
He would needle Ferriss constantly about what was wrong
with him as an athlete and what was wrong with Mississippi,
Ferriss's home state. Finally, Ferriss would explode. "You said
it! You said it," Harris would joyously proclaim. "Mickey," Ferriss would answer, "I did not say what you thought I said—I
merely said 'John Brownit.'"

Pitching was a perennial problem with the Red Sox, however. Fenway's short fence encouraged better-than-average
hitters to think they were *very* good hitters, but it worked psychic damage on the team's pitchers. In spring training, 1946,
Red Sox veterans paid particular attention to the young pitchers—namely, Ferriss and Tex Hughson—who had been pitching well, albeit during the war years. Ferriss, for example had
won 21 games and lost only 10 in 1945.

But in spring 1946 Ferriss had to face Williams in batting
practice. Williams was the most passionate hitter in baseball,
and the philosopher king of hitting as well. He was always discoursing on the science of it; pitchers, he thought, were
"dumb by breed." When Williams stepped up to bat, suddenly,
Ferriss realized it was as if spring training had stopped altogether and something different and tougher had started.
Most of the other players stopped whatever they were doing
to watch. Much depended on this. World Series checks might
ride on how good this young pitcher was.

Williams, it was well known, liked batting-practice pitching to approximate the real thing. He liked to be challenged.
Ferriss was in a delicate position: He had to throw well but
also be careful not to be a hot dog. So he tried to put as much
movement on the ball as he could while not throwing too
hard. Williams took the requisite swings, getting some hits and
hitting some balls into the ground. When he left the cage, the
Boston writers immediately gathered around to find out what
he thought of this young right-hander. Was he the real thing
or was he, in a phrase appropriated from the Germans during
the war, ersatz? "He'll win," Williams said, "he can pitch."
That was immediately relayed to Ferriss, who felt that God
had spoken on his behalf. Later Williams went over to Ferriss
and said: "Kid, I told those writers that all you have to do is
throw it like you threw before and you'll be all right." Ferriss

now felt he could count those 21 victories of 1945 as real; it was as if an asterisk had been removed from beside them.

That had signaled the emergence of a new Red Sox team, one with young pitchers who could match the powerful, if slow, regular lineup. In 1946 the Red Sox veterans regained their skills more quickly than did the returning Yankees and ran away with the pennant. Ferriss won 25 games and lost only 6 that season; Tex Hughson won 20, and Mickey Harris, another young pitcher seemingly on the edge of stardom, won 17. Some people were talking of a dynasty.

But the dynasty did not take place. Ferriss developed serious arm trouble in the middle of 1947; Hughson had two thirds of a good season in 1947, and then *he* developed arm trouble; and Harris, also plagued by a sore arm, never again won more than 7 games. That so many strong and talented young arms could go bad so quickly seemed to indicate what fans had long suspected: that the Red Sox were dogged by the fates.

Another team watching three of its best pitchers come up with sore arms might have been finished. That was almost too much to ask even of such teams as the Yankees or the Dodgers, with their formidable farm systems. But this misfortune did not stop the Red Sox. In those days, weak teams with owners perched on the brink of bankruptcy could always be counted on to part with a good player for a number of lesser players and a considerable amount of cash. St. Louis, Philadelphia, and Washington were such teams. Late in the 1947 season, Joe Cronin, who was then still managing Boston, took aside Birdie Tebbetts, his catcher. "I don't have the pitching, do I, Birdie?" Cronin asked. "No, it's not there, we're coming up short," Tebbetts answered. "That's what I was afraid of," Cronin said. When the season was over, Red Sox owner Tom Yawkey engineered a massive trade with the St. Louis Browns, a trade so complicated that it had to be accomplished over two days. Boston traded away nine marginal players for Jack Kramer, a star pitcher, Vern Stephens, a slow but powerful shortstop, and then, almost as a throw-in, a veteran pitcher named Ellis Kinder. In addition, the Red Sox gave the Browns nearly $400,000 in cash, an immense sum in those days, more than enough to save a bad franchise's existence for yet another year, while, of course, destroying any remaining shred of credibility it had with its fans. When the deal was consummated there was a feeling that the Red Sox had virtually bought themselves another pennant.

With the trade completed, Williams and Dom DiMaggio argued with each other over which of the two new pitchers was more valuable. Williams, a great authority on pitching, insisted that Kramer was; but DiMaggio, whose intelligence Williams greatly admired, said that Kramer was a finesse pitcher, which was not ideal for a small ball park like Fenway. Kinder, DiMaggio added, was interesting, much better than his reputation. Kinder was already thirty-four years old at the time of the trade, had been in the major leagues for only two years, and had won a grand total of 11 big-league games. Some thought that his best pitch was his change-up: that is, a pitch thrown seemingly with the full force of the fastball, in which the pitcher deliberately masks the fact that he is taking off some of the speed. The object, of course, is to throw off the hitter's timing. "A pitcher who depends on a change can't win," Williams said. It was valuable, he argued, only if supported by another major pitch: "A good hitter sees a change, and he can step out of the batter's box, count the crowd, and still hit it out."

Certainly the deal helped the Red Sox immediately: In that first year Kramer won 18 games while losing only 5; and Kinder, showing that DiMaggio was at least partially right, won 10 games and lost 7. Stephens hit 29 home runs and drove in 137 runs. The three of them played a critical role in bringing the Red Sox to the playoff game with Cleveland, and the very brink of the pennant, in 1948.

That year saw another important addition to the Red Sox: Joe McCarthy came to manage them. He was sixty-two, a blunt old-fashioned man who had been a dominant figure on the Yankees in the thirties and forties. He was largely credited for making the Yankees the elite organization of baseball. They traveled first-class; they always wore jackets and ties. He wanted them, whenever they were in public, to look like professionals. Before they came to the ball park, they were to shave at home, or, if they were on the road, at the hotel. "You're a Yankee," McCarthy would tell his players. "Act like one." In 1946 during spring training a rookie pitcher named Frank Shea was trying to lose some extra weight, so he created an extra-heavy sweat suit in which to run extra laps. He was proud of how hard he was working to get in shape. One day he came back to the dugout soaked with sweat and pleased with himself for staying with so ambitious a program. But his cap was turned sideways. McCarthy took one look at him and said, "Young fellow, if you can't wear that uniform right, don't wear it at all."

McCarthy even extended his idea of class to lectures about the use of hard liquor. He did not want his players to drink, he would tell them, but he knew that on occasion they needed to relax, and that liquor helped. Therefore, if they had to drink, they should drink what he drank: White Horse Scotch—because it was the best, and the real danger in drinking came from using cheap, off-brand stuff. It was said that while managing Chicago in the twenties, McCarthy had once lectured Hack Wilson about the seriousness of his drinking. He illustrated his lecture by pouring a shot of whiskey into a glass filled with worms. The worms quickly died. "What did you learn from that?" he asked Wilson. "That if I drink I won't have worms," the slugger answered. Unfortunately, McCarthy's own drinking increased significantly in his later years as a manager. His players had a code name for it. When he was on one of his benders, he was, they said, "riding the white horse."

When McCarthy first became the Red Sox manager there was a great deal of speculation about how he would handle Ted Williams. Williams was famous for his love of hitting, his impetuous relationships with fans and the press, and his hatred of wearing ties. It was said that he owned two ties, a blue one and a brown one, and that once a year, on the occasion of some special charity fund raiser, he would actually wear one. McCarthy showed up for his first meeting with Williams without a tie himself and later explained to reporters that a manager who could not get on with a .400 hitter did not deserve to manage in the big leagues.

McCarthy had strong opinions about almost everything. He was an inveterate smoker of cigars, which he could move nimbly around and through his fingers in various positions. He did not like pipe smokers on his team because he thought they were too contented. (Red Rolfe, the Yankee third baseman, had been a pipe smoker and had tried to hide it from the manager; the other players were sure that McCarthy knew and tolerated it only because Rolfe was so good a player.) McCarthy even had his own peculiar views of history. For example, he liked what he called the "dark-haired Poles" because, he claimed, they came from the south of Poland and had fought fiercely whenever Poland was attacked. But he wanted no part of blond-haired Poles, who he said had not resisted their enemies at moments of crisis.

He liked to tell his players that he knew all their tricks because he had tried them himself. "I know your games," he would say. "I was the one who had the phones taken out of the clubhouse in Chicago. I knew what the players were doing—using them all the time to call their bookies." He hated card games and barred them from his clubhouse. To him they were a waste of time. When he saw his players with cards—the one thing a baseball player had, once the season began, was plenty of time—he would push them to do something else. Why, that man who invented the little wrapper for the sugar cube, he would say, would never have done that if he had been playing cards. Once the players entered the clubhouse they were there to play baseball. Frank Shea once brought a newspaper into the clubhouse during spring training in 1946. "What's this?" McCarthy asked, picking up the paper. "It's a newspaper," Shea said. "Shea, you just throw it in the garbage pail over there. You're here to play baseball, and if you want to read about yourself, you do it in your hotel room," McCarthy said.

Temptation was everywhere. When Clarence Marshall was a rookie, McCarthy called him over just after the club had reached New York. "Hey, kid, where do you live?" he asked, while his eyes looked at a spot of grass about twenty yards in front of him. He is most decidedly not looking at me, Marshall thought. He is talking to me, but it is as if I don't exist. "The Edison Hotel, sir," Marshall said, naming a hotel in midtown. "Don't let the bright lights and the stinking perfume get you," McCarthy said. That was all. His eyes never moved. Rookie dismissed.

He most emphatically did not like the new bonus-baby rules, which allowed teams to sign young players for huge sums of money, but demanded that they skip the minor

leagues and start with the big-league clubs. When Bobby
Brown had arrived as the Yankees' first bonus baby in 1947,
McCarthy had watched him carefully and skeptically. Finally
he took Brown aside and told him, in words that sounded
strangely archaic to Brown, "Bobby, we don't have any rats on
the Yankees."

He was even more resentful when he came to the Red
Sox, which had a weaker farm system. In 1948 the Red Sox
had an eighteen-year-old bonus baby named Chuck Stobbs on
the roster. Stobbs had signed for $35,000—the equivalent of
five years' salary for most rookies—before he had even
thrown his first strike. During spring training McCarthy made
him feel as if he didn't exist. Finally, toward the end of spring
training, McCarthy signaled Stobbs to come over. Stobbs felt a
rush of excitement. Perhaps this was going to be his big
chance. The manager began to talk about how to play second
base. The footwork was critical, McCarthy said. Second base?
Was he going to be transformed into a second baseman? Be-
wilderment showed on Stobbs's face. "You're not Goodman,
are you?" McCarthy said, referring to Billy Goodman, a young
infielder. "No, sir," said Stobbs, "I'm Stobbs." "Get the hell out
of here," McCarthy roared, and Stobbs gratefully did. He
stayed with the team for the entire 1948 season and pitched a
total of nine innings.

As McCarthy saw it, ballplayers were to play hard, and
they were not to take defeat lightly. Once in 1937 the Yankees
split a doubleheader with one of the weaker teams in the
league, losing a game they should not have lost. Afterward,
McCarthy came prowling angrily through the locker room. A
utility outfielder named Roy Johnson, relatively new to the
team, saw McCarthy and complained just loud enough for
him to hear that you could not win every game. McCarthy
heard him. Later that day he called up his superiors. "Get me
Henrich," he said. Tommy Henrich was brought up from the
Yankee farm team in Newark, and Roy Johnson was waived
out of the league. The point was clear to everyone: Even halfway sassing the manager was a very bad idea. But the Yankee
players who had come up while he was managing—such players as Henrich, Charlie Keller, and DiMaggio—had a special
affection for him. He played them regularly, did not jerk

them around, and tried to protect them from the front office and the press.

McCarthy was particularly suspicious of the press. He regarded it as a hostile force, and was as pithy with the Boston press as he had been with the New York writers. When a Boston writer suggested that if Williams played in Yankee Stadium, with its short fence, he would break Babe Ruth's record for home runs, McCarthy looked at him coldly and said simply, "Gehrig didn't." The Boston writers soon learned to deal with him by being provocative. Joe Cashman, a reporter for the *Boston Herald,* decided that the best way to get information was to make a statement, especially a stupid one, rather than ask questions. That so confirmed McCarthy's view of writers as people who did not know baseball, he could not refuse the bait.

To the Red Sox, McCarthy brought his old prejudices, with the exception of the tie rule, which was gone courtesy of Williams. Card playing was still out. The first team lecture was, as far as anyone could tell, primarily about pipe smoking. Billy Hitchcock, the utility infielder, was the only pipe smoker on the team, and he spent much of the season trying to smoke it on the team train when McCarthy was not looking. Once, thinking the manager had gone to bed, he tried to smoke in the small antechamber of the men's room on the train. McCarthy walked in. Hitchcock hid the pipe by cradling the bowl in his hand. Usually McCarthy's visits were brief and his tone curt. But this time he lingered. He was friendly, almost garrulous. Hitchcock's hand got hotter and hotter. Still McCarthy lingered. Hitchcock thought he was going to scream. Finally McCarthy left. Hitchcock was sure he had known about the pipe and had enjoyed squeezing him.

How then to please this gruff old man who sat there all day long saying little, chewing his gum endlessly (and sticking the used gum under the bench where he sat—a McCarthy trademark)? Whom did he like? What did he like? The Red Sox regulars spent much of 1948 trying to figure him out.

For one thing, he liked hustle. He liked toughness. He liked Billy Goodman, the versatile infielder and spray hitter who played first base in 1948. Indeed, McCarthy even said that his mistake, which had cost Boston the pennant, was in not seeing that Goodman was his first baseman until a quarter of the season had passed. He liked Matt Batts, the backup catcher. Batts had been a long shot to make the team in 1948, but Charlie Berry, who had been umpiring some Boston games in spring training, came over to Batts and said, "Hey you, Batts. You want to make this team?" Batts said yes, indeed he did. "Here's what you do, kid. You've got a good arm and you're throwing hard in infield practice, and I know old Joe McCarthy and he loves it. You keep doing it. You throw even harder. I'm watching McCarthy, and every time you do that his eyes light up and he chews that gum a little faster." After that, during the drills Johnny Pesky would complain that Batts was throwing so hard that it was hurting his hand. But Batts paid him no attention; he just threw harder.

Some of the veterans felt that McCarthy looked down on them, that he believed he had inherited a team where the players were too soft, and it was his job to be tougher. With the Yankees, he had been careful never to criticize his players in front of each other; now there was a sense that his patience was being strained. One day when Wally Moses, one of the reserve Boston outfielders, was on the trainer's table being worked on, McCarthy asked what was wrong. "I've got a stiff neck," Moses said. "Probably got it in some fancy air-conditioned bar," McCarthy said acidly, for in those days an air-conditioned bar was something for the elite. "Skip, with the money they pay me, I can't afford to go to any of those. I got it in a movie theater," Moses said.

Some of the pitchers felt that McCarthy was too old-fashioned. According to them he did not understand the changing nature of the game and the importance of relief pitching. He came from a generation, they thought, where if the pitcher was a real man, he would pitch all nine innings. A bullpen in that era was less important, and the men who pitched out of it were not considered specialists who had a particular skill suited to a few innings of late relief work. Rather they were pitchers not quite good enough to be starters. In the spring of 1948 the Boston writers asked McCarthy whether Earl Johnson, who had been at different times in his career a starter and a reliever, would be a starter for him. "He doesn't throw hard enough to be a starter for me," McCarthy said, and it was a revealing moment. He had admitted a player was consigned to the bullpen because his arm was not that strong. On the Yankees, by contrast, the hardest-throwing pitcher on the team, Joe Page, resided in the bullpen.

There was a careful watch on McCarthy in 1948, and some tense moments resulted. Early in the season the Red Sox went into Sportsman's Park for a series with the Browns. During one game a St. Louis pitcher was working on Junior Stephens, who was a notorious bad-ball hitter with a special penchant for going after high balls. As Stephens settled in the batter's box, McCarthy yelled out, "Make him come down." The first pitch came in high and out of the strike zone. Stephens swung and missed. Strike one. "Make him come down!" McCarthy yelled again, a little more emphatically. Again the pitch came in, high and out of the strike zone, and again Stephens swung and missed. *"Make him come down!"* McCarthy yelled even more emphatically. Again the scene was repeated: a high fastball, a Stephen's swing, and a strikeout. Stephens jogged back to the dugout, turned in the general direction of McCarthy, and yelled, *"Make him come down, my ass!"* There was silence in the dugout: It was the first testing of a veteran manager by a veteran player. McCarthy said nothing, but waited while the regulars went back onto the field and took their positions. Then he said, just loud enough for everyone on the bench to hear, "Got a little upset, didn't he?" There was no way to call down to Newark for a Henrich. He would not make an issue of this—Stephens was the best he had. McCarthy was going to have to make do.

As much as anyone on the team, Stephens suffered under McCarthy. As far as he was concerned, McCarthy was always riding him, making snide remarks in the dugout about his fielding and his hitting. "If that toothless old son of a bitch gets on me one more time," he told his friend Billy Hitchcock, the utility infielder, "I'm going to kill him. I'm going to stuff his gum down his throat." That struggle lasted all season to the satisfaction of neither of them.

By contrast, McCarthy continued to cultivate Williams. Early in the season Williams hit a tremendous home run into the bullpen against the Browns. When he came back to the bench, he heard McCarthy's voice, directed at him alone, so no one else could hear it, saying, "If I could hit like you I'd play for nothing." Williams was oddly touched, for the old man was not lightly given to praise. After the playoff game in 1948, Williams was the last to leave the locker room. As he was finally going, he heard a voice behind him. "Well, we fooled them, didn't we?" the voice said. It was McCarthy. "What do you mean?" Williams said. "They all said we couldn't get along and I thought we got along pretty good," McCarthy said. "You're right, Joe, we got along pretty good," Williams answered.

When the Red Sox convened in the spring of 1949, there was a generally good feeling on the team. The players from the Browns, wild though they might have been, had become integrated into the team, and there were no factions or divisions. A few days into spring training there was a contest to decide who was the best-dressed Boston player. Jack Kramer, known as Handsome Jack or Alice because he was a dandy (he not only wore silk underwear but washed it himself—most definitely not a baseball-player–type thing to do), was the odds-on favorite. He was very good-looking, and he worked during the off-season in a men's store. It was said that he once bought a suit because the salesman told him it was the only one of its kind in the world. Later, he saw someone else wearing the same suit, so he immediately gave his away. Kramer arrived in camp with many suitcases filled with newly tailored clothes, and he showed them off to his teammates, including (this was his greatest mistake) Birdie Tebbetts. Tebbetts was a world-class needler, and he decided to sting Kramer. He brought Parnell and Matt Batts in on the joke. "Whatever I say," he told them, "you agree." So as Kramer unveiled one suit after another, Tebbetts would look carefully at it and then say, with a touch of regret in his voice, "It's a great jacket, Jack, but it's just a little bit off on the left sleeve." Batts and Parnell would quickly agree. Visibly upset, Kramer would look in the full-length mirror, and yes, the left sleeve *did* look a little off. So it went. No matter what jacket he tried on, Tebbetts spotted a flaw in the left sleeve, and the other two players agreed. The following morning Kramer took his entire wardrobe to a tailor, delighting Tebbetts and incurring needless tailoring bills. That, thought some of the players, was just Tebbetts getting back at Kramer for the previous spring, when

Tebbetts had arrived in camp with an enormous trunk filled with clothes and announced that he, the lowly Tebbetts, had as many jackets as Kramer. "Yeah, Birdie, but my jackets fit me," Kramer had answered. But to Tebbetts it was all in good fun; he had played on winning teams in the past in Detroit, and this felt like a winning team.

Much of the good feeling in the Red Sox camp seemed to come from Ted Williams. He was at once a star and a little kid, eager to be back at that which he loved best after some six months away. Like many of his teammates he was a serious fisherman, but unlike them he didn't use the time in Florida as a means of getting out on the water. For him, when spring training started fishing ended; he became a full-time baseball player. This spring he seemed more at ease than ever. When writers pressed him for his goals, he talked about leading the American League in hitting, which he had already done four times. "No one but Cobb has done it more than four times," he said. "If I can win it this year I'll be ahead of Harry Heilmann [who also had done it four times]. I'll be second in the record book. There's no point in even thinking of catching up with Cobb."

Matt Batts caught a lot of batting practice that spring, and he loved catching when Williams was up. Batts had barely made the team as a rookie the previous year, and yet here he was with the great star, talking to him as though they were equals. "Goddamn Batts, did you see that," Williams would say as he lashed a ball on a line to right. In would come another pitch. Again a swing, again a line drive. "Batts, I'm going to tell you a secret—I'm good and I'm getting better." In came another pitch. Again he swung, again the ball hurtled deep into the outfield. "I can't stand it, I'm so good," he said. Then, as the pitcher got ready, he would say, "Batts, I'm going to show you something." This time he swung and the ball sailed into left field. "See that, Batts—I can hit to left field. I can hit there any damn time I want. But my money's in right field— that's what they pay me to do." He would take one more swing, Batts remembered, hit it again, and leave the batter's box most reluctantly. "Goddamn, but this is fun," he would say. "I could do this all day—and they pay me for it." Batts thought: He makes it easier to remember that baseball was supposed to be fun.

CHAPTER 2

The Yankee camp in spring training that year was not nearly
so harmonious. There was a new manager, Casey Stengel, and
the veteran players were suspicious of him, in part because
they were still angry that Bucky Harris had been fired (George
Weiss, the general manager, had thought him too lax in his
control of the players). Also, Stengel brought with him a reputation as something of a buffoon. He came by that reputation
honestly, for as a young man he had blended love of laughter
with love of the game. There were many famous Stengelisms.
One was the time he had barnstormed with a team dressed up
as a hayseed, to mix in with the rural crowd watching the
game. Suddenly the hayseed came out of the crowd, claiming
he could do better. An argument ensued between him and the
uniformed players. Reluctantly the players let him bat. The
pitcher grooved the ball, and Stengel *did* do better. On another occasion he was playing the outfield when he spied a
bird near him. He caught it, put it under his hat, and waited
for the appropriate moment, which came when he made a
good running catch. As the crowd cheered, he tipped his hat
and the bird flew out. But his most memorable moment of all,
perhaps, occurred during the 1923 World Series; playing for

the Giants, he hit his second home run against the Yankees. That was astonishing since he was not known as a power hitter. As he trotted around the bases he thumbed his nose at the Yankee bench, for the Yankees had never treated him with great respect. Then, as he rounded third, he blew them a kiss.

The appointment of a man who was famous for his practical jokes was not popular with the staid Yankees. Joe DiMaggio told Arthur Daley of the *Times,* "I've never seen such a bewildered guy in my life. He doesn't seem to know what it's all about." Curt Gowdy, a young broadcaster, found himself in the men's room with the Yankees' new manager, and he introduced himself. The manager, hearing that Gowdy was a broadcaster, immediately put in a pitch for a friend of his as an announcer. Gowdy answered that he was so new himself, he doubted he could help anyone else. "Hey," said Stengel, then fifty-eight years old, "we're both rookies."

After suffering through years of McCarthy's disdain, the sportswriters saw Stengel as a blessing. He always wanted to talk. During spring training he played along with a gag on John Drebinger of the *Times,* one of the more senior writers. Drebby used a hearing aid. The writers held a special press conference with Stengel, at which the manager mouthed the words instead of saying them. The other writers dutifully took notes. Soon Drebinger was cursing his hearing aid, shaking his head, and saying, "And I just got new batteries." It was something that would never have happened in the McCarthy era.

If the veterans were having a hard time trying to feel their way around Stengel, then for the rookies in camp it was even worse. Jerry Coleman, a young second baseman, was a rookie that spring, and he lived in constant terror. He had been a marine dive-bomber pilot in World War II, flying fifty-seven missions in fighters in the Solomon Islands. But spring training was harder on his nerves. He was both married and broke. He and his wife, Louise, were desperately short of money. They had driven to Florida in the flashy yellow Buick convertible of Clarence Marshall, a teammate who was just as broke as Coleman. Coleman carried in his pocket a cashier's check for three hundred dollars, which represented his entire savings from his winter job selling clothes in San Francisco. That was to last through six weeks of spring training, augmented by a weekly stipend of twenty-five dollars. By bringing his young wife to training camp, Coleman was violating tradition: Wives were family, families were pleasure, and a rookie at the Yankee camp was engaged in a life-and-death proposition—he was not yet a member of the team. Charlie Silvera, a young catcher who had played with Coleman in sandlot baseball in San Francisco, had been told not to bring his wife to spring training; not until 1950 would his family be welcome.

Coleman found spring training both exciting and frightening. He was with the Yankees off a weak season at Newark, where he had hit only .251, and was trying to play second base, which was a new position. There were not many slots on the Yankees for those who hit .250 in the minors. He was constantly aware of the odds against him, and of how much he had invested in this moment. Here he was at the very edge of his dream. It was as if this were a favorite movie he knew by heart, and now instead of merely watching it he was acting in it as well. He was surrounded by his heroes. There was Tommy Henrich, the consummate professional, taking his time getting into shape, absolutely confident of his skills. At first, all of Henrich's hits were going to left field, and that surprised Coleman because Henrich was a notorious pull hitter. Then he realized what Henrich was doing: He wanted to see the ball at first, and make solid contact. Then he would worry about pulling the ball. All he wanted at first was his stroke.

One thing Coleman felt sure of was that he was in the best shape of his life. He owed that in no small part to Bill Skiff, who had been his manager at Newark. Skiff had told him, "Jerry, if you want to make the majors, you're going to have to do two things: You're going to have to learn how to use your bat—strengthen yourself—and you're going to have to stop smoking." Coleman understood the first suggestion immediately, for he knew he was not very strong, even by comparison with most infielders. But the second part puzzled him. Stop smoking? Why? "Because it's holding your weight down," Skiff said. "None of these guys know it, but it cuts their appetites. It's habit forming, and soon they'd rather smoke than eat, and they lose weight and then they lose power. Some of them can afford it, but you, you're as skinny as they come.

You can't afford it." Skiff gave him another hard, appraising look. "You drink, Jerry?" he asked. "Not much," Coleman answered. "During the season," he said, "drink two beers a day after a game, whether you like it or not. You need the fluid— it'll keep you from losing weight, and it'll help you relax."

So Coleman had immediately given up smoking, and his appetite had improved. In addition, he had a friend make him a leaded bat with four pounds of weights in it. He worked out with it all winter, and when he arrived at spring training, he felt stronger than ever, and, even more important, his hands were already hard and calloused.

Mostly, though, Coleman worried. He had to beat out the regular second baseman, George Stirnweiss, who had shed a good deal of weight over the winter and was having a good spring. In addition, there were other second basemen from the minors, and there was even the possibility of a trade, although the Yankees traditionally traded for pitchers, not infielders. There was also the possibility of a switch of position. One day there was a flurry of stories in the newspapers that Billy Johnson, who had been the third baseman and was being challenged by Bobby Brown, might play at second.

The rookies were emotionally, if not physically, apart from the others in spring training. The Yankee veterans did not treat them like fraternity pledges, the way veterans on some of the other clubs did. But the presence of rookies created certain emotional tensions. On one hand, a rookie might take a veteran's job; on the other hand, a good rookie might strengthen the team, and thereby help ensure a World Series check. That meant that the rookies were watched but not helped; they were spoken to but not with. Once in 1946 during spring training, a group of veterans was talking in the locker room and a rookie joined in. The conversation came to a complete halt. Spud Chandler, the veteran pitcher, turned to him and said, "Fresh fucking rookie." The rookie was silenced immediately and for the rest of the spring.

Bobby Brown was another young player trying to win a regular job—at third and short. Brown's situation seemed even more difficult than Coleman's. Billy Johnson, the man he would replace, was immensely popular with the other players, someone who reflected the old-fashioned verities. Brown was

an early bonus baby, which set him apart from the start; even
before he played his first game he had been given big money
merely to sign—what some players made as salary after six or
seven years. In addition, he had been to medical school, and
he did not drink, smoke, or chase girls. At the press conference where his signing was announced, Larry MacPhail, one
of the Yankee owners, had spoken so extravagantly about his
talents—what a fine young man he was, and what a brilliant
young doctor he was going to become—that Will Wedge of
the *Sun* finally asked, "Larry, are you signing him as a player
or a doctor?"

As it turned out, neither Brown nor Coleman had anything to worry about. The suspicions about Brown quickly
eased because he was a formidable hitter. He and Johnson
shared third base. Joe Page came up with a nickname for him:
"Quack." Coleman was also hitting consistently and had never
felt stronger. He choked up so far on the bat that his teammates named him "Half-a-bat." But he felt he did not know
how to play second base—he didn't know how to make the
pivot. He was certain he was going to be sent back to Newark
with orders to learn to play second. The veterans watching
him were impressed. Phil Rizzuto, the veteran shortstop, knew
from the very start: Coleman was a natural; his play around
second was instinctive, combining exceptional grace with acro-
batic skill. He also threw a soft, feathery ball, which made
things easier for Rizzuto. Even more important, Coleman had
exceptional range, and this augmented Rizzuto's range; it
meant that with certain right-handed hitters, Coleman could
play very near second base, and that allowed Rizzuto to play
deeper in the hole between short and third. Rizzuto was
thrilled by the prospect of playing every day with Coleman
and was amused that the one person who did not seem to
know how well he was doing was Coleman himself.

Rizzuto could understand the rookie terror that seemed
to engulf Coleman. It was always hard on rookies in the
spring, he thought, although in the nine years since he had
broken in, there had been a gradual improvement in the way
veterans treated them. When Rizzuto had first come up, at age
twenty-three, he was the smallest man in camp. They weren't
even going to let him into the clubhouse. Only a last-minute

intercession by Lefty Gomez had saved him. He was perceived as the possible usurper of Frank Crosetti's job, and the Crow was a popular veteran. Rizzuto was given a locker between Red Ruffing and Bill Dickey, two immense, powerful men, particularly in the eyes of someone as small as Rizzuto. Neither said a word to him. Days passed in silence. Even worse, during batting practice no one would let him hit. Whenever it was his turn, some husky veteran would muscle him aside. It stopped after a week only because Joe DiMaggio came to his defense. "Let the kid hit," he said, and the harassment was over. Later that year, after Rizzuto was established as the regular shortstop, Joe McCarthy took him aside and said, "Rizzuto, I saw what was happening out there. I could have stopped it anytime I wanted. But I wanted to see what kind of stuff you were made of. The truth is, you should have been more aggressive. How are you going to deal with these other teams if you can't deal with your own teammates?" Now Rizzuto watched Coleman with sympathy. He'll be the last one to find out, Rizzuto thought.

One day near the end of spring, Joe Trimble, a sportswriter for the *Daily News,* came up to Coleman and asked him to autograph a baseball. It was the ball signed by all the regular players who had made the big club. "Are you sure you want me to sign this, Mr. Trimble?" he asked. "Hey kid," Trimble answered, "relax, you're going to make the club." That was the way Coleman found out he was a Yankee. He would be paid $7,500 a year instead of $5,000 if he was still with the Yankees on June 1, which was the big day. His promotion ended one phase of terror and began another, the haunting fear that at some critical moment in some crucial game he would fail and cost the Yankees the game and possibly the pennant.

The most serious problem for the Yankees in 1949 was that its famous stars were clearly aging. The team had been known to fans and writers in the late thirties and forties by the names of its three great outfielders—Keller, Henrich, and, of course, the greatest of them all, DiMaggio. The three had constituted one of the best and most versatile outfields of modern baseball, and the names were given as one might give the batting order: Henrich-Keller-DiMaggio. But now Henrich was thirty-six, Keller would turn thirty-three during the season, and DiMaggio would turn thirty-five at the end of it. Keller's body was already giving out on him; he had ruptured a disk in his back during the 1947 season, and had not received proper medical care because of management's desire to keep him in the pennant race. His lower body had been allowed to atrophy: in 1949 he was experiencing constant back problems and could play only part-time.

Even more upsetting were DiMaggio's injuries. It was clear that his body was wearing down. He was thirty-four, and had wartime not interrupted his career, this would have been his fourteenth year as a major leaguer. He had played hard, punishing his body more than most bigger men do, particularly in the way he slid into the bases. Now his body was rebelling. His left heel was operated on in January 1947, and a three-inch bone spur was taken out. He arrived at camp that year weak and underweight, with his leg muscles atrophying. Then, in 1948, he started to feel acute pain in his right heel in the second week of the season. An X ray of it showed a bone spur about an eighth of an inch long. Bone spurs are not unusual for people who are on their feet a great deal, nor are they necessarily dangerous. But for someone who could not rest his feet, and who instead aggravated the problem with hard running, stopping, and sliding, they were a source of almost unbearable pain. DiMaggio should have gone to the hospital immediately.

But the Yankees were the defending champions, and DiMaggio was their most important player. So he played. The problems with his feet forced him into compensatory injuries, and his knees and thighs ached by the end of the season. In November 1948, the season finally over, he underwent an operation to remove the spurs. He stayed on crutches for six weeks in order to rest his foot. When he finally tried to walk without the crutches, he felt better. But in February 1949 the pain started to return. As spring training was about to begin, it was obvious that either he was recovering more slowly than in the past, or the operation had not been a complete success. *Times* reporter John Drebinger was already speculating in print whether DiMaggio would ever play again. "It is," he wrote, "a pretty solid conviction that DiMaggio will never again be the DiMaggio of old."

Upon arrival at the Yankee camp in Florida, DiMaggio was in severe pain. He was flown immediately to Baltimore. There his doctor said the pain came from a normal thickening of the heel and would eventually disappear. Casey Stengel, worried for the first time, told DiMaggio to work out according to his own schedule. He played only forty-three innings that spring, and never hit a ball hard. Every day the pain got worse and limited his activities even further. He could not dig in when he came to bat. Because of his inability to put pressure on his heel, his leg muscles were atrophying once again. DiMaggio's doctor and one of the trainers made adjustments on his shoes, and he tried to work out a new schedule, one that would allow him to hit while minimizing the amount of running.

DiMaggio had become a desperate man, yet he kept his desperation to himself, as was his manner. His career hung in the balance. He tried everything: whirlpool baths, heat treatments, sponge rubber heels as special cushions, and, finally, the removal of the spikes from his right shoe. By early April he could not run at all, and on April 13 there was the most ominous headline imaginable in *The New York Times:* JOE DIMAGGIO TO MISS YANKEE OPENER.

As the pain grew worse, mere walking became painful, and the measures to protect him became more elaborate. The Yankee trainers concocted a complicated new device for his street shoes—a leather arch support, nailed between the ball of the foot and the heel on the *outside* of the shoe. As the team swung through Texas prior to going north for the start of the season, it became less a matter of whether he could play, and more a matter of whether he could walk. At a game in Beaumont, Texas, he limped off the field after a few innings, his face contorted by the pain.

DiMaggio was then subjected to four hours of tests. He emerged from the prolonged session with the doctor, in the journalistic vernacular of that day, "solemn and grim visaged." The condition of DiMaggio's heel was "hot," that is, it was hot to the touch. There was much conjecture in the daily newspapers about whether the Yankees, a notoriously cheap organization, would pay DiMaggio's salary for the year. Del Webb, one of the Yankees owners, a man then in his seventies, had flown to Texas for the exhibition games there, and he accompanied DiMaggio to his meeting with the doctor. During the session the doctor took X rays of the backs of both Webb and DiMaggio. Later he showed both photos to Webb. "This," he said, holding up the two photos, "is the X ray of the body of a young man, and this is one of the body of an older man." Webb said that was perfectly understandable. "Unfortunately," the doctor continued, "the X ray of the body of the young man is yours, and the one of the older man is your young player's."

DiMaggio flew immediately to Johns Hopkins, thinking he might undergo another operation. Because of his status as the nation's number-one athletic hero, there was a horde of writers and photographers waiting for him at the airport. He had traveled to Baltimore on a fatiguing series of flights in old-fashioned prop planes; on one leg of the journey he had flown through a terrible series of storms. Almost everyone on the plane, including DiMaggio, had thrown up. When the plane finally landed he looked at himself in a mirror in the airplane washroom. He was shocked by the white-gray color of his face and the hollow look to his eyes. He was in no mood to face either reporters or photographers. The questions were all the same anyway: Joe, how's the heel? Joe, what are the chances of recovery? And the worst question of all: Joe, do you think this is it? Do you think it's all over? Again and again he heard that last question. It was, he believed, like asking a man who had just suffered a heart attack, "When do you expect to die?"

At the hospital they quickly prepared him for emergency surgery, strapping him to a table. Out of the corner of his eye he saw a man in street clothes coming at him. Suddenly there was a camera. Then the pop of a flashbulb. DiMaggio finally exploded. "Look," he yelled, "I've always played ball with you. Why did you have to do that right now? What's my family going to think if they see a picture of me like this?" That was a rare outburst for a man who prided himself on being in control.

*   *   *

Joe DiMaggio was the most famous athlete in America. In fact, he seemed to stand above *all* other celebrities. Soon after he retired as a player, he returned with a group of friends to the Stadium to watch a prize fight. He was with Edward Bennett Williams, the famed trial lawyer, Toots Shor, the saloon-keeper, Averell Harriman, the politician-diplomat, and Ernest and Mary Hemingway. Suddenly an immense mob gathered. Hundreds of kids, a giant crowd within a crowd, descended on DiMaggio demanding autographs. One kid took a look at Hemingway, whose distinctive face had graced countless magazine covers. "Hey," the kid said, "you're somebody too, right?" Hemingway said without pause, "Yeah, I'm his doctor." For even Hemingway, then at the height of his fame, could not compete with DiMaggio. Endless magazines sought DiMaggio's cooperation to place his picture on their covers. Already two hit songs celebrated his deeds and fame: a light ditty about "Joltin' Joe DiMaggio," commemorating his 1941 hitting streak ("Who started baseball's famous streak/That's got us all aglow?/He's just a man and not a freak/Joltin' Joe DiMaggio . . ."); and "Bloody Mary" from the 1949 hit musical *South Pacific* ("Her skin is tender as DiMaggio's glove . . ."). Still to come was a generous mention in Hemingway's *The Old Man and the Sea:* Manolin fears the Indians of Cleveland, but Santiago, the older man, reassures him: "Have faith in the Yankees my son. Think of the great DiMaggio."

His deeds remain like a beacon to those who saw him play. More than thirty years after DiMaggio retired, Stephen Jay Gould of Harvard, one of the most distinguished anthropologists in the United States, was still fascinated by him. He had first seen him play in 1949, when Gould was seven. Opening Day, he wrote in an essay for *The New York Times,* is not merely a day of annual renewal, "it evokes the bittersweet passage of our own lives—as I take my son to the game and remember when I held my father's hand and wondered whether DiMag would hit .350 that year."

Gould discovered that another Harvard professor, Edward Mills Purcell, a Nobel physicist, was also fascinated by DiMaggio. Purcell had run most of the great baseball records through his computer looking for any statistical truths they might produce. The computer responded that all but one were within the range of mathematical probability: that someone (Babe Ruth) would hit 714 home runs, that someone (Roger Maris) would one day come along and hit 61 home runs in one season, and that even in modern times a player (Ted Williams) might on occasion bat .406. But the one record that defied all of Purcell's and his computer's expectations was DiMaggio's 56-game hitting streak in 1941. A .400 hitter, after all, could have a bad day and compensate the day after. But to hit in 56 straight games challenged probability, Purcell noted, because of the difficulty of hitting a small round ball traveling at a great speed with a wooden cylinder—"and where if you are off one eighth of an inch a hit becomes a pop-up."

Purcell's description of the difficulty of batting was strikingly similar to one that DiMaggio himself gave after a game in St. Louis. "You know," he told Red Patterson, the traveling secretary, as they rode to the train station, "they always talk about this being a game of fractions of an inch. Today proved it. I should have had three home runs today. I knew I was going to get fastballs and I got them and I was ready each time. But I didn't get up on the ball—I hit it *down* by that much [he held his thumb and index finger about an eighth of an inch apart and then touched them just above the center of the ball]. If I got under them that much [he lowered his fingers just slightly *below* the middle of the ball], I get three home runs."

DiMaggio had size, power, and speed. McCarthy, his longtime manager, liked to say that DiMaggio might have stolen 60 bases a season if he had given him the green light. Stengel, his new manager, was equally impressed, and when DiMaggio was on base he would point to him as an example of the perfect base runner. "Look at him," Stengel would say as DiMaggio ran out a base hit, "he's always watching the ball. He isn't watching second base. He isn't watching third base. He knows they haven't been moved. He isn't watching the ground, because he knows they haven't built a canal or a swimming pool since he was last there. He's watching the ball and the outfielder, which is the one thing that is different on every play."

Center field was his territory—right center and left center

too—for most of his career. The other outfielders moved into
his domain with caution. At the tail end of the 1948 season
Hank Bauer was brought up from the minors and he chased,
called for, and caught a ball in deep-right center field. Between innings in the dugout, Bauer noticed DiMaggio eyeing
him curiously. "Joe, did I do something wrong?" the nervous
rookie asked. "No, you didn't do anything wrong, but you're
the first son of a bitch who ever invaded my territory," DiMaggio said. It was not a rebuke, but Bauer deeded over more of
right center in the future.

DiMaggio complemented his natural athletic ability with
astonishing physical grace. He played the outfield, he ran the
bases, and he batted not just effectively but with rare style. He
would glide rather than run, it seemed, always smooth, always
ending up where he wanted to be just when he wanted to be
there. If he appeared to play effortlessly, his teammates knew
otherwise. In his first season as a Yankee, Gene Woodling, who
played left field, was struck by the sound of DiMaggio chasing
a fly ball. He sounded like a giant truck horse on the loose,
Woodling thought, his feet thudding down hard on the grass.
The great, clear noises in the open space enabled Woodling to
measure the distance between them without looking.

He was the perfect Hemingway hero, for Hemingway in
his novels romanticized the man who exhibited grace under
pressure, who withheld any emotion lest it soil the purer statement of his deeds. DiMaggio was that kind of hero; his grace
and skill were always on display, his emotions always concealed. This stoic grace was not achieved without a terrible
price: DiMaggio was a man wound tight. He suffered from
insomnia and ulcers. When he sat and watched the game he
chain-smoked and drank endless cups of coffee. He was ever
conscious of his obligation to play well. Late in his career,
when his legs were bothering him and the Yankees had a comfortable lead in a pennant race, a friend of his, columnist
Jimmy Cannon, asked him why he played so hard—the
games, after all, no longer meant so much. "Because there
might be somebody out there who's never seen me play before," he answered.

To DiMaggio, how people perceived him was terribly important. In 1948 during a Boston–New York game, Tex

Hughson, who liked to pitch him tight, drilled him with a fast-ball in the chest. It was obvious to everyone in both dugouts that the pitch really hurt. Even as he was hit, Joe McCarthy, by then the Boston manager, turned to his own players and said, "Watch him, he won't show any pain." Nor did he.

During the 1947 World Series, in a rare outburst of emotion, he kicked the ground near second base after a Brooklyn player named Al Gionfriddo made a spectacular catch, robbing him of a three-run home run. The next day while he was dressing, a photographer who had taken a picture of him kicking the ground asked him to sign a blowup of it. At first DiMaggio demurred and suggested that the photographer get Gionfriddo's signature. "He's the guy who made the play," DiMaggio said. But the photographer persisted, and so reluctantly DiMaggio signed it. Then he turned to a small group of reporters sitting by him. "Don't write this in the paper," he said, "but the truth is, if he had been playing me right, he would have made it look easy."

Ted Williams, himself caught in endless comparisons with DiMaggio, once said that the difference between the two of them was that DiMaggio did everything so elegantly. "DiMaggio even looks good striking out," Williams said.

Theirs was a rivalry that existed in the minds of their fans, in the minds of their teammates, and, though never admitted by either of them, in their own minds. Williams was, perhaps, the more generous of the two. Clif Keane, the Boston sportswriter, once went to New York in the late forties to cover a fight. He was staying at the Edison Hotel, which was DiMaggio's residence. Traveling with him was a friend who was a great fan of DiMaggio. Keane called DiMaggio and asked if they could come up. DiMaggio said yes. "Joe," asked Keane's friend almost as soon as they were inside the room, "What do you think of Ted Williams?" "Greatest left-handed hitter I've ever seen," DiMaggio answered. "I know that," said the man, "but what do you think of him as a *ballplayer*?" "Greatest left-handed hitter I've ever seen," repeated DiMaggio.

Unsure of his social skills and uncomfortable in any conversation that strayed far from baseball, DiMaggio was wary of moving into a situation in which he might feel or reveal his limitations. He did not push against certain New York doors that would have readily opened for him in those years. Some of his close friends thought the reason for his behavior was his sensitivity about being an Italian immigrant's son in an age when ethnic prejudice was far more powerful than it is today. In 1939, *Life* magazine did a piece on him that its editors thought sympathetic but which said, among other things, "Italians, bad at war, are well suited for milder competition, and the number of top-notch Italian prize fighters, golfers and baseball players is out of all proportion to the population." *Life* found the young DiMaggio to be better groomed than expected for someone who was not a Wasp: "Instead of olive oil or smelly bear grease, he keeps his hair slick with water. He never reeks of garlic and prefers chicken chow mein to spaghetti . . ." In fact, he was meticulous about his appearance, and unlike most of his teammates, who dressed casually in sports clothes, he almost always came to the ball park in a custom-tailored dark-blue suit, with a white shirt and tie. His overcoats were tailored as well, and he even took his army uniforms to be tailored during World War II.

He was spared the normal, crude byplay of the locker room. The other players were aware that he did not like it, and they did not dare risk displeasing him. (About the only person who could tease DiMaggio was Pete Sheehy, the clubhouse man, who seemed to be as much a part of the Yankee scene as the Stadium itself. Once when DiMaggio had been examining a red mark on his butt, he yelled over to Sheehy, "Hey, Pete, take a look at this. Is there a bruise there?" "Sure there is, Joe, it's from all those people kissing your ass," Sheehy answered.)

DiMaggio's sensitivity to being embarrassed never diminished. He carried for no short length of time a grudge against Casey Stengel because Stengel, during the 1950 season, dropped him in the batting order from the cleanup position to the number-five slot, and told him to play first base, a position where he was not comfortable. His teammate Tommy Henrich noticed that when DiMaggio came into the dugout from first base near the end of the game, his uniform was soaked with sweat. Henrich knew immediately that it was not the physical exhaustion that had caused the sweat—it was caused by tension from the fear of embarrassing himself.

After a game he would always linger in the locker room
for two or three hours, in order to avoid the crowd of fans
who waited outside the players' entrance. He simply needed to
sit in front of his locker, catch his breath, drink a beer, and
relax. Once he was sure there were no outsiders around, he
would conduct an informal seminar on the game just played.
In those moments he was absolutely relaxed and un-
threatened. He might turn to Shea. "Spec," he would say to
the young pitcher, "you have to stay with the game plan when
you go after the hitters. If you say you're going outside, stay
outside, don't cross us up. Otherwise we're going to end up
with a big gap out there. The other thing you were doing today is you were goosing the ball. Not really throwing it. Pushing it. Just throw it next time." "Phil," he might tell Rizzuto,
"you didn't get over quite quickly enough on that grounder in
the third inning. I know you made the play, but that isn't what
worries me. What worries me is you getting hurt. If you get
hurt, this team is in trouble. We can't afford it."

When he was sure that most of the crowd at the players'
entrance was gone, he would get ready to leave. The call
would come down to the gate people: "Joe's ready to go." A
taxi would be called and a group of attendants would form a
flying wedge so that he could get out with as little harassment
as possible.

Although DiMaggio was largely suspicious of newspa-
permen and reserved with most of them, his relationships with
them were actually rather good. The last line of the last column of the greatest sportswriter of two eras, Red Smith, concluded: "I told myself not to worry: Someday there would be
another DiMaggio." The writers were, of course, wired to
DiMaggio. They treated him as the White House press corps
might treat a wildly popular president. They understood the
phenomenon, what caused it and what made it work, and they
were delighted to be a part of it, mostly because their readers
wanted to know all about DiMaggio. Besides, the writers respected DiMaggio; for many of them he was the best all-
around player they had ever seen. He frequently carried the
team and he always did it modestly.

If DiMaggio wanted them at a distance, they readily accepted that. For one thing, even if he might not have been the

perfect interviewee (when he first came up, he was so un-sophisticated, he liked to recall, that when the sportswriters asked him for a quote, he thought they were talking about a soft drink), he was a gent. As he took his own dignity seri-ously, he generally accorded the writers theirs. On questions about *baseball*, he was generally candid. He was also aware of the uses of good publicity, and he was, if anything, closer to some of the writers, particularly the columnists, than he was to his teammates. He understood that if he gave too little of him-self, the press would rebel. He never upbraided a reporter who transgressed, as Williams did, but he was, in his own way, just as tough. If a reporter displeased him, even slightly, DiMaggio would ruthlessly cut him off.

W. C. Heinz, one of the best writers of that era, thought that his colleagues were different with DiMaggio from the way they were with other athletes. As they entered the Yankee locker room, they were cocky, brash, and filled with self-im-portance. Then, as they approached DiMaggio's locker, they began to change from men to boys. They became reverential, almost apologetic for even asking questions. You could, Heinz thought, hear the rustle of the paper in their notebooks as they steeled their courage to ask him how he felt.

DiMaggio had good reason for being suspicious of the press. In his first two seasons as a Yankee, he had been noth-ing less than brilliant, leading New York back to the pennant after a hiatus of three years. In his second season he hit .346 and 46 home runs, and knocked in 167 runs. He had been paid only $8,000 for his first year, and for his second, $15,000 plus, of course, his World Series checks, which Yankee man-agement viewed as part of his salary. For his third year he decided to ask for $40,000. The Yankees offered him $25,000. Ed Barrow, the general manager, told him that $40,000 was more than the great Lou Gehrig made. "Then Mr. Gehrig is a badly underpaid player," DiMaggio answered. The Yankee management turned its full firepower on him. This was the Depression, and, typically, the ownership did not view the question in relation to how much money the Yankees had made, or to how many millions Colonel Ruppert was worth, but rather to DiMaggio's salary as measured against the wages of the average American.

The assault was surprisingly harsh. He was privileged and spoiled. "DiMaggio is an ungrateful young man and is very unfair to his teammates to say the least," Colonel Ruppert said. "As far as I'm concerned that's all he's worth to the ball club, and if he doesn't sign we'll win the pennant without him." Then Ruppert added: "Is it fair for him to remain home while the other boys are training down South? No! Absolutely no!" DiMaggio himself remained adamant, which made Ruppert angrier. As the holdout progressed he added, "I have nothing new on DiMaggio. I've forgotten all about him. Presidents go into eclipse, kings have their thrones moved from under them, business leaders go into retirement, great ballplayers pass on, but still everything moves in its accustomed stride." Why, said the Colonel, if you included World Series checks, DiMaggio had averaged $20,000 a year since he came up.

Soon Joe McCarthy joined in: The Yankees, he said, could win without DiMaggio. No one came to DiMaggio's defense, not even the writers. The beat reporters, who had coveted his goodwill in the past, proved to be toadies to management. They helped turn the fans against him—he was often booed that year—and he learned the limits of his bargaining power the hard way. Finally, on April 20, with no leverage of his own, DiMaggio surrendered. He would come back at the salary he had been offered. The Yankees even tightened the screw: DiMaggio would have to get back into condition at his own expense and the Yankees would deduct $167 a day, his per diem salary, from his pay until he did. "I hope the young man has learned his lesson," Colonel Ruppert said.

Gradually the scar from the press's treatment of him during that holdout healed. Something of a pecking order developed in the way he treated writers: The beat reporters respected him, but except for Lou Effrat were not his pals; the grander figures of the time—such columnists and magazine writers as Jimmy Cannon, Tom Meany, and Milton Gross—might pal around with him. There was no danger that DiMaggio would cut off Jimmy Cannon. Cannon was at the height of his fame. He was forty years old and a columnist for the *New York Post*. In the late 1940s he was probably the most influential sports columnist in New York. He and DiMaggio were pals.

Unlike the genteel Red Smith, who wrote for the *Herald Tribune,* an upper-middle-class paper favored by Wall Street executives, Cannon was passionate. It was easy reading him, to know who were the good guys and who were the bad guys. The *Post* was blue-collar liberal, and its readers were baseball-obsessed. Cannon was the New York street kid as columnist—salty, blunt, with a style not unaffected by Hemingway. He loved being a sportswriter, he once told Jerome Holtzman of the *Chicago Tribune,* because "[he] spent most of [his] life at glad events as a sportswriter, amid friendly multitudes gathered for the purpose of pleasure." Sportswriting, he also told Holtzman, could be either the best writing or the worst writing in the paper. How do you know when it's bad? Holtzman asked him. "You feel the clink," he answered.

The son of a minor Tammany politician, Cannon grew up in a cold-water flat alongside the docks on the west side of Greenwich Village. He went to high school for one year, never attended college at all, but was a voracious reader, so much so that his family warned him he would damage his eyes. A wonderful sense of the city, the sharpness and edginess of its life, ran through his writing. He loved Damon Runyon, always dapper, with his wonderful collection of suits, and his three carnations—one red, one white, one blue—which were delivered every day. He emulated him, eventually becoming Runyon's hand-picked successor as a chronicler of the raffish side of the city. Indeed, he loved to quote Runyon about a mutual friend: "He's out hustling, doing the best he can. It's a very overcrowded profession now." Runyon had once been a heavy drinker, and he had taught Cannon, the latter said, to drink a bottle of brandy a day. Eventually Runyon stopped drinking and warned his protégé that if he did not stop "you're going to end up a rumpot." For a long time Cannon did not heed that advice. As far as he was concerned he did not have a drinking problem because he did not drink in the morning. That was the dividing line.

By the late forties, though, Cannon did stop, and in his own words, "When I quit I took the title with me." Home, for much of his life, was two rooms in the Edison Hotel. Restless at night, his work done, he often made the rounds with Leonard Lyons, the *Post*'s gossip columnist. Lyons had a proscribed route: Shor's to "21" to Palm Court, and Cannon knew where he would be at all times. It was better than going to bed. Cannon and DiMaggio shared a special palship because they had a lot in common. Both of them were lonely, without family. They were both insomniacs, and they both liked to make the New York scene, Cannon with his regular date, the actress Joan Blondell, DiMaggio with some show girl. Cannon loved the moment they entered a nightclub, when everyone there gawked to get a look at this baseball god.

He wrote often and well about DiMaggio, and in the process he helped create not just the legend of DiMaggio as the great athlete but, even more significant, DiMaggio as the Hemingway hero, as elegant off the field as on it. Cannon was in awe of his friend, and he lovingly passed that on to his readers. The view he provided of DiMaggio was an uncommon blend of genuine intimacy and pseudo intimacy. Only the better qualities were worthy of mention, of course—those allowed near the star knew what to write and what not to write. Lou Effrat once was invited to spend a week with DiMaggio in Florida during the winter. It was a pleasant interlude, but near the end of his stay Effrat asked DiMaggio a question about his contract for the next year. "What are you doing, turning writer on me?" DiMaggio asked him. That ended the subject of contracts.

DiMaggio was not a man who boasted, but once, late in his career, he talked with a group of younger reporters and mentioned, almost shyly, that when he first came to the Yankees in 1936 the local newspapers were constantly criticizing McCarthy for finishing second. "Then we won three times in a row, and four times out of five," he said. He paused for a moment before adding, "I had something to do with that." It was a rare moment, thought Leonard Koppett, then a young sportswriter. DiMaggio had almost dared to be candid about his own abilities, wary as he always was of appearing to boast.

DiMaggio was aware that he was often a virtual prisoner of his own shyness. Some of his friends thought this was due to his fear of embarrassing himself. But it was also an innate reserve.

Once, early in his career, he was sitting with a few writers at Toots Shor's when his friend Lefty Gomez, the most gregarious Yankee of that era, dropped by. Gomez did not join the table but stood and told a few stories, all of which delighted his listeners. DiMaggio watched him leave and then said, "What I'd give to be like that."

On another occasion at Shor's, he told Lou Effrat to stick around. "I've got a date," he said, "and I need company." DiMaggio's date turned out to be a young actress. After Shor's they went to "21" and then on to a few other places. Around three A.M. Effrat finally got away. The next day he asked DiMaggio why he had insisted that he stay around. "Ah, Lou, you know me," DiMaggio answered, "until midnight with girls I'm speechless."

The stories of DiMaggio's reserve were legendary. When he first joined the Yankees, he drove from California to Florida with Tony Lazzeri and Frank Crosetti, two veterans, neither famous for being talkative. They passed the first two days of the trip without talking at all, and then Lazzeri asked DiMaggio if he wanted to drive. Only then did DiMaggio say he did not know how to drive. It was simply not a subject that had come up before.

The three of them hung out together a fair amount that year, and Jack Mahon, a reporter for the old INS, ran into them while they were sitting in the lobby of the Chase Hotel in St. Louis. The three, according to Mahon, were watching the other guests come and go. "I bought a paper and sat down near them and after a while became aware of the fact that none of them had a word to say to the others. Just for fun I timed them to see how long they would maintain their silence. Believe it or not, they didn't speak for an hour and twenty minutes. At the end of the time DiMaggio cleared his throat. Crosetti looked at him and said: 'What did you say?' And Lazzeri said, 'Shut up. He didn't say nothing.' They lapsed into silence and at the end of ten more minutes I got up and left. I couldn't stand it anymore."

His teammates did not resent DiMaggio's need to be private. Watching him play day after day, often under immensely difficult circumstances, they became the true advocates of his greatness. Some forty years later, Henrich, a proud, unsentimental man, would point out that when fans asked him to compare the Mantle and DiMaggio outfields, he always said that DiMaggio's was better "because we had the better center fielder." Then Henrich would point out an astonishing and revealing statistic about DiMaggio: By and large, such power hitters as DiMaggio have a high strikeout ratio. It is in the nature of the big swing. Reggie Jackson, for example, has almost four and a half strikeouts for each home run. Even Hank Aaron, a marvelous line-drive hitter whose power came from his wrists, struck out twice for every home run. Ted Williams, whose eyesight was as legendary as his concentration, struck out 709 times against 521 home runs. But Joe DiMaggio, Henrich pointed out, hit 361 home runs and struck out 369 times.

His teammates understood that he put extra pressure on himself to live up to the expectations of the media and the fans. They knew that he pushed himself to his limits both physically and emotionally to carry the team. That being the case, they appreciated that he was different, that he worked things out for himself. Once when he was going through a prolonged slump, Bill Dickey, by then the hitting coach, explained to Mel Allen, the broadcaster, what he thought DiMaggio was doing wrong. "How does Joe react to what you've just said?" Allen asked. "Oh, I haven't spoken to Joe yet," Dickey answered. "Why not?" Allen pursued. "A player like Joe, when he's in a slump, you don't go to him. You wait until he comes to you. First he tries to work it out himself. Then if he doesn't he'll let you know he's ready," Dickey answered.

DiMaggio rarely dined with the other players on the road, even Keller and Henrich, with whose names his was inextricably linked in a thousand box scores. He led the league, his teammate Eddie Lopat once shrewdly noted, in room-service. He sought out dark restaurants, where he would sit in the back, in a corner, so that he would not be recognized. If DiMaggio palled around with anyone on the team, it was usually the newer or more vulnerable players who hero-worshiped him and ran favors for him: there was Joe Page, the relief pitcher, whose behavior was erratic enough so that his place on the team was rarely secure; then, for a time, there was Clarence Marshall, the handsome young pitcher; and finally, at the end of his career, DiMaggio palled around with

Billy Martin. Martin began his friendship with DiMaggio by violating the most sacred rule of Yankee etiquette: *He* asked DiMaggio out for dinner, "Hey Joe, let's go to dinner tonight" a statement so startling, a presumption so great, that his teammates long remembered it. DiMaggio was so amused by him that he assented, and the two became friends.

Some DiMaggio hangers-on were known as his Boboes, the phrase then popular for caddies. One who was proud to be known as a DiMaggio Bobo was Lou Effrat, the *Times*'s baseball writer. On occasion, Effrat would come in late to Toots Shor's, the main wateringhole of baseball men and sportswriters, to be told by Shor himself that his presence was requested. "The Daig [for "Dago," DiMaggio's nickname] wants you," Shor would say to Effrat. "What does he want?" Effrat would ask. "He wants to go to a midnight movie." Effrat knew the drill. He would finish his meal, give his wife ten dollars to get home, and join DiMaggio for a late movie. Mrs. Effrat was not invited. Women, particularly wives, never were.

DiMaggio himself squired a series of beautiful show girls, but he was very discreet about it. He never participated in the endless locker-room discussions about women. He made it very clear to his friends in the press that he wanted nothing written about this part of his life, and so nothing was written.

There was a contradiction to DiMaggio's shyness: He wanted to touch the bright lights of the city, but not be burned by them. When he made the scene, he was often seen with the most unlikely of his buddies—a man named George Solotaire. Solotaire, for a time, was his roommate and closest friend as well as his gofer. He ran his errands, took care of his clothes, and made sure that if DiMaggio did not want to go out to eat, sandwiches were brought in. Solotaire specialized in knowing where the action and the pretty girls were. He was also one of the city's top Broadway ticket brokers; he liked to boast that he had once supplied J. P. Morgan with a choice ticket for the same show for seven Saturdays in a row because he assumed that Morgan liked one of the show girls. Solotaire was forty-six years old, short, and stocky, and he spoke in his own Broadway shorthand: If he was out of money, he was in Brokesville; a boring show was Dullsville; a divorce was Splitsville; if he had to leave New York, he would tell friends he had to go camping for a few days; when he returned he would say that it was good to be back in the United States. He at one time wanted to be a songwriter, and wrote two-line jingles for the *Hollywood Reporter* that were, in effect, reviews of shows. Of a show with Ethel Merman he wrote: "The show is in infirm/but it's still got the Merm." Of *Fiddler on the Roof* he wrote: "Have no fear about *Fiddler*/This is a triple-A honest diddler." Writing these couplets, he said, was better than sitting around all day with Freddy or Gladys (tickets for rows F and G).

Solotaire was absolutely awed by his friendship with DiMaggio, and they became the odd couple. Those who thought they knew Solotaire well were often surprised to find out that there was a Mrs. Solotaire, who apparently considered herself happily married and was the mother of their son. Instead, friends remembered Solotaire with DiMaggio, sitting at dinner in the Stage Delicatessen, an unlikely father-son act, the meal passing but no words spoken. Once Solotaire called up a young woman named Ruth Cosgrove and suggested that she be part of a foursome for dinner with the Yankee star. When she arrived at dinner she was pleasantly surprised to find that Solotaire, whose manners were not exactly exquisite, was pulling back a chair for her to sit down. Then she realized that Solotaire was not holding the chair for her, he was holding it for DiMaggio.

Dining with Joe DiMaggio, Ms. Cosgrove felt, gave her a remarkable insight into the male animal. The entire restaurant came to a halt for two hours. The chair of every man was angled so that its occupant could keep an eye on her date. Each one, she noted, seemed to come up with an excuse for passing their table at least once. As for DiMaggio himself, she thought him kind and almost unbearably shy. He asked her out again, and she, who knew nothing about baseball, cemented their friendship by asking early in the evening, "Joe, what's an error?" With that he was finally able to talk.

The possible loss of DiMaggio for the season put a considerable chill on the Yankees as they headed north. They were hardly a one-man team, but it was comforting to know that in big games Joe DiMaggio would hit in the cleanup slot and play center field. Tommy Henrich thought his very presence gave the Yankees a considerable edge.

Years later Charlie Keller could still see DiMaggio batting against the best pitcher in the league, Bob Feller. DiMaggio seemed to summon extra adrenaline for such moments: the best against the best. You could actually see the veins and muscles in DiMaggio's neck stand out, Keller remembered. They were like taut red cords. His whole body was tensed. Bobby Brown recalled that on certain occasions when the Yankees really needed a run, DiMaggio would hit a ball that was not quite going to make the gap between the outfielders. Not much of a chance for a double on that one, Brown would think. Then he would watch DiMaggio go into overdrive, legs extended, going for two bases from the very start. He always made it. There might have been players in the league who were faster going to first base, but there was no player in those days who went from home to second or from first to third or from second to home faster, and no one could better calibrate the odds than DiMaggio. Years later, Frank Crosetti, who coached at third for much of DiMaggio's career, said that DiMaggio had never been thrown out going from first to third.

The team had been built around DiMaggio. The question now was how much it depended upon him. During the early part of spring training, before the seriousness of DiMaggio's ailment had been diagnosed, the Yankees and the Red Sox were considered virtually an even pick, with the Red Sox the slight favorite. By Opening Day a poll of 112 major baseball writers showed that 70 favored the Red Sox, 37 the Indians, 4 the Athletics, and 1 the Yankees. Grantland Rice wrote a column saying that, based on McCarthy's assurance that Hughson, Ferriss, and Harris were pitching well, he was picking the Red Sox. Harold Kaese, the *Boston Globe* baseball writer, after watching all of spring training, where the Red Sox looked more powerful than ever, predicted that the Red Sox would win an astonishing 124 games while losing only 30. That, he wrote, would tie them for first with the Indians. He saw the Yankees winning only 86 and losing 68, which put them 38 games out of first place.

For the first time in the DiMaggio years, the Yankees were afflicted with self-doubt, except for Stengel. After years of managing second-rate teams stocked with mediocre players, he could hardly believe the talent around him, even without DiMaggio. The backup outfielders—John Lindell, Hank Bauer, Gene Woodling (Woodling had led the Pacific Coast League in hitting with .385 the previous year), and Cliff Mapes—were good enough to play for most pennant contenders. The pitching staff was the best he had ever managed. "When I think of those other teams [I managed] I wonder whether I was managing a baseball team or a golf course—you know, one pro to a club," he told one friend.

The team arrived in New York for a three-game exhibition series with the Brooklyn Dodgers. Usually exhibition games did not mean much. But the Dodgers were not only intracity rivals, they were now of championship calibre—the Yankees had faced them in the 1947 Series. The Dodgers won all three exhibition games. The Yankees played badly, and the pitching, except in the first game, was ineffective. In the last game, with Allie Reynolds pitching, Jackie Robinson was on third base twice, and he taunted Reynolds with huge leads as if to say he could steal home anytime he wanted. It was Robinson's audacity that Henrich later remembered: He had seemed to toy with a team that, even though it had not won the year before, still thought itself the champions. Stengel was furious when the series was over: "All of you guys, when you get into the locker room I want you to check your lockers. He stole everything out there he wanted today so he might have stolen your jocks as well."

The next day the season was to start against Washington, and Charlie Keller called a team meeting. Keller was one of the quietest Yankees, but an intimidating man physically (given to picking up Phil Rizzuto with one massive arm and stuffing him in an empty locker when Rizzuto dared to call him "King Kong"). He was also a surprisingly gentle man, a farm boy who had gone to the University of Maryland.

After Keller's senior baseball season at Maryland, the scouts had moved in quickly on him. There were other offers, but to Keller there was something special about the Yankees; the mystique because of Ruth and Gehrig was already there. The Yankees gave him a bonus of $2,500, plus $500 so that he could go back to Maryland after the season and get his degree.

He was ticketed to play at a lower-level Yankee team in Nor-folk, but he hit so well in spring training that the Yankees assigned him to their AAA team in Newark.

At Newark Keller was an immediate star and helped lead the Newark Bears to two pennants in 1937 and 1938. On the occasion of the Bears' winning the International League pen-nant in 1937, Colonel Ruppert invited the entire Newark team to New York City for a party. Keller turned to Hy Goldberg, a local sportswriter, and said, "You know, Hy, it'll be the first time I'll have been to New York." Goldberg was stunned. "Charlie," he answered, "it's the greatest city in the world and it's only twenty minutes away and you're here a whole sea-son—how can you not have visited it?" "Oh, you know," Keller replied, "I'm a farm boy—I don't have any need for a city like that." Alien the city was, and alien it remained. There were too many people and there was not enough space. He thought it was particularly hard on his children. "Daddy," one of them said, "there isn't enough grass here, and when there is grass, the people won't let you play on it." That summed up the city as far as he was concerned.

His teammates admired Keller's strength of character. In the absence of DiMaggio, he was a senior player, and he had called his teammates together to exhort them: "If we play like we've played the last three games, sloppy and dumb, we're going to be the laughingstock of this league. We're going to be a joke to other teams because we're one team with Joe and another without him." Such words coming from Keller were sobering. Everyone listened. He is telling us, Henrich thought, that we are in danger of being perceived as a one-man team. There was shame in that.

CHAPTER 3

Tommy Henrich was stunned by Charlie Keller's talk. The burden was his, he decided. He would have to treat every game as if it were a big game. When he was a rookie he had talked about the pressure of World Series games with Red Rolfe, the third baseman. Rolfe had said, "When you play in a World Series, you either accept the challenge and do better than you normally do, or the pressure gets to you and you fall beneath your normal level." More than any member of the Yankees except DiMaggio, Henrich had a reputation for rising to the occasion. His nickname, used again and again by Mel Allen on the radio, was "Old Reliable." Henrich thought often about why he did well in critical situations. Part of it, he was sure, was his ability to concentrate. An equal part was pure adrenaline. The best analogy he knew was driving a car headed for an accident. Suddenly your reflexes were sharper, you saw better, and you had quicker reactions. Some people fell apart under pressure; others could use it constructively. Seemingly by luck, he was one of the latter. So was Bobby Brown, the young bonus player. For a million dollars in a tough situation, Henrich thought, Bobby Brown will not choke. He might cut down on his swing a little, he might protect the plate a little more carefully, but he would also become more determined.

Vic Raschi, a Yankee pitcher, was convinced that Henrich had learned concentration from playing with DiMaggio, and that he emulated DiMaggio's totality of concentration. For Henrich was unsurpassed as a clutch player: more dangerous in big games than small games, more dangerous in late innings than early ones, and more dangerous with men on base than with the bases empty. Just the year before, he had tied a major-league record of four grand-slam home runs in a season, and had almost broken that record when one of his late-season hits was called foul, a bad call in the eyes of most of the Yankees. Within the league he was known as one of the two or three best clutch hitters in baseball, a man who killed fastballs. ("How are you going to pitch to Henrich?" Zach Taylor, the St. Louis Browns manager, had asked Fred Sanford, then pitching for the Browns, in one close game in 1948. "I'm going to give him four fastballs," Sanford answered. "What the hell does that mean?" Taylor asked. "It means I'm going to walk him on four pitches," Sanford answered. "He hits me like he owns me.")

Henrich had always been a good player, one whose value belied the more ordinary quality of his statistics. He had come up through hard times, when Ed Barrow ran the team. After one season Henrich asked Barrow for a raise. Barrow replied by citing Henrich's batting average. It was quite disappointing, Barrow said. In fact, he was thinking of cutting him for the next year. Henrich stood his ground. "What do you want, a higher batting average for me personally or value to the team? Every day, every at-bat, I do what's good for the team, I move runners around, and I knock runners in. But if you want batting average I'll give that to you next year. It'll weaken the team, but you can have what you want." Barrow recanted and Henrich got a raise of $2,000.

But later, after Henrich sustained a serious knee injury, Barrow announced his unilateral decision of what Henrich's salary would be. Henrich protested, but Barrow explained to Henrich that he was damaged goods: "I'm afraid there's no guarantee that you'll be as good as you once were," Barrow said. "I think your job is to try and get yourself in shape and come to us in the spring and prove that you're worth this money we're paying you."

After the war, Henrich became, in his teammate Charlie Keller's view, a much better player. With maturity came confidence and a better sense of the game. Now, with DiMaggio out, Stengel was batting him cleanup. That had not happened before the war. He constantly studied and tried to refine his skills. When it was windy he liked to take extra fielding practice with Frank Shea, the best fungo hitter on the team. Most outfielders hated to practice fungoes on a windy day, because the wind made them look clumsy, but Henrich knew that that was precisely when he needed such practice.

Throughout his career, Henrich could be counted on to get the game-winning hit. There were no statistics kept in that department in that era, but it was an extraordinary performance: a player systematically rising above his level to help his team win. Henrich was not that strong, he was not that fast, and his arm was not that powerful. "You've lost some of your speed, Tommy," one of his teammates once told him. He answered, "I never had the speed I used to have but I get the job done." He had no illusions about himself or his abilities.

He epitomized the ballplayers born and raised in the America that preceded the New Deal. After World War II, in the homes of the large, burgeoning middle class, it was a virtual assumption that even mildly ambitious white males could go to college, even if their parents had not. But Henrich's generation had come from an America where a few people were rich, a few more were middle class, and a vast number were poor. Those who were rich stayed rich, and those who were poor stayed poor, for the most part, so no opportunity to get ahead could be squandered. At the start of the Depression, the average American salary was about $1,300 a year; in 1949, with the new postwar affluence just starting to affect the country, the average yearly salary was $3,000. The salaries ballplayers received were relatively small by comparison with what they would soon make—perhaps $15,000 for an average player on an average team. But this figure represented something dramatic: entry into the middle class.

Money could be saved, homes and farms could be bought, children's college funds could be started. Many of the players did save as much money as possible. In that era the athletes played through injuries for fear that if they stayed out too long, no matter how legitimate the reason, someone else might take their jobs. (Earl Johnson was a rookie with Boston in 1940, and he remembered coming in one morning and seeing Joe Cronin, the player-manager, stretched out on the trainer's table. The team doctor was operating on him—removing hemorrhoids, it turned out. When the operation was finished the doctor bandaged up Cronin, who then went out and played both ends of a doubleheader.)

Tommy Henrich, in his minor-league career, was *always* aware of how lucky he was to have this special skill that had lifted him out of the masses. He never forgot that when he signed his first minor-league contract, he was working at Republic Steel as a typist for $22.50 a week. That was not much, but, he liked to point out, in the Depression there were heads of families who made less. Baseball had been his one chance to get ahead in life. In the middle of his minor-league career, he had played for New Orleans, which even then was a party city. Ballplayers could always find someone to carouse with who would buy a drink for them. Because of that Henrich deliberately went to the ball park each day in his worst clothes, and he wore slippers instead of shoes. That was his way of fighting temptation. It was not about morality, it was about energy. The summer heat in New Orleans was deadly. An ordinary player could lose five or six pounds in one game. It took all of Henrich's energy to play his best. When his teammates asked him to go out with them after a game, he pointed to his shabby clothes; soon they stopped asking.

Of his four grandparents, two had been born in Germany and two were born here. He had been raised in a predominantly German neighborhood in Massillon, Ohio. German was still taught in the schools when he was a boy. His father, Edward Henrich, had been a good sandlot baseball player, and was secretly thrilled when his son Tom decided to try a career in baseball. As a boy Henrich played softball all day long. He later decided that one of the problems with Little League baseball as it developed after the war was that it became too organized and regimented. There was too much emphasis on manager dads and wearing uniforms. Once, after he made the big leagues, he asked his teammate Joe Gordon, "Joe, did you ever get fifty hits in one day?" Gordon thought about it, and said yes he did. "How?" Henrich asked, knowing the answer. "Well, if you were the best hitter, and you didn't have enough kids for two teams, you hit until you were out, so you could get fifty hits." "Same with me," Henrich said.

It had started when he was in first grade. He came out for recess, and his older brother, Eddie, who was in the fifth grade, was playing sock ball with his friends. In a poorer America, the ball was a knotted sock. "Can I get into the game?" Tommy asked. No, Eddie said, for his brother was too young. "Oh, come on, let him play, Eddie," someone else said. So he played and got a hit his first time up. From then on he was always in a game. His parents did not mind—their kids were out of the house all day long. There was no trouble except for the occasional broken window. Tommy and his brother, Eddie, often played right in front of their house, which was fine except that their mother knew exactly where they were and could call them in for dinner whenever she wanted: *Thomas, Edward, dinner!* Those words could break a game off at a crucial moment. Soon they switched to a nearby park, where she could not see them. But if they got back after dinner had been served, it was their job to heat it up and then do their own dishes.

If Tommy hung around long enough, and if they needed a player, he sometimes got to play with the seniors, who were sixteen and seventeen, and even with the adults in their games. Henrich had a clear memory of the first time he was ever let into a senior game. He was sixteen and it was a considerable event. He had asked the captain what position he was going to bat in. "Tom," the captain had said, "You'll bat eighth—you're my second cleanup hitter." "I was so green," he remembered long after, "that I believed him, too."

He played surprisingly little hardball then. He was smart, able, and hard-working, but, because of his background, there was no chance for college. Gradually he became too old for sandlot softball. When he turned twenty he was playing center field for a local hardball team for the first time. It wasn't even a semipro team, for semipro ball around Massillon was good— a lot of former major leaguers who could make more money playing for industrial teams than they could in the majors. Outlaw players, they were called. Henrich's team was the Prince Horn Dairy. They played on Saturdays and Sundays. Prince Horn did not pay the players, and if they practiced at all it was on weeknights after dinner. There was no time for anything else; all of them had jobs during the day.

A scout for the Indians named Bill Bradley saw him play, and in September 1933 he talked to Henrich about signing with the Indians. At first Henrich didn't take him seriously, but Bradley was insistent: This was real. He arranged a meeting with Billy Evans, the Cleveland general manager. Henrich was offered a hundred dollars a month to play at Zanesville in Class C. He was stunned. His only memory of talking was that he said, "Yes, sir." He never dreamed of playing pro ball, and now here he was signing a contract.

Henrich worked hard to stay in shape during the winter by playing basketball and hockey, and when spring arrived he drove to Zanesville, nervous about his tryout. He never forgot his first time up—how tight he was, how much he was concentrating on the need to get a hit. He was sure that the pitcher would be very fast because this was the pros. As a result, he swung way ahead of the pitch. Then he forced himself to relax and just go with the pitch. He was the last player cut from the roster; he had hit well, near .330, but they sent him down to their Class D team in Monessen, Pennsylvania. At Monessen his pay was cut to $80 a month, but he had a good year, hitting .326 and 15 home runs. He knew he was going to go up the ladder. The next year he was raised to $125 a month, played at Zanesville, and did well again. Now, for the first time, there was a real possibility of playing in the major leagues. A player named Lee Gamble from Monessen had made the majors, and Henrich did not think that Gamble was that good. The year after that, 1936, he was in New Orleans, and he loved being there. He played for Larry Gilbert, who was like a father to him. When he went to bat the first time that year, the first pitch was a curve. Henrich thought to himself, Oh a curve on the very first pitch—I'm with the big boys now. He hit .340 that season, and he loved it all—he simply could not wait to get to the ball park. Years later, Red Smith, the great sportswriter, would say of Henrich that he had never

known of any other player who took more sheer pleasure in
playing the game.

There was a mistake in his contract, a glitch. The Indians
were accused of trying to cover him up in the minor leagues.
By chance he became a free agent that winter and suddenly
there were seven other major-league teams trying to sign him,
including the New York Yankees. As a boy he had always
loved the Yankees. When he was eight years old he had
bounced a rubber ball off the front steps in an invented game.
If he caught the ball, the batter was out. If he missed it, the
runner got on. It was the Yankees of Ruth and Gehrig who
always won.

The team that wanted to sign him most desperately was
the St. Louis Browns. They not only offered more money but
guaranteed his father that he would play every day. The Yankees made no such commitment. But it was the Yankees he
chose—it was the team that all the best players wanted to join
because of those magical ingredients: tradition, class, and excellence. The Browns were forty-four and a half games out of
first that year. "The Browns will play you every day, Tom," his
father had countered. "But suppose I'm a good ballplayer and
I end up with the Browns," he answered, "then I'll always be
unhappy and I'll always blame myself for not going with the
Yankees. I'll always wonder whether I should have bet a little
more on myself." His father listened and told him to bet on
himself and sign with the Yankees. Tom Henrich never
doubted that he had made the right choice.

That summer Joseph Lelyveld was a sixth-grader in New
York City. A serious Yankee fan, he owned some thirty books
on baseball. All his allowance went to the *Sporting News* and
assorted baseball magazines, and his most prized possession of
all was an autographed copy of Joe DiMaggio's autobiography,
Lucky to Be a Yankee. He knew all the baseball statistics, past and
present. He collected cards, and in his room, on the bulletin
board, were autographed photos of the Yankee team that were
bought at the Stadium.

When he took piano lessons in 1948, on the Upper West
Side of Manhattan, he found out that his teacher's apartment
was near that of the great Babe Ruth. After his lesson, he

would run outside the apartment building at Eighty-third and Riverside, hoping for a glimpse of the Yankee slugger. Ruth, in failing health at the time, never did make an appearance.

He had become interested in baseball in 1946 when his family had moved to New York from the Midwest. Lonely and unsure of himself, in a new school where the kids seemed to be much tougher, he found order and symmetry in the universe of baseball as he did not in the world around him. Besides, not very far from where he lived was Yankee Stadium. His father, later a prominent rabbi in the civil rights movement, was certainly not a fan. His parents tolerated his obsession, but did not encourage it. They hoped he would grow out of it.

Technically his favorite player was DiMaggio, the greatest of Yankee stars, but DiMaggio was a god, far too great to identify with. So he chose Tommy Henrich as his favorite player. Henrich was clearly one of Mel Allen's favorites—Old Reliable, in Allen's phrase. The articles about him in *Sport* magazine were always complimentary; they told that he was a good family man and that he was respected by his teammates.

That spring, with DiMaggio ailing, Henrich had to carry the team, and Lelyveld tried to help him do it. He did it by creating a ritual in which he could, through fierce concentration, help Henrich to hit home runs at critical moments. He would sit in his room with the radio on, listening to Mel Allen. He was not to be interrupted. He had a calendar with the Yankee schedule, and slowly, as the game progressed, he would ink out a proportionate amount of the small square of that day. If four and a half innings had passed, he would ink out half of the square. As the game progressed he would ink out more. The inking he thought was important, for there was a certain finality to it—he was closing off the game.

When Henrich came up in a clutch situation Lelyveld would put his glove on and bounce a ball off the wall. Then he would look out the window at the New Jersey side of the Hudson. There, right across the river, was a huge Spry factory with the company's name in flashing lights. At the moment Henrich hit, he would look at that sign. Lelyveld used his powers carefully and he was not promiscuous with them; he did not seek unnecessary home runs that merely added to Henrich's statistical prowess. In that sense he was like his hero

himself. But when Henrich came up in the late innings with
the game tied, or when the Yankees were a run or two behind,
Lelyveld turned on his full powers. His eye did not wander
from the sign. He did not drop the ball. His powers were
nothing less than phenomenal. (He tried the same ritual, he
once admitted, with other players, but had nothing like the
success he enjoyed with Henrich's at-bats.) No wonder, then,
that Tommy Henrich had such a phenomenal spring; again
and again he got the game-winning home run or double, carrying the team in the absence of DiMaggio.

On Opening Day, Lou Boudreau, the Cleveland shortstop, once said, the world is all future, and there is no past.
The Yankee season opener was against Washington. There
were 40,000 spectators. Thomas E. Dewey, still a governor
and not the president after his defeat by Harry Truman the
previous fall, was there, but he did not throw out the first ball.
Joe DiMaggio was there, but in civilian clothes. He had gone
out by cab. Nearing the Stadium, he looked up to check the
flag. He always liked to see which way the wind was blowing,
and on that day it was blowing out. A hitter's wind, he
thought. Opening Day and a hitter's wind and I'm not playing. He had been on crutches the day before.
    The Washington pitcher was Sid Hudson, a good pitcher
who had the misfortune to play for one of the worst teams in
the league. He had lost 16 games the year before while winning only 4. Henrich liked Hudson and often teased him
about a game the two had played in a few years earlier. Hudson had been pitching in the ninth inning of a tie game. The
Yankees were up. There were two outs and a man on third.
Bill Dickey, one of the slowest men on the team, was the batter. The third baseman, Bobby Estalella, was back on the grass
when Dickey dropped down a beautiful bunt—a dead fish as
the players then called it—along the third baseline. Estalella
charged from third, but, even as slow as Dickey was, there was
no way he could throw him out. The only hope was for the
ball to roll foul. Unfortunately, Estalella, a Cuban and one of
the first Hispanic players in the majors, spoke little English.
Hudson yelled, "Let it roll." Estalella charged. "Let it roll!" he
shouted again. Dickey touched first base. Estalella scooped up

the ball. The game was over. After that Henrich always teased
Hudson about his Spanish. Hudson loses 15 or 16 or 17 games
a year, Henrich thought, but if he pitched for the Yankees, he
would win that many.

On this day Hudson was making it close. He was pitching
very well, especially against Henrich. In his first four trips to
the plate Henrich struck out once and altogether had
stranded six runners. He was a fastball hitter who wasn't
seeing any fastballs. In the ninth inning, with the score tied
2–2, Phil Rizzuto tried a bunt and was thrown out. Then Gene
Woodling popped up. That brought up Henrich, and for the
first time Hudson fell behind in the count. With 3 balls and 2
strikes, Henrich stepped out and looked at Hudson. All he
could think was fastball. This time, he thought, I'll see one. In
it came, and Henrich hit it into the right-field seats. The Yankees won 3–2. The next day, with Vic Raschi pitching against
Paul Calvert, Henrich hit a ball deep into the right center-field
bleachers to give Raschi the only run he needed. The Yankees
won again.

Thanks to Henrich, the Yankees had gotten off to a quick
start. It soon became obvious that another major asset was
their veteran starting pitchers: Raschi, Reynolds, and Lopat. If
the Yankee lineup was in transition that year, with an aging
outfield built around a crippled DiMaggio, then the pitching
staff had finally stabilized. It was a great starting rotation and
it had to be, because Cleveland, with Bob Feller, Bob Lemon,
Early Wynn, and Mike Garcia, was every bit as good. With
Boston the matchup was power hitter against power hitter, but
with Cleveland it was pitcher against pitcher. In those games
no one gave anyone an edge; both sides pitched tight and
hard. Once Allie Reynolds came in too tight against several
Cleveland hitters. Early Wynn, who was on the mound, sent
the word back through Yogi Berra that he was going to deck
Reynolds. "You tell Early go right ahead," Berra told Jim
Hegan, the Cleveland catcher, "but tell him to remember that
The Chief throws a hell of a lot harder than he does."

On another occasion Frank Shea was pitching for the
Yankees against Bob Feller. That day someone on the
Cleveland bench was riding Shea unusually hard. Without

showing that it bothered him, Shea called over Billy Johnson, the third baseman. "Billy," he said, "find out who it is who's busting my ass." A couple of minutes later Johnson walked over to the mound. "Spec, it's Al Rosen," he said. So when Rosen came up to bat, Shea knocked him down. Rosen picked himself up and Shea knocked him down again. Two innings later, Shea came to bat. "Spec, I wouldn't dig in too much if I were you," Hegan said. "Feller's pitching, Spec." In came the first pitch and it knocked Shea down. He picked himself up and started digging in. "Spec," said Hegan, "I think you ought to listen to me, and like I say I wouldn't dig in." "What do you mean?" Shea asked. "Well, Spec, how many times did you throw at Rosen? Twice, right?" In came the next pitch and it knocked Shea down again. "You're okay now, Spec, but just remember, we give back one for each one you throw."

In 1947, the Raschi-Reynolds-Lopat rotation had not existed. Reynolds had already come over to the Yankees and done well, but Lopat was still in Chicago, and Raschi had been a spot pitcher, a rookie brought up in mid-season, winning just 7 games. Then, in 1948, it had come together: Raschi had been 19-8 on 31 starts with 18 complete games; Lopat, 17-11 with 13 complete games and the lowest earned-run average of the three; and Reynolds, 17-6 with 11 complete games. They were a manager's dream, the power of Reynolds and Raschi contrasting with the soft, tantalizing pitches of Lopat, already known as the Junkman.

Reynolds was a formidable athlete, probably the best all-around natural athlete on the team. At college the track coach had tried to guide him to the track team and had spoken often of the Olympics; the football coach had fawned over him and he had even received a bid from a professional football team; and Hank Iba, the basketball coach, had tried to talk him into playing basketball. Sports always came easily to him—he was fast, strong, and agile. Once when he was a Yankee he drove out with Tommy Henrich for an evening of boccie ball at Yogi Berra's house. Henrich asked him how he thought he would fare. "Quite well," Reynolds said. Why was that, asked Henrich. "Because I'm good at all sports," answered Reynolds without any affectation. He was part Indian, suffered from diabetes ("the classic Indian disease," as he liked to point out), and had problems with his stamina. But his skills were so obvious, the only question was how best to use them.

Some hitters thought he threw as fast as Feller, and others thought he threw a curve almost as good as Feller's. Other pitchers were in awe. Johnny Sain, a wily pitcher short on pure power, came to the Yankees two years later. Once he sat in the dugout with Whitey Ford and discussed what he'd most want for a big game. "I'd like ten of Allie's fastballs." "How would you use them, Johnny?" Whitey Ford asked. "Whitey, I'd make them the first ten pitches I threw in the game," Sain answered, "and then make them guess the rest of the game if I was going to throw any more."

Yet when Reynolds first joined the Yankees, the results were not remarkable. Chuck Dressen, then a Yankee coach, decided that Reynolds was too tense on the days that he pitched. He decided that for his first start he should be given one shot of brandy as he warmed up, another when the game started, and a third in the third inning. That would loosen him up. Reynolds, who did not like to drink, could barely stand up by the third inning. From then on Reynolds wanted nothing to do with Dressen.

The Yankee management soon decided that his lack of stamina was not due to a bad attitude; if anything, Reynolds was too competitive and tried too hard in big games. Reynolds later reflected that he had arrived in New York as a thrower. But pitching and throwing were very different matters— throwers impress, pitchers win. Early on, Spud Chandler came over to him and told him that he was not putting out enough. Reynolds was annoyed by this and argued that he was. "No," Chandler said, "you think you're putting out, but you're not. You're not nearly mentally disciplined enough, and you're not aggressive enough. You could be a lot tougher." What Chandler was talking about, Reynolds soon figured out, was about knowing what to do at all times, so that he, rather than the hitter, set the tempo.

Charlie Keller helped him too. "Allie," Keller asked, "would you like to know the impression I have of you as a pitcher?" "Sure, Charlie," Reynolds said. "Do you remember the triple I hit off you in Cleveland that went down the right-field line?" he said. Reynolds remembered it. "It was hit off a curveball, right?" Keller said. Reynolds agreed. "Do you know I never saw another curveball from you," Keller continued. Reynolds realized Keller was right, that he had never thrown him another curve and that Keller was saying he had to vary his pitches more. Slowly but surely he learned to think, to use his curve, and to set hitters up. Soon he became one of the foremost pitchers in the league.

Eddie Lopat came over from the White Sox in a trade. Having him for a teammate, Reynolds thought, was like having an additional pitching coach. Many of his teammates thought Lopat was the smartest pitcher of his generation in the big leagues, a master at keeping hitters off-balance and using their power against them.

He was a converted first baseman who had become a pitcher in the minor leagues during the war. His friend Reynolds thought, and he did not mean it pejoratively, that if not for the war years, Lopat would never have made it to the majors. He did not throw particularly hard, and in normal times he would have been weeded out for lack of a fastball. At one point, in 1942, after six years in the minor leagues, Lopat had thought of quitting; he had been sold to the Chicago Cubs but the deal had not gone through. His wife talked him into giving it one more year. By that time he had done it all, traveled on every bad train in the South, and been paid a pittance again and again—$275 a month in Oklahoma City, where he knew he would not last very long because the team was so poor, always selling its players just to keep afloat. Then in Little Rock he held out for $400 a month, finally got it, and won 19 games.

That brought Lopat to the promised land, the Chicago White Sox in 1944. There, he learned the slow curve from Ted Lyons, and also how to throw both short-arm and long-arm versions of his pitches (by either extending his arms or holding them in), which gave him four basic pitches instead of two, allowing him to vary motions and speeds. He mastered the way to look as though he were driving off his legs with full power while actually he was taking much of the power off.

The batter's eye, after all, was on the ball and the pitcher's upper body; he did not see the pitcher's lower body, which was the key to a pitcher's power. And he picked up an additional deception: how to reduce the power in his pitch by taking the edge off the snap of his wrist.

Lopat was an even better pitcher in the major leagues than he had been in the minors. The more strengths the hitters had, the more he could use his intelligence and wide assortment of pitches against them. Ted Williams listed Lopat among the five toughest pitchers he ever faced, along with Whitey Ford, Bob Lemon, Bob Feller, and Hoyt Wilhelm. Invariably he referred to him in conversation not as Lopat but as "that fucking Lopat." Lopat was very proud of that. When he pitched against the massive Walt Dropo, the confrontation took on a certain circus quality. Because Lopat looked so easy to hit, Dropo was determined to crush his pitches. So Lopat threw him even softer stuff, and Dropo would be out seconds ahead of the pitcher. As, time and again, his at-bat was terminated by a weak grounder or strikeout, Dropo would curse Lopat. This occurred so regularly that Bobby Brown, the Yankee third baseman, could barely keep from breaking up with laughter every time Dropo came up.

Lopat took a special pride in his ability to pitch at a high level with none of the natural gifts of most front-line pitchers. From time to time Joe Page would needle him about his lack of speed. "Cutty-thumb," Page would call Lopat, the pejorative term for a slow-ball junk-ball pitcher. But since Lopat was probably the foremost of the team's needlers, these were verbal battles that Page rarely won. "Goddamn, you're right Joe, I do throw junk. But hell, anyone can go out there on the mound with the stuff you've got and win. But Joe, if you can get 'em out with the stuff I've got . . ." Here Lopat tapped his head. "That takes *brains,* Joe. Real brains. I'm sorry about it, Joe, I really am." Soon in deference to the sharpness of Lopat's tongue, Page stopped teasing him about his lack of power.

In February 1948 Lopat came home to find out that he was supposed to telephone a George Weiss.

"I don't know anyone named George Weiss," he told his

wife. "The only one I know is general manager of the Yankees."

He called Weiss. "Ed," said *the* George Weiss, "we have just traded for you and you're a Yankee."

"I guess that's all right," he said, which later struck him as a less-than-brilliant answer. Thereupon Weiss immediately suggested that Lopat come to spring training and sign a contract there. Lopat said that was fine as long as they agreed in advance on his salary.

"I don't want to go all the way down there and not sign and then come back," he said.

"That has never happened," Weiss said.

"Well, I would hate to be the first," Lopat answered. Lopat had made $14,000 the year before and asked for $20,000. After several days of hard negotiating they got quite close. Weiss wanted him to sign for $18,500 plus $1,500 in expenses, which at least kept his base-salary level down.

"That's more than a lot of pitchers here are making," Weiss said.

"Mr. Weiss, I don't care what they're making," Lopat said.

Weiss named a pitcher who had completed sixteen games the previous year and was making less.

"Mr. Weiss, I completed twenty-two games and was second in the league in earned-run average," Lopat said.

"How do I know you can pitch like that for a contending club?" Weiss asked.

"Mr. Weiss, I heard that kind of talk when I was a rookie. I can do it, and I'll keep on doing it," he answered.

"Well, what if our other pitchers find out how much you're making?" Weiss asked.

"Sir, if they find out it'll be from you—not from me," Lopat said, and got his salary.

With the Yankees, Lopat was helped by Carl Hubbell, the great Giant pitcher. Hubbell's own career had finished five years earlier; he was somewhat at loose ends and often came out to the Stadium to watch games. Lopat introduced himself, and the two became friends. Hubbell had thrown a brilliant screwball, a pitch that Lopat did not have in his repertoire, and which there was no point in learning now. But Hubbell taught him something very important: "Ed," he said, "when I was ahead I would sneak the fastball in, but when I was behind I threw the breaking ball, or the screwball." It sounded simple, but the idea lingered with Lopat. Brilliant, he began to think, absolutely brilliant in its simplicity. It was the complete reverse of what you are supposed to do. Every other pitcher in the league came in with the fastball when he got behind. That meant that hitters thought fastball. But Hubbell had been confident enough of his control to reverse the order. So Lopat reversed it too, and his success grew significantly. ("The trouble with that fucking Lopat," Williams said, "is that he selects his pitches ass-backwards.")

There was a wonderful cockiness to Lopat. Once during a pennant race with Cleveland, with the bases loaded and the Yankees ahead by one run, he faced Al Rosen with a 3-and-2 count. Rosen was a legendary fastball hitter, and he yelled out to Lopat, "You haven't got the guts to throw me your fastball, you sneaky little son of a bitch." Lopat reared back and fired his fastball. In it came, getting to the plate just a little behind time. Rosen swung mightily and missed. He was still righting his body when Lopat walked past him on his way to the dugout. He turned to Rosen and grinned, "That's my blazer."

The ace of the staff in 1948 might well have been Vic Raschi. On the days he pitched, even his own teammates were afraid to go near him. He seemed, in Lopat's phrase, like a bear who had missed breakfast. Allie Reynolds once said, "Vic pitched angry." He spoke to no one. Before the game he sat by himself getting angrier and angrier at whichever team he was supposed to face. He hated it when his infielders tried to talk to him during a game. He intimidated his catcher Yogi Berra. If Raschi was missing the plate, Berra was supposed to go out and talk to him. Raschi would have none of it. Even as Berra approached the mound, he would angrily wave him away. "Yogi, you get your Dago ass the hell back behind the plate," he would say. Or, "Yogi get the hell out of here with your goddamn sixth-grade education."

Raschi's sense of purpose had always been exceptional. In high school in Springfield, Massachusetts, he had been a prominent three-sport athlete. Despite his success as a school-boy pitcher, he was determined to go to college, and the Yankees were able to sign him only by promising to pay for his education. In his own mind his best sport was basketball, which he played at William and Mary. One of the conditions of his Yankee-endowed education was that he not play football. Basketball, the Yankees said without much enthusiasm, was permitted. In his freshman year he played center at six feet one and a half inches and did well, although he tore a tendon in his ankle near the end of the season. He was named All-State center after his freshman year. A member of the Yankee organization called him up, congratulated him on the award, and then mentioned the bad ankle and said, "Vic, that was a wonderful year, but no more basketball. The Yankees can't risk those injuries." Raschi had not been pleased—he had a vague sense that the Yankees were controlling him. He continued his education and contented himself by playing minor-league baseball at the same time. He did reasonably well in the Yankee farm system, served as a physical-fitness teacher for three years during the war, and got out in 1945.

In 1946 he was called up to the Yankees for the final days of the season. In his first appearance in the majors he pitched against the Philadelphia Athletics in the Stadium, and in the fourth inning he found himself in trouble with two men on and a tough batter up. Suddenly he heard a voice coming from somewhere nearby saying, "He can't hit a high fastball." Raschi stepped off the rubber and turned around, wondering who had said that. In those days there were only three umpires and so one of them had to go between second and the pitcher's mound with men on base. Bill Summers was bent over behind the mound. Raschi looked at him. Summers's head never moved. But the disembodied voice spoke again. "Yeah, you heard me right—he can't hit a high fastball." Then there was a brief pause, and he heard the voice again: "We Massachusetts boys have to stick together." So Raschi went to his high fastball and got the batter out.

The three pitchers were each other's friends, a team within a team. Reynolds and Lopat were particularly close:

They roomed together for seven years, though oddly enough, they did not know everything about each other. When Reynolds became player representative, it was his job to hand out the paychecks. At the first meeting Lopat ambled up to him. "Allie, you got one there for Lopatynski?" he asked. Reynolds thumbed through the checks. "Yeah," he said. "Who's Lopatynski?" "Me," said Eddie. The three reinforced and taught each other. They also shared a mutual concern for what they at times called "The Project," known to the others as "Bringing Up Yogi." As a rookie, Lawrence Peter Berra was subjected to unmerciful teasing because of his odd, chunky body to which arms and legs seemed to have been haphazardly attached. In 1946, when Berra came up at the end of the season, there was a Yankee–Red Sox game, and Charlie Keller started joking around with Red Sox pitcher Mike Ryba. Ryba, who was considered to be a less-than-handsome figure himself, had created what he called his All-Ugly team. Its playing captain, he had always claimed, was Charlie Keller, so powerful and hairy that his nickname (which he hated) was "King Kong." Keller took the ribbing from Ryba because he believed Ryba even uglier than he. When their teams played they always argued about who was on the All-Ugly team. "I've got a new playing captain for you," Keller told Ryba.

"There's no way, Keller," Ryba said. "There's no one uglier than you in baseball."

"Yes, there is," Keller said. Just then Berra came out of the dugout and walked past the two players. Ryba stared at him.

"I take it back, Keller," he said, "it's all over for you. You're off my team. You're no longer ugly enough."

He was the son of Pietro and Paulina Berra, Italian immigrants who lived on The Hill, which was the Italian section of St. Louis. The small houses there were well kept, and almost every one had a vegetable garden in back. The language spoken in his home was Italian, not English. His mother never learned to speak English. She called him Lawdie, which was her version of Lawrence. Pietro, who had come to this country as a bricklayer, had found work in a brick factory in St. Louis. Like many other immigrants, he

hated the idea of his son playing baseball, which, as far as he
was concerned, was a totally useless endeavor. He was convinced it was the cause of his son's poor grades in school.
Yogi played regardless, but he tried to keep his clothes
clean—his father would slap him if his clothes were dirty; if
he had gotten too grimy he would stop at a neighbor's house
and wash up, and, if necessary, change his clothes. His boyhood was an odd combination of life in the old world and
life in the new world. One of his primary responsibilities as a
boy was to have a fresh bucket of draft beer ready for Pietro
when he got home from work. When he heard the factory
whistle blow, he would race from his ball game to the
kitchen, pick up his father's can and fifteen cents, and dash
over to the local tavern. Berra did poorly in school—he had
almost no interest in it. His love was baseball. For a time he
took a job on a Pepsi truck, making twenty-five dollars a
week, all of which he turned over to his family and from
which he was given back two dollars.

People had always looked at him and had their doubts.
He didn't look right, didn't look like a ballplayer. When he
had wanted to turn pro as a boy, despite his success as a
schoolboy and sandlot player, his looks had been held against
him. He attended as many pro tryouts as possible, and
though his physical power was considerable, it was well
enough concealed by his odd physique that the scouts were
not impressed. Branch Rickey, usually brilliant at spotting talent, took one look at him and said, "That boy is too clumsy
and too slow." A triple A ballplayer at best, Rickey decided.

Still Berra was offered a contract and a bonus of $250 to
sign. He turned it down, and eventually signed with the Yankees for $500. When he played in his early years at Norfolk
he made $90 a week. He was still growing, and desperately
hungry all the time. His mother sent him a small money
order regularly so that he would have more money for food,
but warned him never to let his father know, or he would
make him come home.

Even when he finally proved that he could hit through
the minor leagues, his looks seemed to work against him.
There was a constant cruelty to the way he was treated. Rud
Rennie of the *Herald Tribune* once turned to Bucky Harris

and said, "You're not really thinking of keeping him, are you? He doesn't even look like a Yankee." Harris kept him but called him The Ape. He bore it all. He had heard the jokes before, and the one thing that had saved him was his ball playing. He was good at that, and because of his skill people had been forced to respect him.

Fortunately for Berra, Stengel fell in love with his talents, and realized he had to protect him before the locker-room baiting, which had a cruel edge, got out of hand. This was remarkable, for Stengel had a quick and sometimes cruel tongue himself. "My assistant manager Mr. Berra," is what he often called him to writers and other players, and there was no sting to it. One time, writers surrounded Stengel and started talking to him of recent Yogiisms. "I wish I had gone to college because then I could have been a bonus player," was one he had just told one of the writers. Normally Stengel encouraged banter of this kind. This time he cut it off. "He talks okay up there with a bat in his hands," Stengel said. "A college education don't do you no good up there."

Berra needed all the help he could get. He eventually became an All-Star catcher, and a Hall of Fame player, but in those days he was extremely unsure of himself. If he was batting and took a called strike, he would look over at the bench to see what Stengel thought. If he swung and missed, he would look over at Stengel as if to apologize.

Of his usefulness as a hitter, a left-hander in Yankee Stadium, there was no doubt. The Yankees gradually broke him into the lineup, but they could not figure out what position he should play. In 1947 it appeared that his future would be as a catcher. But then in the World Series Jackie Robinson humiliated him by stealing, it seemed, at will, and he did not seem to want to catch anymore. In 1948 he alternated between the outfield and catching. He hit 14 home runs and drove in 98 runs. But in one game he went into right center on a ball that was clearly DiMaggio's, and there had almost been a major collision. Since one of the unwritten laws on the team was that DiMaggio's body was precious, a decision was made not to risk another such accident. Berra would be a catcher.

Management brought Bill Dickey back to tutor him, for

Dickey had been a masterful catcher. He worked long hours with Berra, particularly on his footwork. Sometimes from a distance they looked like two dancers at an Arthur Murray's studio. Gradually Berra improved. The Yankee management was pressuring Dickey to give an answer, for if Berra could not do the job, they would probably have to engineer a major trade. "Can he do it, Bill?" George Weiss kept asking, and Dickey seemed to equivocate. Finally Dickey told Weiss, "Yes, he'll make it, and he'll be a pretty good catcher."

But there was so much to learn, and he was learning in the middle of a pennant race. In addition, the pitchers were uneasy with him. There were so many things he did wrong. For one thing, he did not know how to catch the ball. He tended to stab at the last minute, carrying the ball, in the eyes of Allie Reynolds at least, out of the strike zone. He was supposed to do the reverse—scoop the ball into the strike zone. "Don't stab, Yogi," Reynolds would say. "Reach out and bring it in." It was as bad with low curves—Berra seemed to grind them into the dirt. The pitchers were sure they were losing calls because of Berra, and they were not happy.

Then there was his throwing. To the dismay of the pitchers in situations where an opponent might steal, he called not the pitch that would work but rather the pitch that might help him throw out the runner—a high outside fastball against a right-handed hitter. Since opposing players were very much aware of this, it was like a death warrant to his own pitchers. Eventually the pitchers met among themselves and decided that *they* would call the pitches. One day he might be experienced and confident enough to call his own game, but for the moment they would teach him. They tipped off Yogi in different ways: Reynolds, for example, would go to his glove, or his belt, or his hat—changing signs regularly in a game. Yogi seemed agreeable. The only problem was that Casey Stengel, aware of Yogi's insecurity, also wanted to call the pitches in tight situations. This meant that at critical moments, Yogi might start looking at the dugout. The pitchers did not want that. For one thing, Stengel had not been a pitcher, and he did not necessarily know the right pitch at the right moment. But even worse, it broke Yogi's concentration. The pitchers wanted Yogi to see the game through *their* eyes, and to learn their reasons for each pitch. Reynolds told the others he would break Yogi of the habit.

Early in the season, late in a game against Philadelphia, there were runners on second and third. Reynolds could hear Stengel yelling from the bench, obviously wanting to give Berra a sign.

"Yogi," Reynolds yelled, "if you look over to the bench I'm going to cross you up."

That was no small threat: A fastball from Reynolds coming in to a catcher who was expecting a curve was a terrifying thought.

"You listen to me, Yogi," he yelled. "I'm dead serious."

In the background they could hear Stengel yelling even louder.

"Don't listen to him, Yogi," Reynolds yelled.

On the bench Raschi and Lopat were trying to keep from breaking up. But Yogi was paralyzed. It was as if he could give no sign, caught between these two powerful pulls. Everyone in the park, Reynolds thought, understood the test of wills going on. Stengel's voice seemed louder.

"Look at me, Yogi!" Reynolds shouted.

They could all hear Stengel yelling now. "Yogi, if you don't look over here I'm going to fine your ass."

What Yogi could not see, because he did not dare to turn, was that Stengel was holding up some dollar bills.

"Don't turn, Yogi," Reynolds ordered. "Just keep looking at me." Berra squatted down, seemed to take a final look at Reynolds, and nodded slightly. He did not turn to the dugout. All color was gone from his face. The fastball came in. The hitter struck out, the inning was over. The pitchers had won. It was, thought Raschi, a great moment of independence for the pitchers. The catcher was theirs, the rhythm of the game was theirs. It was also, thought Raschi, a major step in Berra's coming-of-age, liberating him from the manager.

Another source of tension was whether Yogi would be allowed to signal Stengel if he thought a pitcher was losing his stuff. He was supposed to pick up a small handful of dirt. Then Stengel would come out to the mound and eventually the pitcher would leave. But Reynolds and Raschi would have none of it. Reynolds told him, "Yogi, if I ever see you

give that sign again—ever, even once—I'll kill you. I mean it,
Yogi, I'll fight you in the clubhouse." Raschi was just as
tough: If Berra thought he was slipping a little and tried to
go out to the mound, Raschi would come right at him. "I
think you're losing it, Vic . . ." Berra would begin. "Yogi,
you'll lose your sorry ass right here if you don't get behind
the plate," Raschi would answer.

CHAPTER 4

The Red Sox started slowly. They opened in Philadelphia and lost to the A's when Lou Brissie beat Joe Dobson 3–2. The next day Ellis Kinder pitched against Joe Coleman. Both Kinder and Pesky made throwing errors, and the Athletics won again 3–2. Poor fielding had hurt Boston. It was an old story for the Red Sox: When their hitters hit, they won big, but if it was a close game, if the other team's pitching was good, then Boston's defense and its lack of bullpen were liabilities. They won the third game only because Mel Parnell pitched a shutout.

McCarthy was still wrestling with his lineup. All spring he had vacillated between Billy Goodman, whom he loved because of his attitude, his versatility, and his ability to hit to all fields, and the giant rookie Walt Dropo. Dropo had gone north with the club from Florida, but McCarthy's preference for Goodman was obvious to everyone. Dropo might be the power hitter of the future—some of his hits in the spring had been tape-measure jobs—but no one accused him of having soft hands. McCarthy was not sure whether Dropo was really ready for the majors, whether his power was an asset on an already powerful team, and whether his lack of defense skills would detract from an infield that was already weak. But in the end McCarthy's decision was made easier: Goodman's shoulder was hurting and so the manager went with Dropo.

It was not an easy beginning; Dropo did not hit at the start. His strike zone was large and the veteran umpires did not seem eager to give him the benefit of the doubt. In the second game of the season he complained to Bill McGowan, the veteran umpire, about a called strike. "Get back up there, Busher," McGowan said, "we haven't even been formally introduced." Warned by McCarthy that McGowan might make his life miserable for the rest of his career, Dropo apologized to McGowan the next time up. "That's all right, kid, now we know each other," McGowan said.

Dropo was undergoing another kind of test, and that was trial by media. Every day, it seemed, he read in the newspapers that his stay as a major leaguer would be brief. Stories about his imminent return to Louisville had hounded him all spring. Now it was starting again. In the ninth inning of the second game of the season, Dropo headed up to the plate for his turn at bat. Suddenly he was called back. McCarthy was going to use Goodman as a pinch hitter. The next day there was a flurry of articles that Dropo was doomed. After eleven games, hitting .141, Dropo was sent back to the minors. A story in the *Globe* seemed to be right out of Ring Lardner: DROPO SAYS CURVE HAD NOTHING TO DO WITH REMOVAL. In the last sentence Dropo addressed the fans: "Please tell them I can hit a curveball—honest I can."

Early in the season the Yankees went up to Fenway for a three-game series with the Red Sox. A series like this was always special, the two top contenders checking each other out. It was an article of faith that the Red Sox should win at least two out of three at Fenway, a park to which they had tailored their team.

The wild card in this series was pitching. Both managers were still uncertain of it. For the Yankees, the basic rotation was Raschi, Reynolds, and Lopat. The question of who would be the fourth starter—Fred Sanford, who had been picked up over the winter from the Browns, Tommy Byrne, Bob Porterfield, or Frank Shea—was still unanswered.

For the Red Sox the question of pitching was even more

complicated. Mel Parnell, off his 1948 performance, was a sure bet. Jack Kramer, a pickup in the big Brown trade, looked like another. Joe Dobson was also a likely starter. But the qualities that made Joe McCarthy so effective with his everyday players—his traditionalism and his certitude—hampered him with pitchers, who were more complicated physically and emotionally. They were, by the nature of their jobs, more vulnerable. A career-ending injury was like a death threat to any player. But pitchers, even when they were young, lived closer to that threat than other ballplayers. Managers who understood that were more successful with their pitchers than those who didn't.

For the first game in Fenway, McCarthy had intended to start Jack Kramer but Kramer was not feeling well, so instead he chose Tex Hughson. Hughson was a calculated risk at that point. He was from Kyle, Texas, by his own description a simple country boy who had worked his way through the University of Texas at Austin (he later went on to become immensely successful in real estate, turning his ranchland into housing units as the town of San Marcos expanded). From 1942, when he was twenty-six, until 1946 he was one of the premier pitchers in the American League, with a fondness for throwing in tight on right-handed hitters. He was even willing to come inside to DiMaggio in Fenway—to keep this powerful man from extending his arms. It was a dangerous proposition, and it terrified most pitchers. If you missed the spot, even by a little, DiMaggio would kill the ball. In that brief four-year period, Hughson won 72 games and lost only 37, with an earned-run average of under 2.60. There seemed to be no limit to his future.

In 1947 Hughson was enjoying another good season when his right arm began to give him terrible pain. He visited several doctors who diagnosed that the sympathetic nerve was not relaxing properly and was cutting off the circulation of blood to his arm. The pain soon became paralyzing. One doctor wanted to operate immediately. There was no guarantee that he would be able to pitch again after the operation, so Hughson held back. Another doctor said he could relax the nerve with a shot of Novocain. He took out the longest needle Hughson had ever seen, filled it with Novocain, and inserted

it. The pain was almost unendurable; Hughson remembers
trying to turn the wooden table to sawdust with his hands. As
the Novocain ran through him, he felt lighter and lighter—
like a balloon about to fly. But it did nothing for the pain in
his arm. It became clear that an overdeveloped muscle was
cutting off the circulation in his pitching arm. (About fifteen
years later, Whitey Ford, nearing the end of his career, came
up with a similar injury, and more recently, J. R. Richard, a
talented young Houston pitcher, almost died from the same
problem.) Hughson finally checked into the hospital for an
operation to remove part of the muscle. A young nurse took
his blood pressure. She looked at him and said, "Man, according to this you ain't human—you're dead." "Young lady,"
Hughson answered, "try my left arm—I think you'll find I'm
still alive."

In 1948 he rejoined the team somewhat warily. He could
only work under certain conditions—he needed a lot of rest
between starts, and if he worked from the bullpen, then he
had to pitch once they started to warm him up. He could not
get up, warm up, sit down, warm up again.

Hughson realized that somehow Joe McCarthy had seized
on him as a symbol of what was wrong with the Red Sox. He
had been kept on after he developed problems with his arm
by Joe Cronin, the general manager, not McCarthy, and
Cronin had asked him, "Tex, can you help the team?" "Yes,"
he had answered, "in relief and if I'm used right." But McCarthy regarded him as a malingerer. Probably McCarthy was in a
dilemma. He had been told to shape up the Boston operation,
that the players were soft and coddled. But McCarthy worked
for Tom Yawkey, who was second to none in coddling. Therefore he could not come down on any front-line ballplayers.
Hughson, nursing his arm as he tried to recover, was a perfect
target. McCarthy was suspicious of pitchers in general,
Hughson decided. They were never quite rugged enough,
and a wounded Boston pitcher was the worst kind. Hughson
tried to explain to Larry Woodall, the pitching coach, the
physical limits of his condition. "You can't get me up, let me
throw, sit me down for a few innings, and then get up again.
I'm not a troublemaker, but I can't do it," he said. Woodall
reported Hughson's problem back to McCarthy, who became

enraged. "Fuck him. He's not going to help us anyway," McCarthy said.

So McCarthy's decision to start him surprised Hughson. He had been matched against Allie Reynolds, and both pitched well. Reynolds singled in the sixth inning to put the Yankees ahead 2–1. But the Red Sox rallied and Hughson went out leading 3–2, having given up only five hits in six innings, a worthy performance for a pitcher in his situation. The Yankees went on to win 5–3, but Hughson was pleased with his outing and was sure he would get more spot starts. He did not, however, start again for thirty-three games, and when he did, it was his last of the season.

Fred Sanford started for the Yankees against Chuck Stobbs, the young Boston bonus baby, in the second game of the series. It was one of those typical Fenway Park games, which are murder on the earned-run averages of pitchers. At one point in the fourth inning the Yankees were ahead 6–2. In the bottom of the fourth, it was 7–6 Red Sox. In the top of the fifth it was 8–7 Yankees. In the bottom of the fifth it was tied 8–8. In the sixth inning McCarthy summoned Ellis Kinder in relief. McCarthy had his doubts about Kinder, particularly about his heavy drinking and his failure to observe even the most basic curfew rules during spring training. There had been one bitter showdown between the two of them in 1948 during spring training, in which McCarthy had threatened to send Kinder home to Tennessee unless he reformed.

Also in 1948, there had been a memorable scene in the second game of a twi-night doubleheader. Kinder was supposed to pitch the second game. His teammates were accustomed to seeing him arrive at the ball park in varying stages of disarray, but they had never before seen him like this—just gone. He smelled, thought Matt Batts, like a distillery. Kinder threw the first pitch over the backstop, the second over Birdie Tebbetts's head. He couldn't catch the ball when it was thrown back to him. After walking two men, he was relieved. Over the public-address system it was announced that he was leaving because his arm hurt. Kinder, who was right-handed, walked off the mound holding his left arm.

*   *   *

Ellis Kinder was an old-fashioned, unreconstructed carouser, cavalier in the extreme about training rules and curfews. "To the degree that Ellis trained at all," one of his oldest friends in Jackson, Tennessee, once said, "he trained on the hard stuff." He did not like lectures from friends, wives, or managers on what he could and could not do in his off hours. That was his business. He believed that baseball and alcohol mixed. At least *he* had always mixed them. He could drink hard all night and pitch hard the next day without any signs of deterioration or fatigue. In fact, carousing was an essential part of his pregame preparation. It was, his friend Matt Batts thought, almost a ritual. "Sooner or later, my friend, it's going to get you," Batts would say. "Matt," Kinder would answer, "I don't figure I have a chance of winning unless I do it—it's my way of getting loose." Normally, he explained, he might have a few beers at night. But the night before a game he needed to stay out all night, drink hard, find a woman. "When I first started pitching I would be a good boy, you know," he said. "And I took good care of myself, and I went to bed early. But I'd stay awake half the night worrying and I pitched like crap. So I changed. And it worked." It was hard, Batts thought, to argue with the man.

Several years later he was on the Red Sox train from Chicago to Cleveland, and Lou Boudreau, by then the Red Sox manager, tried to get him to go to bed. Boudreau was drinking Coke, and Kinder was drinking bourbon. Kinder was resolute in his determination to keep drinking. "I'll have another," he told the bartender. "Same as him?" asked the bartender, indicating Boudreau's Coke. "No, goddammit, same as before," Kinder said. He felt it was time for *Boudreau* to go to bed. "Good-night, Skip," he kept telling Boudreau. Eventually Boudreau decided that this was not one battle he was going to win and went to bed. Kinder stayed up, drinking through the night. When the train arrived in Cleveland he was so drunk they had to call for a wheelchair. Curt Gowdy, who had witnessed the scene the night before, looked at Kinder, who was unconscious, his head rolling back and forth like a rag doll's.

"I don't think we'll see Ellis for three or four days," Gowdy said to his assistant.

That afternoon Boston played a doubleheader in near 100-degree heat. In the seventh inning of the first game Gowdy looked down and to his surprise saw Kinder amble in from the bullpen. He looked as if he had slept like a log the night before. He retired nine men in a row. Boudreau thanked him and told him he could take the rest of the day off. "I'll stick around, Skip," he said. "I've got nothing else to do." Stick around he did, coming in to pitch several innings of shutout baseball in the second game on this brutally hot day.

He was, thought his teammates, a physiological miracle. They teased him that when he retired they should ship his glove to the Hall of Fame in Cooperstown and his body to Harvard Medical School. "Old Folks," based on his late entry into the big leagues, was his official nickname; "Old Grand-dad" was his unofficial one. There were periodic attempts to make him go on the wagon. When Kinder was sober, he was very polite about these efforts. He did not argue; he simply walked away. On the occasion of his posthumous election to the Madison County Tennessee Sports Hall of Fame in Jackson, his widow and childhood sweetheart, Hazel, recalled, "Bless his heart. Ellis *did* love a good time."

Kinder was to emerge as one of the league's very best pitchers, and probably its single best relief pitcher. The change-up was his best pitch. Before 1949 he was known only as a pitcher who had shown flashes of talent, with no consistency. No one knew at that time how smart he was, and how remarkable his physical endurance was. He was the kind of man, one teammate thought, who did not seem unusually big or powerful in the baggy uniforms of that era. But when he was stripped to the waist in the locker room, it was apparent how thick his chest and shoulders were. He was, thought Ted Williams, probably the strongest man on the team, stronger even than Junior Stephens. In addition, there was a toughness to him. He had been a rookie at thirty-two, by which time he had already seen a lot of life. That set him apart from the other rookies.

Kinder was born in the small town of Atkins, in northwest Arkansas. He was one of six children. His father, Ulysses

Grant Kinder, was a poor sharecropper who worked at best one hundred acres. It was a region that had always known hard times, and during the Depression those times were even harder. Ellis Kinder made it through the seventh grade, and then dropped out—he could not afford the time away from farming, and there seemed little reason to stay in school. Years later, when he was in Boston, he worked for a time selling cars at a large Chevrolet dealership; the idea behind the promotion was, come meet Ellis Kinder, the famous baseball player, and buy a Chevrolet from him. Nathan Shulman, the dealership owner, found Kinder easygoing and totally unaffected by his fame. He was eager to hire him. There was only one hitch: When it came time to finalize the contract, Ellis could barely read or write, it turned out.

In every rural small town in America there is a local baseball team, and the strongest boy or the strongest man is always the pitcher. From the time Ellis Kinder was thirteen years old, he was the best pitcher. He could throw the ball harder than anyone else in Atkins. He played in all the local games, although it wasn't always easy. Ulysses Kinder was a deeply religious man, and he did not believe in playing sports on the Lord's Day, the one day most other boys had off. Ellis had to sneak away on Sundays to play. He would go to church with his family, and then afterward he would secretly change from his good clothes to ordinary ones. Then he would play ball most of the afternoon, sneak back, take a bath in the nearby creek to get rid of the sweat and dirt of the game, change back to his Sunday clothes, and show up fresh and starched to join the family for Sunday night services.

He dreamed of playing in the major leagues, but his chances were slim. Atkins was buried deep in rural Arkansas, far away from the eyes of potential scouts, and there was almost no way of showcasing his talent. There was no American Legion ball, and he did not go on to high school or college. Over in Scottsville, some twenty miles away, they had heard of him, however, and although Scottsville was technically smaller than Atkins, there was a big sawmill over there called Bigler's. All the boys in the region wanted to work there because Bigler's paid well—ten dollars a week—and it was a lot easier than farming. The people who ran the mill came over to see

Ellis Kinder. They wanted him to pitch for the Bigler's Sawmill team, which played against the surrounding teams and also the local Civilian Conservation Corps team from Scottsville. Kinder, now twenty, took the job. He pitched on Saturday and Sunday, sometimes for both ends of a doubleheader, and sometimes—just in order to make things even—he pitched for both teams.

He seemed destined for a career as the best semipro pitcher in that part of Arkansas—a local legend. But he dreamed of something bigger. He often talked to Hazel about how if he could only save up enough money to go up to St. Louis and get together with Paul and Dizzy Dean, both Arkansas country boys, they'd help him get to play with the Cardinals. "Hazel, I believe I could really get on with those Dean boys, I believe they'd understand me," he would say.

But the years passed, and no scout showed up on his doorstep. He seemed to have slipped through the net that major-league baseball teams employ to find talent in America's small towns.

Then one day in the summer of 1938 Preacher Gilliam drove through Scottsville. Preacher Gilliam was the brother of Hartley Gilliam, who was, as everyone in Jackson, Tennessee, knew, the owner of the Lakeview Cabins, the Lakeview Restaurant, the Lakeview baseball field, and, most important of all, the Jackson Generals. Preacher was a conductor on the railroad, and, in his spare time, he was Hartley's chief scout, working the small towns in the South. He stopped to watch the semipro game in Scottsville. At first, it was said, he did not even get out of his car. But finally he did, and saw a young man with an exceptional curve. After the game he approached him and asked whether he would like to play for money. "Depends on how much," Ellis Kinder answered. Preacher Gilliam figured out how much it would take to get a boy out of this town. "Seventy-five dollars a month," said Preacher Gilliam. "Sounds good," said Ellis. There was one other question Preacher Gilliam wanted to ask. "Boy, how old are you?"

"Twenty-four," said Kinder.

"That's too old for a rookie," said Preacher Gilliam. "From now on you're twenty-one."

So Ellis Kinder turned pro, and shed three years from his

age. He and Hazel moved to Jackson, where they found an apartment for fourteen dollars a month, and Ellis pitched with great success in the Class D Kitty League. The Kitty League was one of the best Class D leagues in baseball. It fielded teams in Tennessee and Kentucky, well stocked with country boys who were not very different from their fans. In 1939 he won 17 and lost 12, and in 1940 he won 21 and lost 9 and led the league in innings pitched with 276, in strikeouts with 307, and in earned-run average with 2.38. The Jackson team was unaffiliated, so Kinder was not part of a system that had a vested interest in promoting him. Rather, the Gilliam family had a vested interest in holding on to him, or selling him only if there was a considerable offer. Also, while he was a very good minor-league pitcher, he did not have a blazing fastball. Finally, his friends believed, the major-league teams were sure to have heard about his carousing. At one point the Gilliams sent him to the Binghamton, New York, farm team of the Yankees. The deal was simple: $1,000 if he showed up in Binghamton, and $2,000 if he lasted through the season. His record there was 3-3. He was soon back in Jackson, and his Binghamton teammates, including Ralph Houk, later a Yankee catcher and manager, believed that the Yankees had been wary of him because of his reputation. They apparently feared he would corrupt the younger players in their farm system. He ended the year back in Jackson, where his record was 11-6.

In 1943 the Kitty League folded, and Kinder worked as a pipe fitter for the Illinois Central. In 1944 he managed to land a job with the Memphis Chicks in the Southern Association. There he began to blossom, winning 19 and losing 6. His contract was purchased by the St. Louis Browns for $19,000. He went into the service for a year, then joined the Browns in 1946, and eventually, along with Jack Kramer and Junior Stephens, was sold to Boston in time for the 1948 season.

Kinder was hardly an overnight sensation. By 1949, his second year with the Red Sox, he had won a grand total of 21 games in three previous major-league seasons. But in the second half of the 1948 season he had pitched well. As the Red Sox battled the Indians and the Yankees, Kinder became one of the most dependable pitchers on the team. In the first three of his last five starts of the season he beat the White Sox 6–2, the Athletics 5–3, and the Yankees 9–4. Then he lost to the Yankees, lasting only three innings of a 9–6 game. He pitched one more time, with four games left, and beat the Senators 5–1. But McCarthy still had his doubts about him. Thus the disastrous choice of Denny Galehouse in the one-shot playoff game against the Indians.

Now, in the second game against the Yankees, McCarthy brought in Kinder, and he pitched beautifully. Not perfectly, for he gave up three hits, but beautifully. He did what great pitchers do—kept the hitters off-balance, made them react to him, kept them in doubt. He pitched four innings of shutout baseball and the Red Sox won 11–8. McCarthy, desperately short of pitchers, frustrated by the injuries to Ferriss and Hughson, had found something.

The next day the Yankees decided to use Eddie Lopat. He started poorly and fell behind 4–0 because of some poor Yankee fielding. But a 3-run homer by Gene Woodling pulled the Yankees ahead to win. Two out of three in Fenway without DiMaggio was a lovely way to spend a spring weekend.

CHAPTER
5

For the Yankees, the train ride out of Boston was sweet. Only later, as airplanes replaced the special trains, did the players realize how wonderful they were. The train waited for them in the station: two sleepers and a dining car. It left on the team's timetable, not according to any other schedule. Players who spanned both the era of the team train and the era of the team airplane thought that the cohesiveness of the team suffered dramatically when the train was replaced.

Obviously, train travel took a lot longer. When the Yankees got on their train, the players would be together for six hours if it was a trip to Boston, or twenty if it was to St. Louis. They ate together, played cards together, and talked endlessly. If it was an especially long trip, they invented games. There was the game of cows, in which players had to match cows by color as the train swept through the farmland: If your cow was brown on one farm, then you needed a brown cow on the next farm to increase your score. A game that the writers liked was called "L. Peter B." L. Peter B. stood for the initials and middle name of Lawrence Peter Berra, and in order to play it, one writer would give out a name—H. Benjamin G., for example—and the others would try to guess: H. Benjamin

G. being Hank Greenberg. (On the Red Sox, Rudy York, who had been traded in 1947, had been one of the more inventive game players. York specialized in the game of batting averages, among others. In this game he would position himself in the center of the lobby of his hotel when the team was on the road. Watching the activity of the lobby, he would announce batting averages: "Two-twenty . . . two-forty . . . three-seventy . . . two-ten . . . one-eighty . . . four-oh-seven." "Rudy," a rookie once asked him, "what in hell are you doing—just mumbling to yourself?" "No," he answered, "I'm rating the women who come through here.")

The train was not only an opportunity for game playing—it was the center of an ongoing seminar about hitting and pitching. One of the ways in which the modern baseball player differs from the old-time baseball player, some veterans think, is in the area of single-minded devotion to the sport. The modern player is probably more talented physically, often has more education, and is paid much more money. During the off-season he works out more efficiently in a modern weight room to strengthen his body. But his attention is divided; he has an agent, a stockbroker, and he often has one eye on Wall Street and another on public appearances and endorsement opportunities. He spends less time actually thinking baseball and talking baseball with his teammates, and even reading box scores.

The train was where the peer groupings took place, and where the subgroupings—by class, education, age, and position of importance on the team—were revealed: People who had been to college tended to hang out with each other, the pitchers with other pitchers, the rookies with other rookies. Compartments were awarded on the basis of a player's value to the team and on seniority: stars and veterans in the center of the car, which was quieter; rookies and utility players at the ends of the cars, where you got a harder ride over the wheels. Years later Bobby Brown liked to tease his boyhood friend, Charlie Silvera, that it was amazing that Silvera, the perennial backup catcher, did not have a broken back after all those years of riding directly over the wheels.

One of the most famous features on the Yankees' train was the bridge game. (Poker, starting in the McCarthy years, was a no-no, even a low-stake game. Tensions that already existed could have been exacerbated by the loss of money. "For sure the best poker player will be the utility infielder and he'll be taking money off my All-Star shortstop. It always works like that," McCarthy once said. "Always tears the team apart. My rule against poker is real—don't break it.") In the thirties the bridge game had included Gehrig; Dickey, the catcher; Red Rolfe, the third baseman; and Arndt Jorgens, the third-string catcher. Charlie Keller watched the game closely when he first came up, edging closer to it all the time. When Gehrig finally retired, Dickey, who was fond of Keller, asked him if he played. "A little," said Keller, showing that he was properly modest. They asked him to join them. When the game was over Dickey turned to Keller and said sardonically, "Well, C, you didn't lie. You said you played a little, and you play a little." That meant that Keller was in the game, although it also meant that he had to start taking lessons from Dickey, the acknowledged master. Eventually, as the team changed, Henrich joined in, as did Curt Gowdy, a rookie broadcaster.

Gowdy was a country boy from Wyoming who hunted and fished, and that helped him bridge the gap between the players and the press. In addition, a broadcaster, hired as he was by the team, was considered more trustworthy than a writer. Gowdy loved his new job and was thrilled by his easy acceptance by the players. He had almost blown it earlier in the season when the players were sitting around the bridge table late at night talking about McCarthy. He might be the Red Sox manager now, but their reverence for him remained. "Wasn't he a bit of a drinker?" Gowdy asked, for he had heard that at the end of his New York tour McCarthy had gone on terrible three- and four-day benders.

Even as the words came out of his mouth, he knew he had made a serious mistake. A quick frown came over Keller's face. Gowdy excused himself and went to his compartment for the night. Keller followed him, and grabbed him. Keller was probably the strongest man on the team, and while there was no physical violence implicit in his action, it was a terrifying moment for the much smaller Gowdy.

"I never want you to make another remark about Joe McCarthy like that," Keller said.

"I didn't mean to say anything wrong," Gowdy said.

"Listen," Keller said, "there might have been some trouble with drinking—I'm not saying there wasn't. But he always protected us from the front office, and he protected us from the writers. He never said anything bad about us to the writers. There isn't anyone on this team who wants to hear you say anything against him."

Then Keller told Gowdy a story. It was his rookie year, 1939. DiMaggio had been hurt in the spring and was unable to start the season. So Keller started and played brilliantly. He was hitting near .340 when DiMaggio was finally ready to return. That day McCarthy penciled DiMaggio in on the lineup, and Keller was crushed. It signified to him that there was no place on the Yankees for him. He went back into the locker room and started to cry. McCarthy was hardly a gentle man, but he nonetheless had sensed that there would be a problem. He went into the locker room to look for Keller and took him into his office. "Charlie," he said, "you're going to be a great Yankee star, believe me. You have to work on pulling the ball more, particularly in this ball park, because this is not a good park for you to be an opposite-field hitter. I'm not playing you today. I'm sitting you down for another player who's the greatest player I've ever seen. But it's there for you and it's going to be a wonderful career. All you have to do is wait your turn and work on pulling the ball." McCarthy had kept his word: Keller soon became a regular. He had been touched by this rough man's sensitivity, by the fact that he had spoken to him in private, with no witnesses.

When Keller finished telling the story, he patted Gowdy on the back, letting him know that there were no hard feelings. Nonetheless Gowdy was shaken because he knew that he had broken the unwritten rules of the inner club.

The writers and players were friends but never peers. The players were apart: They were the ones who with 60,000 people watching had to stand up to the Bob Feller fastball, or had to pitch to Ted Williams with the bases loaded. That was the line, the line between doing it, and being the best in the world, and writing about it. Certain things could be written about—on-the-field activities, mostly. But other things, even if they clearly affected on-the-field behavior—for instance, serious drinking—could not be written about. Rather, it was the writer's job, if the player was drunk, to get him safely back to his room (and it was the player's job, if the writer was drunk, to get him back to *his* room). The writers observed the code because they cherished their jobs and considered themselves immensely privileged. They knew about the personal lives of the players, but that information was never to be used. Yet there was always a line separating them. Among the players there was the fear that perhaps some writer might write something unwelcome one day, the fear that although the writer might observe the code, he was outside it. He might slip and talk to his wife—and wives were outside the code. One spring Clare Trimble, the wife of Joe Trimble, seemed to be spending a lot of time with Vi Dickey, who was Bill Dickey's wife. Soon the word came down that this was not a good idea, the wife of a player being too close to the wife of a writer.

The tensions were always there. Lou Effrat remembered one time when he had been a young reporter and another writer named Bill Slocum got sick from eating a bad hot dog. The Yankee doctor gave Slocum some medicine. Someone mentioned it to Lou Gehrig, a man about whom it was believed nothing critical had ever been written. Gehrig said, "A writer sick—good, I hope he gave the son of a bitch rat poison."

Occasionally, open hostilities broke out. Joe Trimble of the *Daily News* was a constant critic of Nick Etten. One time Etten left his glove near first base during an inning and a foul ball rolled into it. Trimble wrote, "Etten's glove fields better without Etten in it." Another time Etten was so angered by what Trimble wrote that he tried to throw him off a train. John Lindell also hated Trimble, who had once informed his two million readers that Lindell was a plain, unadulterated bum. Lindell cut out the story and kept it in his wallet so he would never forget. But generally the relationship between the New York writers and players was amicable. It was a far cry from the Boston locker room, which was sometimes seen as an open war zone, mostly because of the way some writers harassed Williams.

But that was largely the extent of it. It was not an icon-
oclastic era, in the coverage of sports or other news. There
had been serious debate about whether *Life* magazine should
publish photos of the American dead scattered on the beach
of Tarawa. Sports reporting was even more timid. The writers
were not even truly independent of the club, which bought
their meals and paid for their hotel rooms and train rides.
The writers were beholden to the players, and even more so to
management. A writer did not take lightly a player's side
against management.

In January 1949, when the sportswriters were preparing
for their annual dinner, which was a major event in those
days, they included a song about George Weiss, the Yankee
general manager. They all loathed him, not just because
he treated them badly but because he was perceived as a
cold, petty, cheap man who treated the players badly. But
they were afraid of him. Weiss had recently fired Bucky Harris, whom the writers liked, and Lou Effrat wrote a song for
the show, to be sung by an actor playing Harris. "Lord of the
House," he would sing, "you turned out to be a louse." It was
too strong, the writers said, and finally it was toned down.
When the actor sang it, he merely mouthed the word. With
luck, the audience would guess it. Tame stuff, Effrat thought,
and they kill it.

The sportswriters loved the game, their jobs, and the
prestige it gave them on the paper. They were not about to
make waves. There was much talk when they were together
about whether a certain story "hurt baseball," an odd phrase
for it implied that they not only had to cover the sport but
protect it as well. There was a quiet consensus that such stories
were to be avoided.

They were an odd mix, the players and writers. The players were more often than not rural Southern Protestants; the
writers were urban Irish and Jews. The writers were fifteen to
twenty-five years older than the players. Some were even older
than that. In 1949 Dan Daniel was fifty-nine. He had been
covering baseball for forty years, and he was, in his own mind,
if not in the minds of his colleagues, the official oracle of the
sport. He had started on the old *New York Herald* when a
stringer who covered the Dodgers in spring training wanted

five dollars a day instead of three. That had angered the *Herald*'s sports editor, who, rather than pay such outrageous wages, wired back that he would send a college kid to cover the Dodgers. When Daniel started out, most reporters wrote their stories in pen and ink. He was one of the first men at the *Herald* to go to a typewriter. His legal name was Daniel Markowitz, but he did not use his last name at the injunction of his editor because of the era's anti-Semitism. His byline was simply "By Daniel." Soon that became "Dan Daniel." When he asked his father if it was all right to change his name legally to Dan Daniel, his father had no objections. "Markowitz isn't your real name anyway," he said.

By 1949 Daniel had been around so long that he had stopped going to the clubhouse to get quotes, since he had heard them all before. He *knew* with unfailing accuracy what a manager or a player would say. Once Joe McCarthy complained about some quote, claiming he had not said it. Daniel was hardly flustered—"Well, it's what he should have said," he noted. There was, his younger colleagues noted, no way to scoop him, even when they might beat him by a day on a story of a major trade. For the next day there would be a Daniel story and it would begin: "It came as no surprise to this reporter yesterday when the Yankees traded for . . ."

To the other young reporters he was somewhat self-important and pompous, his use of language outdated. As Red Smith once noted, the people he quoted in his stories did not *say* things, they *exuberated* or *vehemed*. Once when he was discussing an earlier pennant race, his friend Frank Graham said, "Oh, Dan, stop veheming." In 1946, when the American League had crushed the National League 12–0 in the All-Star Game, he wrote that this proved the National League was in danger of becoming a minor league. Then in October, when the Cardinals beat the Red Sox in the World Series, he wrote that this showed that the American League was second-rate. When a colleague noted the inconsistency, Daniel was not at all disturbed. "That's okay," he said, "I've warned them both. Now they're on their own." By 1949 his age was beginning to show. Daniel sometimes fell asleep at games. "Shall we wake Daniel?" a reporter once asked Will Wedge of the *Sun.* "No," Wedge replied, "he's busy interviewing John McGraw."

In those days the job of a baseball writer was a cherished one. To the young journalists of the era who had not gone to college and who did not want to cover politics or foreign affairs, or who worked on papers that lacked foreign or Washington correspondents, it was the best job on the paper. Everyone coveted it. Trying to get a position as a beat baseball writer was like waiting for a Supreme Court justice to retire. It was a position held for life.

John Drebinger of the *Times* was fifty-eight in 1949, and immensely proud of the fact that for twenty years he had written the *Times*'s page-one stories on every World Series game. He still had fifteen years to go until retirement, and when he did finally retire in 1964, at age seventy-three, he told Clifton Daniel, the *Times*'s managing editor, that there was no other job he had ever wanted. "No other job?" asked Daniel incredulously, for he was a former London and Moscow bureau chief who thought the jewels of the *Times*'s kingdom were its foreign posts. "No," said Drebinger, "and I surely wouldn't have taken yours."

When a beat job finally opened up, the new reporter became, overnight, the star of the paper. When he walked into the city room, all the other reporters clustered around him: He knew the stars of the baseball team, and he was full of the inside dope, even if he did not always write it. He was also the source of tickets for big games, something of which senior editors were always aware.

But the job also had its drawbacks. The endless travel separated the writer from his family. (Effrat was away so much that his children called him Uncle Lou.) And he was loath to take vacations for fear that some younger member of the staff might come in and prove to be a better writer. Of Dan Parker, sports editor of the *Mirror,* it was said that he deliberately hired mediocre writers so that none would outshine him.

The writers did not make a lot of money, but their salaries went surprisingly far because of the perks. In the late forties the base annual salary for a writer was perhaps $5,000 or $7,000. But thanks to the clubs, they stayed at the best hotels and ordered from room service. At spring training they went to Florida for two months. In truth, it was two months of sitting in the sun doing what they liked best—talking baseball—and then deciding among each other what the day's story was. If their families were coming down, the club found them small houses and picked up the tab.

They were catered to by the fans as good friends of the ballplayers. Once, Harold Rosenthal, a swing reporter for the *Herald Tribune*, wanted to wire his apartment so that his neighbors could hear his children if he and his wife went out for the evening. That way they wouldn't have to hire a baby-sitter. This required a relatively complicated electrical procedure at that time. Rosenthal was given the name of someone at New York Bell, and he made the call. Harold Rosenthal? The baseball writer? Of course it could be done. By the way, how did the Yankee pitching look?

Joe Trimble frequently experienced the same phenomenon. If he took his car to be repaired, the garage owner would look at the name. Trimble . . . not the same one who covers the Yankees? We'll have your car ready in an hour, Mr. Trimble.

In any city with a halfway decent baseball team, nothing was more important than the box scores. The *Daily News* had a circulation of more than 2 million, and though its predominantly blue-collar readers did not thrill to its editorials bashing Franklin Roosevelt and Harry Truman, they lived and died by its sports reporting. Its editors knew this. The great years of the *News*'s growth had coincided with the ascendance of Babe Ruth. The paper had made him its personal property, and that had set a tradition. Whenever there was a star athlete in the city, the *News* would assign a reporter to him full-time. And the *Mirror*, of course, would take up the challenge.

In the early evening, the *News* and *Mirror* delivery trucks raced through the city to make their drops. During the baseball season men and boys would eat their dinners early and leave home to line up at the candy stands, which were near the drops: Fifty-seventh and Eighth Avenue, Seventy-second and Broadway, etc. As they waited they argued the merits of the

best players on the three local teams. At around seven-thirty
P.M. stacks of paper would be thrown off the trucks and
quickly unbundled. The fans would pick up their papers, argue a bit more, and head home, usually before eight-thirty.
The papers recounted what they had often already heard,
and, even more important, gave the box scores.

Among the people who waited faithfully by the candy
store in Flatbush at Avenue M and East Seventeenth Street
with his two cents for the *Daily News* was a boy named Maury
Allen, who was sixteen and a half in 1949. Maury Allen was a
passionate baseball fan, which was not unusual, although as a
Yankee fan in Brooklyn he was unusual. Allen, who later became a prominent sportswriter, would recall those days with
wonder. His boyhood was about baseball. He and his friends
played ball all day, listened to radios on the front steps, and
argued endlessly about which team was better, or which player
was better—DiMaggio or Williams. But the arguments did not
end there: They ranged beyond the question of the ballplayers themselves to the question of who was the best broadcaster, Mel Allen or Red Barber, or the best reporter, Dick
Young or Joe Trimble or Milton Gross. If you rooted for the
Dodgers you rooted for Young, who was the liveliest and most
irreverent sportswriter of his day, and Barber, whose voice
was Southern and crisp and whose use of language was elegant. If you liked the Yankees you spoke of Mel Allen, Trimble, or Ben Epstein, a former wrestler who wrote for the
Mirror.

In retrospect, the singularity of the baseball connection in
those days struck Allen. No one on his block had a television
set. His friends were baseball fans. Football fans, with the exception of those who rooted, with some help from the arch-
diocese, for Notre Dame, were rich people who had been to
college, and who rooted for their college teams. They did not
live in his neighborhood. Nor were Allen and his buddies interested in singers. They did not argue the relative abilities of
Frank Sinatra and Bing Crosby. A generation later, young
people were more hip and more affluent. They were linked by
their feelings about rock and roll stars, about the television
shows they watched, and about the cars or motorcycles they
drove. But in these simpler times it was only baseball. Proba-

bly, he thought, it meant that boys were more separated from girls in that era.

Monday, May 2, 1949, was the worst day of young Maury Allen's life. He was the local baseball bookie, and he had to pay out. He had been beaten and beaten big. Small baseball pools were not unusual in that era. The idea was quite simple. Other kids, usually friends, would each put down a dime and pick three hitters. If one's chosen hitters got six hits among them, Allen would have to pay back sixty cents. Generally such pools were quite profitable: About thirty kids might bet, and it was rare that more than one or two would beat the system. Allen usually made about eight or ten dollars a week, which was a nice sideline. It was easy to figure out how his clients would bet. The Yankee fans would invariably offer up the three best Yankee hitters. The other kids, the Yankee haters, would bet on whichever team was in town playing the Yankees.

On the previous weekend, the Red Sox had been in town, and there had been a lot of betting, particularly on the four best Red Sox hitters: Dom DiMaggio, Pesky, Williams, and Stephens. Maury Allen had a little spiral notebook and he had dutifully written down the bets: Goldberg—Pesky, D. DiMaggio, Williams. The Yankees had won the Friday game behind Vic Raschi, and while Dom DiMaggio had gotten three hits, Raschi had closed off the middle of the batting order. There was heavy betting for Saturday and Sunday as well, but Allen was not worried—on Saturday Eddie Lopat was pitching. Lopat was a bookie's delight, and a good hitter's nightmare. On Sunday Allie Reynolds was pitching. The odds could not have looked better. The Yankees did indeed win on Saturday. But on Sunday everything came apart for Maury Allen. Dom DiMaggio opened the game with a single and then Pesky hit a home run into the right-field seats. That was a bad omen. Dominic went on to have three hits that day, Pesky also had three, Williams two, and Bobby Doerr and Junior Stephens one apiece.

Allen was cooked. Almost everyone who bet with him had beaten him. He owed fifteen dollars, far more than he had in reserve. He could not afford to go to school that Monday, and had to spend the day borrowing from every member of his family, particularly his brother. That Red Sox victory, 11–2, did not derail the Yankees from first place, and it left Boston still in sixth place. But it ended Maury Allen's career as a bookmaker.

CHAPTER 6

The Red Sox had gone on a hitting rampage in New York—all of them, it seemed, except Bobby Doerr, their All-Star second baseman. He had ended up with two hits in twelve at-bats for the three games. It was typical of the way the season had been going for him so far. As April passed, he thought it was merely a slow start. By May it was a slump. In June, he was still hitting only .207. It was especially humiliating because in the spring he had predicted not only a good start for himself but also for the entire team. Now the team was dragging, and he was one of the main reasons.

Doerr found himself confronting the secret fear that haunted all ballplayers: that this was something serious, the first signs of the end of his career. He was thirty-one. Previously he could count on hitting about .290, with between 90 and 110 runs batted in each year, and he could field well. He was so steady that his career was exceptional for that reason. By the time his career was over he ended up playing fourteen years of major-league ball, all with one team, Boston—1,865 games in all. He had never played any position other than second base. Now, at the peak of his career, he was slumping and he had no idea what was wrong. He was not seeing the ball well against ordinary pitchers, against whom he normally hit well. It got so bad that Birdie Tebbetts, the catcher, suggested that Doerr have his eyes examined. Doerr went to an ophthalmologist in Malden, Massachusetts, who assured him that whatever it was that was going bad, it was not his eyes.

Doerr was easily the most popular member of the Red Sox, and possibly the most popular baseball player of his era. He was so modest and his disposition so gentle that his colleagues often described him as "sweet." He was the kind of man other men might have envied had they not liked him so much. In 1929, when Doerr was an eleven-year-old growing up in Los Angeles, someone had told him that baseball players made $10,000 a year. The sum had been beyond his comprehension. He thought to himself, Wouldn't that be something, to make big money like that doing what I love best.

Doerr was a child star in baseball, so good in high school and with the American Legion that when he was only sixteen he was offered a contract to play with the Hollywood Stars of the Pacific Coast League. (By the time he showed up, they were the San Diego Padres.) Doerr was so excited that he could barely think of anything else. His older brother was already playing with the Portland team in the same league. Because he was being asked to give up high school, his father, who worked for the telephone company, had to grant permission. The Hollywood Star people offered a two-year guaranteed contract at $200 a month. His father thought about it a great deal, and finally said yes, he would give his approval, if Bobby agreed to come back in the winter to continue studying for his high school degree. "I want you to save all the money you can," the elder Doerr said, "and buy stock in the telephone company," a suggestion that the young Doerr heeded for his entire career. Then Bobby Doerr and his father, in what was the most exciting moment of Doerr's life, went to Sears, Roebuck and bought a suitcase for his new life.

In San Diego he looked too young to be a professional baseball player and on occasion was barred from a clubhouse or two. Once he took batting practice using Fred Haney's bat, a mistake he would *not* make again because Haney was so angry. His time with the Padres was remarkably happy. He met a player almost as young as he, but in some ways even less grown up. His name was Ted Williams. As the two youngest members of the team, they hung out together, and when the 1936 season was over, Doerr, who loved the outdoors, introduced Williams to fishing (which, of course, Williams denies; as he remembers it, he introduced Doerr to fishing). That began a fifty-year friendship.

Doerr was as comfortable with himself as Williams was not. He knew he was talented (he was to enter the Hall of Fame in his sixties, driving across the country in a van with his family, including his ninety-three-year-old mother, to attend the ceremonies), but he did not push himself obsessively, as did Williams. The difference on occasion drove Williams crazy. For Doerr often could not pass the Williams Test—the oral exam Williams administered after any hit, and with particular urgency after a home run. Williams would want to know exactly what kind of pitch Doerr had hit. Sometimes Doerr did not know. Instinct had won out: He had swung, the ball had left the park, it had worked. Williams would start cursing him, "Jesus, Bush, how can you not know? You're too goddamn dumb to play in this league." Doerr never minded— that was just Ted being Ted. Indeed, even when he *did* know he would tell Williams that he didn't, in order to infuriate him. "I can't understand it," Williams would tell Doerr. "You could be a three-hundred hitter—it's all there for you." "Ted, damn it," Doerr would reply, "I take as much extra hitting as you, I love to hit as much as you do, but I'm a middle infielder, and I'm in the game on every pitch, and it drains you terribly—and affects your concentration on hitting." There would be a grunt from Williams, neither of assent nor dissent, and the subject would be closed, for the moment at least.

In South Hadley, Massachusetts, in that summer of 1949, Bartlett Giamatti was taking Bobby Doerr's slump almost as hard as Doerr was. Bart, son of Valentine and Mary Giamatti, was eleven years old, and Bobby Doerr was his favorite player. The son of a professor of Italian at Mount Holyoke, and one day to be a professor himself, he identified powerfully with Doerr.

He had chosen Doerr carefully. Ted Williams was beyond
his reach as a role model; it was all right for a devoted Red
Sox fan to admire him, but it would have been immodest, indeed improper, to emulate him. That was left to those boys
who were the best hitters in their towns. Bart Giamatti was not
that good a hitter. So Williams was out. Since he had not been
blessed with a great arm, Bart liked to play second base, which
was the shortest throw in the field. That was Bobby Doerr's
position. From careful reading of the newspapers and listening to Jim Britt, the Red Sox broadcaster, Bart knew that
Bobby Doerr was extremely popular with his teammates and
not a carouser. Everyone on the team was said to look up to
him. That made him a perfect role model, especially for a professor's son.

Life in South Hadley was very quiet: There were no
movie theaters, no television yet. Home video games were
still forty years away. Even though Giamatti had visited Fenway Park only once, he saw it in his mind every day as he
listened to the games on the radio—they were as immediate
as if he were actually there. He had converted his room into
a baseball museum, with pictures of players that he had
drawn himself. In that sanctuary, he had become expert at
turning the radio in different directions in order to pick up
the signal, which was especially weak when the weather was
stormy.

He was not sure whether baseball had more meaning for
him because he was the son of immigrants—the sport could
have been seen as a shortcut to the center of American
culture. But he did keep his own all-Italian all-star team:
catcher, Berra; first base, Camilli; second base, Lazzeri; shortstop, Rizzuto; third base, Crosetti; outfielders, Dom DiMaggio,
Joe DiMaggio, Mele, Zarilla, and Furillo; pitchers, Raschi and
Maglie. That he was starting as many as six Yankees did not
bother him. There are loyalties, and there are loyalties; sometimes they intersect, sometimes they do not.

Years later, as president of Yale University, and soon to
become Commissioner of Baseball, Giamatti would try to ana-
lyze why baseball had meant so much to him. Baseball was, he
thought, the first comprehensible topic for a young person of
that generation. Sex, God, war, and politics were strictly adult

topics; but with baseball he could read the newspapers and listen to the radio and know that this was important and that these men were great. Then he could go out and emulate their acts. He could *be* Bobby Doerr.

He had already learned that being a Red Sox fan brought a certain amount of pain with the pleasure. Three years earlier he had sat with his friends in Frankie White's garage listening to Country Slaughter score ahead of Johnny Pesky's throw. There would be more to come, but he would endure. In the meantime, he was still worried about Bobby Doerr's slump. He knew all about the trip to the eye specialist. He feared that the career of his hero might be coming to an end. Then slowly and steadily, starting in late June, Bobby Doerr began to see the ball better and to hit. And then Bartlett Giamatti also began to see the ball better, and they both began to breathe easier.

The Yankees continued to play well. Henrich's clutch hitting was extraordinary. It was important in understanding the Yankee strength in those days to know that they did not win so much on power, though many people thought they did, nor even on pitching. They won by playing well in tight games, by not beating themselves with mental errors, and by sheer concentration, both in the field and at bat. One of the first things Joe McCarthy told Mel Allen when the latter began broadcasting Yankee games was, "You've heard all that stuff about Murderers' Row. Don't believe it. We don't win on power. We win on defense and good pitching."

Another strength of the team was turning out to be the rookie second baseman, Jerry Coleman. His play around second base was the best that many of the Yankees had seen since Joe Gordon had been in his prime. At the start of the season Coleman had thought his transition from minor to major league would be gradual, that George Stirnweiss might play the first seven innings or so, and then if the Yankees were way ahead he might come in. But early in the season Stirnweiss bruised a nerve in his hand and the job had become Coleman's.

To Coleman's mind there was glory in being a Yankee— you were the best; but there was also a monstrous quality to it, in the need to live up to the almost unbearable expectations of others. He thought of his skills as marginal. He was not a great spray hitter and he certainly lacked power. He was there only for defensive reasons. If he blew a play in the field and cost them a game, then he was a liability. He was playing with less room for failure than almost anyone else on the team. He lived in terror of making the key error that would cost the Yankees not just a game but a pennant. It was not so much the fans he feared as his teammates. He desperately wanted their approval. For Coleman was not just a rookie, he was a *Yankee* rookie. As a result, he felt overwhelming tension from the moment he woke up each day.

He began the season batting at the top of the order. He would wake up every morning thinking of the game they were going to play that day. Should he hit the first pitch or should he wait? That question would hang on him all morning— whether or not to go after the first pitch. Finally Stengel understood the pressure he had placed on Coleman, and switched the batting order, putting Coleman at the bottom. When the season was over, Coleman realized that he had not enjoyed a decent breakfast all season. All his stomach could handle was boiled eggs and cream of wheat. In a very short time he developed serious ulcers. He was amused when fans and writers told him how cool and confident he looked out on the field. The release from the pressure came only once the game began. Then his own inner doubts receded as instinct took over. Those were the blessed hours of his day. He gradually came to realize that he was doing all right, perhaps even better than anyone expected. But he also knew there would be no real acceptance until he had shown that he could do as well in his second year. Only then would he be a real Yankee.

Coleman finally understood that most of the other Yankees, rookie and veteran, felt the same terrible pressure: DiMaggio smoked cigarettes and drank coffee between innings and developed his own set of ulcers; Tommy Byrne got up at three A.M. on the days that he was going to pitch and wrote letters to his wife; Bobby Brown ground his teeth like a machine gun; Vic Raschi behaved like a bear on the mornings he was going to pitch.

Coleman did not feel that he had the natural skills to be a second baseman. In addition, he was learning in front of the largest audience imaginable—40,000 people every day. It was the Crow who probably saved him, he thought. The Crow was Frank Crosetti, the veteran Yankee infielder who had retired after the 1948 season. With seventeen seasons behind him, he dated back to the era of Ruth and Gehrig. Not many outsiders understood Crosetti, a reserved man who carefully removed himself from anything outside of the game itself. Other players did not necessarily like reporters, but they understood the uses of publicity. Crosetti was different. He made no bones about his dislike of them. They, in turn, quickly grew to resent him. Why bother interviewing him, they decided, since he had nothing to say. Crosetti did not mind at all: They were not ballplayers; what they did was, in his mind, absolutely extraneous.

The Yankees were not just a family to Crosetti, they were a religion. Within that religion, arrogance was a sin. He was always on guard against it. If the Yankees won three in a row and the players started celebrating in the locker room, the Crow would look at them coldly and say, "Don't be so gay when you're all full of shit." He did not congratulate batters who hit home runs except, it was said, Maris on the occasion of his sixty-first and Mantle on the occasion of his five-hundredth. He did not congratulate them because they had merely done what they were supposed to do. Coleman understood that Crosetti was probably the last of a generation to whom the idea of the Yankees would mean so much; Coleman's own generation of Yankees, serious though the players might be, had enjoyed greater advantages in childhood, and their loyalties were more complicated.

Crosetti knew everything about Yankee baseball, and almost nothing about anything else. He had no time for the ancillary pleasures of the season. He did not attend the victory parties that celebrated World Series wins. His car was already packed as the Series wound down, and the moment the last game was over, he left as quickly as he could and drove back to California. In 1949 one of the rookies asked Crosetti if he had *ever* attended a victory celebration? Yes, he answered, once—in 1932, his rookie year. Why not since then, Crow? the player wondered. "No need to," Crosetti answered.

That spring and summer of 1949 Crosetti was assigned to work with Bobby Brown and Jerry Coleman every day in infield practice. He was like a drill instructor, thought Coleman, who had already served one tour of duty in the marines. Their habits had to be perfect, he would tell them, because if their habits were perfect then they would become instincts: They would do things right during the game without even having to think. There might be 20,000 fans already in the stands waiting for a big game while Brown and Coleman took infield practice, but Crosetti would yell at them nonetheless: "*Set yourself! Set yourself!* How many times do I have to tell you to set yourself!"

Do it the right way, he would insist. That meant catching a ball with two hands. He hated one-handing the ball—that was for showboats, not Yankees. Sometimes near the end of a workout, with the stands already filling and the last round of batting practice almost finished, Brown and Coleman would needle him by taking throws one-handed. He would yell, "*That's it! That's enough!* You guys are screwing around! You're nothing but screw-offs!" And he would stomp off the field, leaving them giggling yet embarrassed in front of the huge crowd.

The hardest part for Coleman was the pivot—learning how to take the ball from the shortstop and then move toward first on the throw. It had not seemed natural at first. But Crosetti understood this and advised, "Just catch it and throw it. Do it by instinct. Don't think about it. Just do it, do it, do it! Catch it and throw it."

Coleman slowly realized that Crosetti approved of him. But privately Crosetti worried about Coleman. He told Coleman's friends on the team to make sure that he had a beer before dinner to help him relax. He told them to keep him from eating just bread and butter (out of sheer nervousness Coleman would devour the bread and then not eat dinner).

That season Coleman had another mentor as well. Tommy Henrich had emerged as the team leader. He was very helpful to the younger ballplayers, and equally hard on them if they failed to live up to his expectations. Once in an early season game, Coleman took a pop fly. He had been quite pleased with himself, but later, when they were in the dugout between innings, Henrich came over to him. "Jerry," he said, "this is the Yankees. We're a family. We don't have any secrets among us. If you want the ball, *yell* for it."

To Coleman, with DiMaggio out and Keller still limited physically, Henrich was the symbol of the Yankees. He desperately wanted to please him. But Henrich was not easily pleased. When they talked, Coleman always had the sense that Henrich was peering inside him. Perhaps, Coleman thought later, that ability to withhold his approval was how Henrich made others live up to his standards.

More than anyone else, Phil Rizzuto, Coleman's second-base partner, knew how tense Coleman was. He saw that he was constantly popping some kind of antacid pill. Several times that summer Coleman spiked Rizzuto at second base, not during plays but afterward, when they were talking to each other near the bag. When Coleman drove, he would constantly fiddle with the rearview mirror, adjust it, readjust it. The man, Rizzuto thought, could not be wound tighter. "Jerry," Rizzuto would say, "relax. You and I don't have to hit. We're here for our fielding, not our hitting. You're a good fielder. Be yourself. The rest will come."

Although the addition of Coleman immediately solidified the Yankee defense, the Red Sox, on paper, remained a far better hitting team. That meant that the Yankees' edge was slim indeed and that a great deal depended on relief pitcher Joe Page. In the major leagues most of the pitching records are held by pitchers who played early in the century; yet the top fourteen relief pitchers, in terms of saves, all played after 1970. In the late forties the art of relief pitching was relatively undeveloped. If a pitcher was good he was a starter. If he was not very good he might be a relief pitcher. Teams did not have bullpens in the modern sense of the word—rather they had several pitchers who were viewed by the manager as dubious starters. A star relief pitcher was someone who got 10 saves a year. Johnny Murphy, a reliever with the Yankees, got the nickname "Fireman" based on 8 or 9 saves a year.

Joe Page was a left-hander with an exceptional fastball—it was not only fast but lively. When Page had first come up with the Yankees, he had been considered a pitcher of great promise. But given a choice between the pursuit of pleasure late at night and serious training, he always chose the former. Clarence Marshall, who roomed with Page in 1949, noted that Page slept in his room twice during the entire spring. Often there was a late-hour phone call from Page to Marshall: He had discovered a wonderful party in another hotel. Would Marshall like to join him? There was a lot of action going on.

When Marshall declined, Page would put a young woman on. In the most seductive way possible she would repeat the invitation: "Clarence . . . Joe . . . says . . . *you're* . . . even cuter . . . than . . . he . . . is . . ." Then Page would come back on. "Joe," Marshall would tell him, "somehow you're the kind of guy who can go through the hotel lobby at three A.M. and not get caught, and even if they catch you, your fastball is so good that they won't do anything. But me, if I try it just once they'll catch me and I'll be on my way to Kansas City."

When Whitey Ford joined the Yankees in 1950, the first person to take him out on the town was Joe Page. The team was in Chicago. They went to a fight and then to dinner, and then, at about midnight, to a nightclub, and then, at one-thirty, to another nightclub. People complain about Page's stamina on the field, Ford thought, but he's showing me plenty of stamina tonight. At three-thirty Page took him to yet another club, this one called the Airline Club. There, to Page's astonishment, a voice from inside announced that the club was closed. "But I'm Joe Page," Page shouted, as if it were inconceivable that a nightclub could close with him on the outside.

The next day Eddie Lopat asked Ford, "What'd you do last night, Whitey?" "Oh, I went to the fights with Joe and then had dinner with him," Ford answered. "Get back early?" Lopat pushed. "Sure, about one o'clock," Ford lied. "Then what the hell were you doing at the Airline Club at three-thirty?" said Lopat. "And don't bullshit me—we were there."

Such lack of discipline was bound to infuriate Joe McCarthy. In 1946, early in the season, McCarthy exploded at Page after a series in Detroit. They were on a team plane and McCarthy sat next to him. He asked Page when he was going to shape up. He told him he was on the brink of failure, and wasting exceptional talent. As McCarthy lectured, Page seemed not to care. McCarthy grew angrier. "You know what I'm going to do with you?" he told Page. "I'm going to send you back to Newark—you can make your four hundred dollars a month there if you want." But even that didn't work. "You want to send me to Newark, send me to Newark," Page answered. "Maybe I'll be happier there, anyway." But the next year McCarthy quit as manager.

In 1946 Page won 9 and lost 8 despite his obvious talent. Then in 1947 he became a relief pitcher. On one memorable night he was called into a game against Boston in relief, with the sure knowledge that if he failed he would be either sent back to the minors or traded. With the bases loaded and a count of 3-and-0 on Rudy York he was one pitch away from the minors. He struck out York, and Doerr, and got Eddie Pellagrini on a soft pop. He had found his calling.

Page seemed to blossom in his role as bullpen specialist. He even began to pal around with DiMaggio, though little of DiMaggio's work ethic rubbed off. DiMaggio, more than anyone else on the team, seemed able to control him. Page absolutely revered DiMaggio; DiMaggio, in turn, was sympathetic. He understood the insecurities that turned off many of Page's teammates. If they were at a restaurant and Page started boasting, showing his need to let the world know that he was Joe Page of the New York Yankees, DiMaggio would give him a cool look, and more often than not he would settle down. "Joe's shadow," the other Yankees called him. For a time they roomed together, and years later Mel Allen liked to tell the story of the day the news arrived that DiMaggio was going to marry Marilyn Monroe. The writers debated whether this was good for DiMaggio, until one of them said, "Well, it's got to be better than rooming with Joe Page."

In 1947, Page proved he was able to pitch for two or three innings as he could not for seven or eight. He came in, took charge, and simply overwhelmed the hitters. That season he started only 2 games but relieved in 54 others. His earned-run average was 2.48, and he led the league in saves with 17, and in wins for a relief pitcher with 14. The Yankees won handily that year, and he had been a key part of the team's success. In the seventh game of the World Series against the Dodgers, he simply blew the Dodgers away, pitching five innings of one-hit ball. After the game, reporters crowded around his locker and the first thing he said was, "What did the Dago say?" "Forget the Dago, Joe," said writer Jimmy Cannon, "this is your day."

But Page was not a man to handle success well, and in 1948 he relapsed. Something was missing, a certain edge, an instinct to dominate. He appeared in almost as many games, 55, but his earned-run average ballooned up to 4.26, and he won only 7 games. In that season, when three teams had finished in a virtual tie, there was a belief among many Yankees that Page had cost them dearly. George Weiss put private detectives on him that summer and found out what he expected, but it made no difference. On certain matters Page was incorrigible.

In 1949 they needed him badly and he seemed to be bouncing back. If anything happened to Page, it might mean trouble. Nothing brought that home better than a three-game series with the Athletics in Philadelphia on May 14 and 15. Philadelphia was a weak team, more often than not in the second division by then. The glory days of Connie Mack were long past. Going into Philly, the Yankees wanted nothing less than a sweep. They were playing well, three games ahead of Detroit and four ahead of Cleveland. Boston was still stumbling. But instead of a pleasant rest stop, Philadelphia turned into a nightmare. In the first game, on Saturday, Vic Raschi was a little wild, but the score was 5–2 Yankees when Page relieved in the bottom of the sixth. He made it through the sixth, although his control was obviously a problem. In the seventh he gave up three runs, and the score was tied. The A's went on to win 8–5. To lose to a weak team would have been bad enough. To do it by blowing a big lead was worse, particularly when the game had been given to Raschi, the ace of the staff, and neither he nor Page, the team's best reliever, could hold it.

Sunday was even worse. It was a doubleheader. The first was started by Tommy Byrne, the talented left-hander whose only problem was chronic wildness. He was pulled and replaced by Frank Shea, who had a 7–3 lead in the seventh. Then it all began to unwind. Shea was hit hard, Page was brought in again, followed by Frank Hiller, and then Fred Sanford. Nothing worked. Philadelphia tied the score with 2 home runs in the ninth, the second coming with two out. Another lead had been squandered, and in the bottom of the eleventh the Athletics won it. It had been a hard game to lose: The Yankees had outhit the A's 12–7, had left 11 men on base, and their pitchers had walked 11 men.

In the second half of the doubleheader Allie Reynolds started. That was reassuring because he was a great money player and they needed a win badly. At the end of four innings the Yankees led 5–0. Reynolds was being hit, and had given up five walks, but nonetheless it appeared that the Yankees' main problem was fighting the clock. There was a curfew on Sunday baseball in Philadelphia in those days and an inning could not be started after six P.M. With their fat lead the Yankees were desperate to make it legal and then get out of town. They got to the fifth but it was not yet six P.M. The sixth would be the final inning. The Yankees led 6–0 in the bottom of the sixth. Then it all disintegrated. It began with a single to Elmer Valo. Then a walk, then a hit. Then Reynolds walked in a run. A single brought in another run, and the Yankee relief pitchers started a procession to the mound—Bob Porterfield, Fred Sanford, and, finally, Joe Page. But the Athletics continued to walk and hit. Suddenly Valo was up again, singling off Page for a 7–6 Philadelphia victory. The game was over; the Yankees had lost.

For the veterans, the train ride out was pure misery. Worst of all, Joe Page had failed in every appearance. Some of the younger players did not know how much that could mean, and they were playing a game of Twenty Questions. Suddenly Stengel walked through the dining car. Angry at Page, angry at himself for somehow not picking the right pitcher, and angry at the Athletics, Stengel said, his voice full of scorn, "I'll give you the perfect question for it. Which one of you clowns won't be here tomorrow?" That ended the game of Twenty Questions.

Near the back of the dining car Tommy Henrich was having dinner with Mel Allen. If anything, Allen, the broadcaster, was more of a Yankee than the Yankees. He took losing very hard.

"Three games to *Philly*," Mel Allen was saying.

"Can you believe Valo? Two hits in one inning? Criminy," Henrich added, for he was a rare ballplayer who did not swear. They were both thinking that at the end of a season you can sometimes look back, remember a series like this, and see where it all slipped away. Just then Gus Mauch, the trainer, joined them.

"It's not so bad," he said. "It's just a ball game."

"No," said Henrich, "it's not just another ball game. It's three games to a lousy club and we could have won all three. We blew those three games—we gave them away. It's the way to lose a pennant."

"I don't agree with you," Mauch said. He was having a steak and cut into it. He had ordered it rare, but it was well done. He called the waiter over and sent it back.

"Oh," said Henrich, getting angrier by the minute, "you've got troubles. Your steak isn't rare enough. That's hard. That's a bad day. I'm glad you sent it back. I'm sure they'll cook you a better one." Mauch saw how angry he was and let it pass. He had clearly joined the wrong table. It was the kind of night, Henrich decided later, when people could get in fights if they weren't careful.

Joe DiMaggio did not hang around with the team, for he could not bear to feel utterly useless. The pain in his foot had not gone away. He had been told by the doctors that nothing could be done for it except to rest. Patience was easy for a doctor with a forty-year career.

DiMaggio lived in a hotel apartment in Manhattan. When he went out on crutches, he was immediately set upon by well-wishers. In the days before television, baseball players were not as recognizable as they are today, but DiMaggio was always distinctive—tall, powerfully built, with wide shoulders and a slim waist. He had a long, oddly handsome face with a prominent overbite.

He took refuge at his favorite restaurant: Toots Shor's. It was the great sports-celebrity hangout of its day. Bernard Shor (it was said by his patrons that only his mother had briefly called him Bernard before calling him Toots—short for Tootsie, the name derived from his long curls) was huge, boisterous, and aggressive, and seemed to come straight out of Damon Runyon. He had run Billy LaHiff's, a speakeasy in the days of Prohibition and a favorite hangout of Runyon's. In the tamer age of legalized drinking, this gave him a certain raffish reputation. In the forties New York was famous for cab drivers and waiters who had hearts of gold under rude and insulting exteriors. Certainly no one mastered the style better than Toots Shor, who was, by nature, both sensitive and abrasive, and who raised it to an art form. He charmed by insulting. Shor loved to boast of a letter he had received from a patron from the Midwest who had praised the food and service but added, "however, if you hope to make it [the restaurant] a success, you'd better get rid of that fat slob of a headwaiter who spent most of his time insulting patrons."

If he insulted someone, that person was welcome. He was particularly skillful at using the technique with some of his more serious celebrities. It allowed them to shed some of the burden of their fame and relax—while being treated as VIPs. Shor was surprisingly nimble, indeed almost delicate in knowing how far to go, and when to stop.

No one had ever been known to praise the food excessively, and if truth were known, the writers often spent several hours drinking there and then went on to eat elsewhere. That did not bother the proprietor, who made fun of fancy cuisine, anything that had *sauces*. Shor would sit down at select tables with his favorites and have a drink or two, sometimes quite a few more. The only night of the year he did not drink, Shor like to boast, was New Year's Eve. "That's amateur night," he would say. The draw was the crowd and the proprietor himself, who would introduce athlete to politician to Broadway or Hollywood star. It was at Shor's, after all, that someone introduced Yogi Berra to Ernest Hemingway, "an important writer." Berra, in one of his Hall of Fame Yogiisms, said, "Good to meet you. A writer, huh. What paper you with, Ernie?"

Toots Shor's was actually a men's club, one that reflected the age, a time when New York still had three baseball teams. It was white, male, and boozy—hard-liquor boozy. It's patrons ate red meat. No one, in the proprietor's view, was ever drunk; they were half loaded or three-quarters loaded. It was about baseball first and foremost—the players, the writers, and the executives, in that order. If a few professional football players happened to be hanging around, Shor would ask them if they would like to be introduced to DiMaggio—protocol demanded it.

Shor placed great emphasis on having customers who, in his words, had class and behaved with class. DiMaggio had class. Joe Louis had class. Red Smith and Jimmy Cannon had class. Hemingway had it. Some of his customers, usually those who had been exiled for some transgression, took a somewhat more jaundiced view. In a long profile in *The New Yorker,* John Bainbridge quoted one dissident as saying of Shor, "He's exactly the kind of guy who he would throw out of his own place." Tourists, those who had read about this legendary New York spot in the newspapers, waited in line. The wait itself was something of a floor show. The masses could ogle while Shor bustled around the room, dropping in at tables and insulting new arrivals. *"Whitey, Yogi,* you bums, you guys are playing lousy but I'll feed you anyway."

The local writers loved going there, for Shor had a good ear and an instinct for talent. He could sense when a journalist was on the rise. When Shor welcomed—or insulted—a writer, it meant that he had made it into the big time. It was virtually a rite of initiation; now he was a member of the city's best sporting club. Drinks were somehow almost always free. Shor was almost as good to sportswriters who accompanied the visiting teams as he was to the New York writers. "What are you guys doing here?" he would ask. "It's amazing you still got your jobs when you can't even write a sentence in English." Raymond J. Kelly, the *New York Times* sports editor, was not pleased by the skill with which Shor seemed to be able to maneuver himself and his restaurant into the *Times*'s columns. He once upbraided Effrat, a Shor's regular, about it. "You are not supposed to use our columns to publicize your personal friends," he said. "I just used his name, I didn't say it was his restaurant," Effrat answered in what was not one of his strongest defenses.

When there was a Yankee–Red Sox game or a World Series in town, the first place to be was the game and the second was Shor's—at a good table afterward. Everyone seemed to be there. Earl Warren was there. Sinatra—Sinat to the owner— went there, although one time Shor must have gone too far. There was a moment that regulars remember of the proprietor running into the street after a furious Sinatra and shouting, "Sinat, Sinat, I didn't mean it, Sinat, I didn't mean it." Jackie Gleason was always there early in his career, mostly on the tab, although when he tried to borrow two hundred dollars from Shor, the owner was outraged. Why, he yelled, did Gleason need to borrow money when he was already eating free? "To tip your waiters," Gleason answered. "You don't want them to think I'm a cheapskate." When Shor died almost penniless in 1977, Gleason was among those who spoke. "Save me a table, pal," he said, presumably turning to that big saloon in the sky.

There was always action. Once Shor was sitting at a table with Hemingway, Cannon, and Leonard Lyons, the gossip columnist. Suddenly he broke into laughter. "What's so funny, Toots?" Cannon asked. "I just realized I'm the only guy at this table who doesn't think he's the greatest writer in the English language." No wonder writers loved it. For men like Red Smith and Jimmy Cannon, it was confirmation of one's fame: Either man could walk in and be seated at Table One, which was the first table hard to the left after the giant circular bar. There they'd receive compliments on a column just printed and, while the sports world passed in review, pick up material for two or three more columns. "The mother lodge," Smith called it.

Women were most decidedly not welcome. A regular could bring, on rare occasion, his wife—the Missus, as wives were called. But if he brought her too often, he lost status. For women were not considered good customers. If they were ladies, they did not drink enough and they inhibited the men; if they drank, then they might be "lushes," and that was worse. This misogyny was evident at the door. "You know I hate going there, Tommy," Eileen Henrich once told her husband. "That maître d' looks at you if you're a woman and looks right through you. Can't we please go to Sardi's. They treat me as well as they treat you there."

The proprietor himself had a strict sense of propriety, though: He did not like men who told dirty stories in front of women, and he did not like men who cheated on their wives. If a regular came in with a woman other than his wife, he received icy treatment. This club was about being pals, what one regular called palship. The rituals observed were on the order of lending money to a guy who was down, or making sure that the children of pals got handsome presents on their birthdays (though such children were rarely seen, and certainly not known).

A sense of Our Guys and Their Guys was pervasive. Our Guys were the regulars, the writers who were at the bar and who were favored by Shor. They knew each other and the code of the place—what you did and didn't do, whom you avoided. Their Guys were in effect the tourists who lined up for tables, and who clearly did not know the drill. Their Guys could also be celebrities who did not know Shor or who failed in their initiation rites, by being either too proper, too subservient, or too abrasive. Shor himself liked to boast of how he had kept Charlie Chaplin, the great actor and comedian, waiting for a table. Chaplin and entourage had shown up without any prior notification, and Chaplin finally complained to Shor about the wait. "Let's see you be funny for the people [in line] for the next twenty minutes," Shor had said. There was a lesson here: There was fame outside Shor's, and there was fame inside; sometimes the two were the same, and sometimes they were not.

Red Smith and Jimmy Cannon were the star writers, but there was no doubt who the ultimate celebrity was in those days: DiMaggio. Shor was a fan at heart; he loved being surrounded by sports stars. Above all, he loved DiMaggio. He was immensely proud of the fact that they were close, and that DiMaggio favored his place. He helped DiMaggio in contract negotiations one year when the Yankees offered DiMaggio a performance-attendance clause. Shor told DiMaggio to go with the simpler contract and to avoid the attendance clause. DiMaggio followed his advice and it ended up costing him about $25,000.

While DiMaggio waited for his heel to improve, he found the restaurant a very different place. It was one thing to go there after a satisfying day at the plate; but now that he was separated from the team, the atmosphere there seemed only to underline his new, vulnerable status. Even when people meant well, even when they were scrupulous about not asking questions—Joe, how's the foot? Joe, when are you gonna come back?—those questions hung in the air. And, no matter how hard Shor tried, it was hard to stop the well-wishers, both old friends and strangers. Everyone seemed to know someone who had been rescued from a bone spur by a doctor with a secret treatment. Others simply wanted to exchange symptoms. Finally, in desperation, DiMaggio retreated to his hotel room. More alone than ever, he did not want to see anyone. He told the switchboard to let through calls from only two people, Shor and George Solotaire.

By his own admission he was becoming unhinged. He tried to watch baseball games on television, thinking that it would help hone his batting eye. But television baseball was different from the real game. The pitcher would rear back and deliver. The ball would come in. Watching it, DiMaggio would decide a pitch was right down the middle. The umpire would call it a ball. DiMaggio would wait for the catcher or the manager to protest. But they did not. For a while, he thought he was losing his eye. That made him even crazier. Finally he decided it was the fault of the camera, which distorted angles. Because he was tense, he drank more and more coffee. Then he would stay awake until four in the morning, thinking of new careers. When he woke up in the late morning, he could never remember any of them. It was the worst time in his life.

Only one message brought any kind of relief. Rogers Hornsby, the great hitter from another age, dropped by Shor's. He had suffered a similar ailment, and it had threatened to end his career. Knowing how close Shor was to

DiMaggio, he passed a message to him: "Tell Joe, just be patient. The only thing that can help one of those things is rest." Hornsby was right, DiMaggio imagined. Meanwhile, a third of the season was gone. Mercifully the Yankees were still winning. In late May they went on a long road trip, not to return until mid-June. They were in first place when they left and in first place by three games when they returned. The Red Sox were more than seven games back.

"April 14—Yankee Outfield Hopefuls: Charlie Keller, Gene Woodling, Johnny Lindell, and [Hank] Bauer, left to right, are fighting for places in the 1949 outfield of the New York Yankees," notes the Associated Press caption.

Left to right: Charlie Keller, Joe DiMaggio, and Tom Henrich, as pictured in 1949

Allie Reynolds

Vic Raschi

Tommy Byrne

Yogi Berra

Phil Rizzuto

Joe Page

Ed Lopat

Bobby Brown

Yankee second baseman Jerry Coleman showing his athletic ability early in the season, against Chicago

New York Yankees Johnny Lindell (left), Joe DiMaggio (center), and Jack Phillips arrive at Pennsylvania Station, New York City.

Joe DiMaggio (right) as he signs his 1949 contract in the Yankees' office in New York. At left is Dan Topping, one of the owners and president of the Yankees. George Weiss, the club's general manager, stands between them.

Family photo: Joe and Dominic DiMaggio pictured eating at home with their mother. "The boys can't wait to go to work on that platter of steaming ravioli," the caption notes.

Another family photo: The baseball celebrity of their sons made the senior DiMaggios newsworthy as well. Here they drink a toast after taking out first citizenship papers in February 1942.

The DiMaggios cut their golden wedding anniversary cake. Left to right: Dominic, Mrs. DiMaggio, Joe, Joe Sr., and Tom.

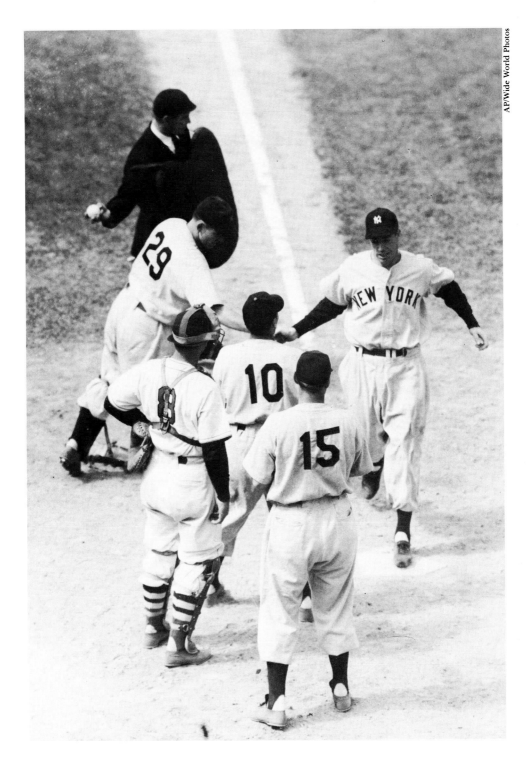

Three days in June: Joe DiMaggio crosses the plate after hitting one of his four home runs against the Red Sox. This was the first of two in the 9–7 Yankee win. Greeting him are Charlie Silvera (29), Phil Rizzuto (10), and Tommy Henrich. Boston catcher Birdie Tebbetts watches.

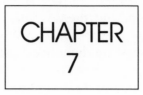

CHAPTER
7

The Yankees had a tradition of playing in big games and winning. Mental toughness was enforced by the team leaders, and a succession of leadership had been established from generation to generation. The one word Henrich thought described those Yankee teams was *tough*. They pushed themselves and each other. It was as if everything they did advertised that this was a serious business. They were accustomed to being the best, and they expected to be the best. Besides, in addition to the glory, they needed the extra money. If they played hard, they would make the World Series, and the additional money in those days was enough to buy a house. A player's salary might be $9,000 or $12,000, and a winner's share in the World Series as much as $5,000.

The Yankee players, not the managers, became the keepers of their own tradition. The harshness in the locker room was a reflection of the economic coldness of the world outside. If a young player came up and did not play hard, the veterans would get on him. "That's my money you're playing with," they would say, and they meant their World Series checks. Usually that was enough. When Eddie Lopat joined the Yankees after several years with the White Sox, he was stunned by the more serious attitude of the Yankee players. Right from the start, in training, they were talking about the need to win the pennant in order to play in the World Series. Nothing was to come between them and their rightful postseason bonus.

"It was a very tough team," Gene Woodling later said. "It was a team where everyone demanded complete effort. It was not a team where anyone ever said 'nice try' when you made a long run after a fly ball and didn't get to it. I played on a lot of other teams and they *all* did that. But not on the Yankees. I think someone might have hit you if you said it—nice try, my ass. You weren't supposed to try, you were supposed to do it. We led the league in RAs—Red Asses—that's the baseball term for very tough, hard guys. We had more than anyone in the league. Even DiMaggio—elegant as hell, beautiful clothes, always a suit, a gent, but on the field a real RA."

Henrich himself had once felt the sting of the veteran players who served as the enforcers of tradition. In his rookie season one day he had fooled around in batting practice, not quite taking it seriously. Suddenly Arndt Jorgens, the third-string catcher, was annoyed. "Come on, Tommy, knock it off. Let's get serious!" The third-string catcher, Henrich thought—this is a tough club. You don't mess around here.

In 1949 Henrich got on Hank Bauer, the intense young outfielder, for not anticipating plays properly. On occasion Bauer would mumble, "How come he's always getting on me, I'm busting my ass out there." The answer was simple: Bauer was a strong and driven player, but there was room for improvement. When Henrich first joined the Yankees, the older players were the enforcers, Then, in the late forties, he, Keller, Lindell, and Billy Johnson took over. DiMaggio was above it; it was out of character for him to push others, although he could on occasion cast a cold glance at a malingerer.

In 1948 Yogi Berra did not yet seem to understand that baseball as played on this team was a deadly serious matter. The Yankees had been playing against Detroit, and Berra had not run out a pop-up; he had made it only to first. That cost the Yankees a run, and, as it turned out, quite possibly a ball game. After the inning Berra came in to strap on his catcher's equipment. Charlie Keller came over to him. "You feeling all right, Yogi?" he asked. "Yeah, I'm fine," Berra said. "Then why the hell didn't you run it out?" Keller asked. Those were hard words from a man who did not waste words. Lindell immediately joined in. Berra looked over to DiMaggio as if to ask for help, particularly because he was a fellow Italian. DiMaggio gave him a withering look. Eddie Lopat, who had watched the entire scene unfold, thought to himself, Now I know why this team is special.

Later that season the Yankees went to Washington for a doubleheader. By then DiMaggio was exhausted by the season and the pain, but he insisted on playing both games. He was so tired that by the end of the second game Lopat and Allie Reynolds virtually carried him off the field. Berra, claiming fatigue, had begged out of the second game, and in his place Gus Niarhos played. Niarhos came up several times with men on base and drove none of them in. Later in the locker room, DiMaggio turned around and said, loud enough for Berra to hear, "Jesus Christ, a twenty-year-old kid and he can't play both ends of a doubleheader when we're fighting down the stretch. What kind of bullshit is this?" From then on Berra's work habits began to improve.

The Red Sox were still looking for that kind of tradition. Yawkey had purchased aging stars from the Athletics and other weak teams in the mid-thirties. These veterans brought their talents, which were still considerable, but they also brought their bad habits. Jimmie Foxx, a great power hitter near the end of a magnificent career, delighted at walking into bars and yelling, "The drinks are on the house—old Double X is here." Often a day at the ball park began by trying to figure out in which local hotel he might still be asleep.

Lefty Grove, one of the greatest pitchers in the history of the sport, had also come to Boston near the end of his career. Grove kept a bottle of whiskey in his locker. He was given to tantrums, though as Ted Williams noted, his tantrums were always beautifully controlled. If he smashed his locker after a tough loss, he always did it with his *right* hand. When Grove was pitching no one wanted to make an error. When he was still with Philadelphia, he had been close to setting a record for consecutive wins. He had fifteen in a row and was going for his sixteenth. A Philadelphia outfielder had gone onto the field without his sunglasses, and had lost a ball in the sun. Grove, according to the story, never spoke to him again.

His Boston teammates could easily believe such stories. Bobby Doerr had a very clear memory of Grove's temper. Early in Doerr's career, Grove was pitching batting practice, and Doerr, in his last swing, hit the ball hard toward the pitcher's mound. He thought nothing of it and left the batting cage to pick up his glove, which was lying near first base. As he bent over to pick it up, a baseball whistled by about two inches from his head. Doerr looked up, and there was Lefty Grove screaming at him, "Don't you ever hit it at me again, you little son of a bitch." Unfortunately, such antics were more about preserving the dignity of Grove than they were about making Boston a better team, Doerr realized.

Some of the older players not only drank harder, they even had their hangover rituals down pat. Joe Dobson, the pitcher, was always amazed at the way they worked off bad nights. They would come out to the ball park early the next day and put on old uniforms and windbreakers. Then they would run very hard, sweating out the booze. When their old uniforms were completely soaked, they would go into the locker room, strip, and just drop their soggy clothes on the floor. Then they showered and dressed in their real uniforms.

That generation had graduated now. But none of the younger men was by nature a leader. Dominic DiMaggio was too reserved; Pesky was feisty, but he was small, and in baseball small men were not often leaders; Doerr was laid back; and Williams wanted no extra responsibilities—striving to be the best hitter in the game and living up to the expectations of the fans and his teammates were quite enough. The Yankees admired the sheer talent of the Red Sox, but thought they lacked mental toughness.

In fact, the Red Sox were a team that looked better on paper than on the field. They were the kind of team that excites a neophyte fan but worries a professional baseball man. They not only lacked depth both on the bench and in the bullpen; they lacked defensive skill and team speed. The Yankees seemed to be strong, fast, and deep at every position. No one took an extra base on any of the Yankee outfielders, Mel Parnell once noted. By contrast, the Red Sox flexed their muscles at the expense of their overall defense.

That was particularly true at shortstop. At this most critical position, Boston was deficient. Junior Stephens played adequate shortstop, although in no sense was he one. When a ball came to him, he often dropped down to one knee to take it. The first time Jerry Coleman saw Stephens, he thought to himself, That is a man who's scared of his job. There were those on the team, including Doerr, who thought the ball was coming in to second awfully late, and Doerr was going to get killed by a base runner if Junior did not speed it up. Pesky had played shortstop before the trade, but McCarthy had moved him to third because he had better hands and was quicker.

Shortstops were the glue of a good team. One reason the Yankees and the Dodgers were perennial pennant winners in that era was that they had the two best shortstops in baseball: Phil Rizzuto and Pee Wee Reese. In 1949 both were in their prime. The great irony was that Reese had been a Red Sox farmhand, the final piece, some of the players thought, in cementing a great team. But he had been traded while he was still a minor-league star ten years earlier, not because he wasn't good enough but because he was too good. Joe Cronin, the player-manager and shorstop at the time, wanted to play five more years, and he wanted no part of Pee Wee Reese.

Unfortunately, Cronin was Tom Yawkey's closest adviser. Here was the real virus in the Boston organization: cronyism. Yawkey had bought the Louisville Colonels for $195,000 for one reason—to gain the rights to its young shortstop. But Cronin managed to ignore Reese's obvious talent. What he saw instead was his size, or lack thereof. The first thing he said when he saw Reese was, "So that's the guy who's going to take my place. He's too small." From then on he kept up a steady drumbeat with Yawkey to get rid of Reese. Reese started the 1939 season slowly, and orders came down from Boston for Billy Evans, who was in charge of the Boston farm system, to sell Reese. Evans resisted as long as he could. Soon Reese began to play well, and Evans begged Cronin to send someone down to look at him. "I'm not interested in Reese," Cronin told Evans. In Brooklyn, Larry MacPhail, a shrewd judge of talent, was watching these events, his mouth watering. He finally bought Reese from Boston for $75,000. Yawkey, who did not need the money, had virtually given away a diamond of a player without even giving him a shot at the major leagues.

Not long afterward a very drunk Yawkey called Evans one night and fired him. Evans told friends that Cronin had been behind this move as well. Had I been out that night at the movies, or had I called him the next day when he was sober and asked for my job back, I could have had it, he told friends. Instead he was pleased to leave. Enough was enough.

Such stories were typical of the Red Sox at the time. It was, for better or worse, an extension of owner Tom Yawkey's whims. If a group of business-school professors might have chosen the Yankees as an exemplary model of cold-blooded organizational skill, then they would have been equally appalled by the Red Sox organization. George Weiss was a hired hand who ran the Yankees as a business; he had a vested interest in maximizing the profit. With very few exceptions he treated his athletes as potential adversaries who would take advantage of any kindness bestowed upon them, and who performed best only when they were hungry. He had no desire to get close to them, and there was no doubt in his mind that he was more important to the success of the Yankees than they were.

If Weiss paid below the going rate, Yawkey, one of the richest if not the richest owner of his generation, made sure that he paid above it. The implicit motto of the Red Sox was that whatever happened, the ballplayers should never be made unhappy.

Yawkey, the heir of a Michigan timber and mining family, had come into a large part of his inheritance when he was thirty, and four days later he bought the team. He was the last of the breed of wealthy owners known in the press of the day as "sportsmen." He idolized his ballplayers. A shy, rather lonely man, his life was simple. He lived during the winter months in the Pierre Hotel in New York. When the baseball season started he moved from New York to Boston, and took up residence in his apartment in the Ritz. There he adhered to a basic routine. He would get up late, eat in his room, then be driven to the ball park by his chauffeur. He would go to his box at Fenway with a few of his close associates, watch the game, start drinking in the later innings, particularly if the Red Sox were losing, and then be driven back to the hotel by his chauffeur, where once again he would eat in his room. Those times when he actually appeared in the Ritz dining room were rare indeed.

Clif Keane, the Boston sportswriter, watched him with fascination all those years. Yawkey was a man, he thought, who loved sports, loved baseball, and loved the people who played it, yet was utterly afraid of them. In 1975, during the memorable World Series between the Red Sox and Cincinnati, Keane turned to Yawkey after one game. "Hey Tom, I'm going over to the Reds' dressing room to talk to Sparky [Anderson]. Want to come along?" "They don't want to meet me, Clif," he answered. "Of course they do, Tom," said Keane, and so they went. Anderson, possibly the most charming and ebullient man in baseball, went out of his way to be gracious to Yawkey. The latter was thrilled. "Clif," he kept saying when he left, "that was grand—just grand. What fun! What a grand fellow!" "Come on, Tom," Keane wanted to say, "what's it all about? Why can't you just be a real person, go out and talk to the baseball people all around you, be human, be natural. They'd all like you, you know."

But Yawkey's shyness, almost pathological, had profound organizational consequences. He drank quietly but steadily in his solitude. He had very few friends, and those with whom he was truly close were such men as Eddie Collins, Joe Cronin, Haywood Sullivan, and Mike Higgins, all of whom worked for him. Obviously, this situation was unhealthy. There was a constant blurring between professional matters and friendship. Yawkey's management staff became small and incestuous. They made him, as he once said of Sullivan, laugh. Some of them became expert at playing to him, at knowing what he wanted to hear, what subjects were forbidden, and how to get what they wanted from him. He liked, for instance, to arm wrestle with Mike Higgins, and Higgins knew when to lose and when to win. It was a matter of instinct and survival.

In notes to himself in the mid-sixties, a time when such

problems seemed even more severe, Boston sportswriter Harold Kaese wrote, "Who would ever advise a friend to take a job under the present alcoholic axis of Yawkey and [Mike] Higgins?" A few years later, Higgins, who had held virtually every job in the Red Sox organization, was sentenced to a four-year prison term in Louisiana for negligent homicide after his car hit and killed a Louisiana state highway department worker and injured three others.

Yawkey was a generous man, but on his own terms. He was quick to reward players for exceptional performances. Boo Ferriss in his rookie year made $700 a month for five months, or a total of $3,500. He was also pitching brilliantly. He won his first eight starts. Cronin kept telling him, "Don't worry about the money—whatever you do, that's not a problem. Mr. T will take care of you." At the end of the season Yawkey called Ferriss in and gave him a bonus of $10,000. There were endless stories like that. He handed Mike Kelley, the head of his Minneapolis farm team, an envelope after Ted Williams had spent a year there. Inside the envelope was a note that said, "Thanks, Mike, for making a ballplayer out of Williams," and $10,000 in cash.

But Yawkey could also act like a spoiled child. Once when a Boston sportswriter mentioned some of the things about the team that bothered Boston fans, Yawkey's temper quickly flashed. "Just remember, I have the last word," he said. "I always have the last word." Generally, if a sportswriter wrote a story that annoyed him, he would rant that by God the next day he was going to buy the paper and put the SOB out of work.

Some thought Yawkey was merely trying to have a belated childhood by playing with grown-up toys. When Earl Johnson first arrived at spring training in 1940, he noticed a heavy-set man dressing at the locker next to him. How can that fat guy play baseball? Johnson thought. That's disgraceful— he's way out of shape. Just then the man spoke. "Aren't you Earl Johnson?" "Yes," answered the rookie. "I'm Tom Yawkey," said the man. He stuck out his hand. "Nice to meet you, Mr. Yawkey," mumbled Johnson. "Cut out that Mister stuff, my name's Tom," Yawkey said. In fact, the owner liked nothing better than to put on a Red Sox uniform and, with a handful of substitute players helping out and local urchins running down the balls in the outfield, take batting practice. At these times no one else was around in his own ball park, and there was a hard rule: No photographers were ever to capture this moment. The batting-practice pitchers were under orders to groove the ball on all occasions (according to Kaese they substituted tightly wound, hopped-up balls—Phillips 99 balls they were called—so that the ball would carry and hit the wall). The ball boys were handsomely tipped for their efforts. The scorer was at best biased: Anything Yawkey hit, no matter how flagrant the mishandling in the field, was a hit; anything hit by others and mishandled by others was an error. The bench players who participated were considered sycophants by their teammates (the "ass-kisser all-stars" was the exact nickname).

Though he loved his players and the idea of being a part of the game, Yawkey became increasingly reclusive. He had been close to Grove and Foxx and that generation of stars, for they were his own age and would go on hunting and fishing trips with him. But by the time of the Williams-Pesky generation, he was close only to Williams, the superstar. Dick O'Connell, one of the front-office men, would push Yawkey to get out and visit with the other players, which he did, though somewhat reluctantly. He would invariably spot Eddie Pellagrini, a utility infielder. "Eddie, how are you," he would say. "Gee, he really likes me, doesn't he?" Pellagrini would say, beaming, to Dick O'Connell after one such visit. "Eddie," answered O'Connell, "you're the only one he knows."

All of this showed in the attitude of the team, and also in the bottom line. The Yankees in those days were, by outside estimate, making an annual profit of about 5 or 6 million dollars. In 1948, despite the feverish pennant race and the fact that Boston set an attendance record, the Red Sox showed a profit of only $55,000. That meant that without the profits from the playoff game, the Red Sox might have run in the red. In only four of Yawkey's sixteen years did the team show a profit. Perhaps Yawkey did not want to make a profit because he would only have ended up paying more income tax. But the statistic says something important: He never regarded baseball as a business.

*   *   *

Despite their encouraging victory over the Yankees in May, in June the Red Sox continued to slip. McCarthy was becoming irritable. He could not wait to unload Sam Mele, who had played a fair amount for him in right field in 1948. After one game the previous year in which Mele had not gotten to a ball, McCarthy turned to the bench and said, "Henrich would have stuck that in his ass." The criticism had stung, for it was an unfavorable comparison with the Yankees. The next day Mele went into McCarthy's office to order some bats. "I thought you might want to order a glove, not bats," McCarthy said.

In May, still looking for a right-fielder, Boston bought Al Zarilla, a skilled outfielder, from the hapless St. Louis Browns. Zarilla was following in the footsteps of Kramer, Stephens, and Kinder. The price tag was said to have been between $125,000 and $150,000. THE BOSTON BROWNS, the Red Sox should now be called, the *Globe* said in a headline. Luke Sewell, a former Browns player and then manager with the Reds, said of the Red Sox, "They must have the most profitable franchise in baseball. It's the only club that's supporting two teams in the same league—their own and the St. Louis Browns." But even the purchase of Zarilla did not seem to improve the way the Red Sox were playing. They were impressive at home and in games where they established big leads early, but they had trouble in close games.

McCarthy responded by spending more time at the end of the bench with Gus Froelich, the trainer who had come up with him from the Yankees. One of Froelich's jobs was to keep a towel discreetly wrapped around a bottle of whiskey and, when things were going badly, to make himself available to the manager.

In early June the Red Sox went on the road and lost two of three to the Indians. Nothing seemed to go right. Lemon beat Kinder 8–3. Kinder had given up ten hits and didn't even make it through the third inning. With a record now of 4–3, he seemed on his way to a most ordinary season. The next day Early Wynn beat Dobson 8–1. On the train from Cleveland to Detroit, McCarthy walked through the Pullman cars to find his players slumped and asleep in their seats in

broad daylight. "What the hell is this?" he shouted with reporters within hearing distance. "If they had to play a doubleheader after a night game there might be some reason for
this—for sleeping in the daytime."

Detroit turned out to be even worse. Parnell started in the
first game and at one point Boston led 7–1. But, bothered by
what he felt was a flat mound, Parnell lost his control. McCarthy went to Tex Hughson, whom he did not like. By the
eighth Boston was still ahead, 9–6, and McCarthy called on
Earl Johnson. Johnson was one of the better relief pitchers on
the Red Sox—a sinker-ball, screwball pitcher who made hitters hit the ball down. In 1948, he had been 10-4. But McCarthy had never, in Johnson's view, hidden his contempt for
him. On this day Johnson was sick with an intestinal flu, and
had not even wanted to come to the ball park. When McCarthy told him to go down to the bullpen, Johnson felt he could
barely walk. He gave up a hit to George Vico, and then walked
three men in a row, forcing in Vico. That made it 9–7, with
the bases loaded. He had never walked three men in a row
before in his life. As Johnson walked to the bench, McCarthy
never looked at him. But his voice was very clear: "Big-league
pitcher my ass! Can't even get the goddamn ball over." Having
your manager talk like that in front of your teammates,
Johnson thought, was like dying a little. Next, Ellis Kinder
came in from the bullpen. He gave up an outfield fly, which
scored a run and made it 9–8. Then he walked a man, and the
bases were loaded. He gave up a single, which made it 9–9.
Up came a pinch hitter named Connie Berry, who was hitting
.085 at the time. Kinder walked him on five pitches and the
Tigers had the lead and the game, 10–9.

The next day there was a doubleheader. Joe Dobson
asked to pitch the first game and won 5–3. But in the second
game Mickey Harris started. His arm hurting him, he gave up
7 runs in the first six innings. By the eighth inning it was 7–2.
With the game virtually gone, McCarthy again called on
Johnson, who was still sick. He stood out there, weak and fee-
ble, and, in his own words, pitched as if it were batting practice. He gave up 6 hits and 4 runs in one inning. McCarthy
left him out there. When Johnson walked back to the dugout,
again he heard McCarthy's voice: "Christ sake, if you kept

them from scoring we might actually win a game sometime."
This time Johnson turned and said, "I'll tell you one fucking
thing—at least I didn't walk anyone this time." Johnson knew
he was finished on the team.

McCarthy could not control himself. He was furious at
Johnson. He was furious at Kinder. Kinder was always breaking rules; he was always the last man on the bus and he looked
like the party had been going on all night and was still going
on. He was going to learn. A day after the Detroit defeat, Mc-
Carthy imposed a midnight curfew, the first curfew he had
ever given the team. Kinder was hardly bothered by it. He had
decided that McCarthy ruled by a double standard: one for
the stars and another for the other players. He had no in-
tention of observing the curfew.

Within a week Sam Mele and Mickey Harris were gone,
traded to Washington for Walt Masterson. The *Boston Globe*
was underwhelmed. Its headline said: SOX TRADE ENDS SENTI-
MENT FOR POSSIBLE PENNANT.

CHAPTER
8

In mid-June Joe DiMaggio got up one morning and stepped cautiously on the floor, expecting the pain to shoot through his foot once again. Miraculously, the pain was gone. He touched his heel with his hand. Until then it had felt hot to the touch. Now it felt normal. He began to smile. He walked around the apartment and felt no pain.

That day, for the first time in weeks, he went out for both lunch and dinner. On the street when people recognized him he was pleased. He was delighted to sign autographs. Soon, he decided to take batting practice. The team was on a western trip, but Gus Niarhos, a backup catcher who was injured, and Al Schacht, a former pitcher known as The Clown Prince of Baseball, were available. Schacht could still throw reasonably hard. For fielders they got a bunch of neighborhood kids who hung around the Stadium. The workout lasted an hour.

Soon DiMaggio expanded the workouts. He had Niarhos hit fly balls to him, and he would run them down. He was easily winded, and his legs were not in shape, but there was no pain. The Yankees came home from their road trip, and he showed up at the park in uniform. No one asked questions about whether he was ready. One morning he called Curt

Gowdy, who lived in the same hotel, and they drove out to the Stadium together so that Gowdy could watch him take batting practice. When he finished, Gowdy took a look at his hands. They were completely covered with bloody blisters caused by the batting.

"Jesus, Joe, look at that," Gowdy said.

"Oh, that's nothing, forget about that," DiMaggio answered. "I took too much batting practice, but that doesn't matter. There's no pain in my foot. That matters."

Cleveland was in town for the first series of the home stand and Lou Boudreau, the Cleveland manager, was also the manager of the American League in the All-Star Game. It was still two weeks away and Boudreau told DiMaggio he hoped he would be able to play. "I'm not even in the running," DiMaggio said, for the fans voted then.

"I think it could be arranged," Boudreau said.

After the first game with Cleveland, when everyone else had left the park, DiMaggio asked Niarhos to hit fly balls to him in the outfield for half an hour. Then he ran around the outfield a few times. Again there was no pain. After the Cleveland series, the Yankees had an exhibition game with the Giants at home before going up to Boston for three games. Stengel told DiMaggio simply to let him know when he was ready, and DiMaggio decided to try the exhibition game.

Before the game there was a home-run–hitting contest, and by far the biggest cheers were for DiMaggio. He hit only one out, but it drew even wilder cheers from the crowd. He went hitless in four trips during the game, but the Giants had used Kirby Higbe, who was throwing a knuckle ball at the time. It was not the optimum pitch to return against. The next day the team left for Boston, and until the last minute DiMaggio did not know if he would make the trip. He was torn between the desire to play and the fear that he wasn't ready for real pitching. He did not want to embarrass himself and hurt the team. The other players went up by train in the morning. He waited and then finally jumped on a 3:15 plane. On the plane he saw a friend who asked if he was going to play. "I don't know," he answered. At 5:15 he arrived at the clubhouse. Stengel was surrounded by writers who were asking for the lineup. He was still waiting to hear from DiMaggio.

DiMaggio was dressing slowly, pondering what to do, and Stengel was stalling the writers. Finally DiMaggio said yes, he could play, so Stengel put him in the lineup.

In their dugout the Red Sox watched DiMaggio come out to warm up. One of the younger Boston players predicted that DiMaggio would have a hard time running out an infield hit. McCarthy, a great DiMaggio fan, immediately interrupted him. "You don't know him. You watch him the first time there's a chance for an infield hit. Watch how he runs," he said. There was an ominous note to the way McCarthy said it, one of the Boston pitchers thought, as if he were saying, "*They* are the real professionals."

In the first game Mickey McDermott was pitching for the Red Sox. He was young, skinny, and wild. In the second inning DiMaggio led off. McDermott was very fast, one of the three or four fastest pitchers in the league. DiMaggio found it hard to adjust his batting eye to McDermott's speed and he fouled off six or seven pitches. Each one went off to the right, which meant that he was swinging late. Finally McDermott came in with a fastball, belt-high, and DiMaggio slapped it over Junior Stephens's head for a single. That was a hit well earned. Then Lindell walked and Hank Bauer hit a home run. The Yankees were up, 3–0. In the third Rizzuto singled to start the inning, then DiMaggio came up again. That man, McDermott thought, does not seem to me like a player who has missed two months of play, that looks to me like the real Joe DiMaggio. On the mound he said a prayer: "Please, dear God, help me get this man out. I won't ask anything else from you today." Then, he remembers, "I heard this deep voice answering me: 'I'll help you get him out, Maurice, if you've got a really good fastball today. Other than that, son, you're on your own.'" He was, it appeared, on his own. This time DiMaggio put his body into a pitch and hit it over the wall. How sweet the feeling was. Rizzuto jumped up and down like a little kid as DiMaggio crossed home plate. The Yankees won 5–4 behind Reynolds and Page.

Ellis Kinder pitched the second game against Tommy Byrne. Byrne, a lefty, was intimidated by Fenway. He never made it past the first inning. He walked three and gave up three doubles in a row to Williams, Stephens, and Doerr. In the second, with the Yankees playing deep, Williams bunted for a hit and then Stephens hit a home run. The Red Sox took a 7–1 lead into the fifth. Even in Fenway, that was a huge lead against a tough pitcher. But in the fifth, Kinder seemed to lose his control. He walked Rizzuto and Henrich, which brought up DiMaggio. Kinder was a hard pitcher for DiMaggio, who preferred a fastball pitcher; Kinder usually relied on subtlety instead of power. This time, though, DiMaggio got the pitch he wanted and drove the ball over the fence in left center. The score was now 7–4.

In the seventh Gene Woodling doubled off Earl Johnson with the bases loaded. In the eighth, with the score tied 7–7, and with two out and no one on, DiMaggio came up again against Johnson. The Boston fans, aware that something remarkable was going on, had started cheering for DiMaggio as well as for their own team. Johnson, the top Boston relief pitcher, was determined not to give DiMaggio anything good to hit. He was aware that Williams and DiMaggio were in a dead heat for the title of best hitter in baseball. A few years earlier, with a game on the line, Johnson had pitched to DiMaggio with two out and men on second and third. Joe Cronin had come out to the mound. "Whatever you do, Earl," he had said, "don't throw him a strike. Don't let him beat us." Johnson had placed the ball exactly where he wanted it, about six inches on the outside, but DiMaggio had pounced on it and, even more remarkably, pulled the ball past third for the game-winning hit. A few months later Johnson ran into DiMaggio at a postseason banquet. "Joe, how in the hell did you pull that ball?" Johnson asked. "I figured that when Cronin came out he told you not to give me anything good to hit. I was sure he told you to pitch on the outside. So I waited, and I was ready," he answered.

Johnson decided to give DiMaggio a low inside curve, a hard pitch for a hitter to get in the air. He put the ball exactly where he wanted it. To his amazement DiMaggio reached down and golfed the ball way over the wall and onto the screen. It was the hardest kind of swing for a good hitter, particularly one who was out of tune. As DiMaggio neared the dugout, Stengel, never one to miss an opportunity for theater, came out and starting bowing toward him like a Muslim to Mecca.

Even before the Boston game, DiMaggio's return had become, day-by-day, an occasion of national drama. Now it was a national sensation, so much so that he later sold his account of it to *Life* magazine for $6,000, a very large figure for the period. DiMaggio's own memory was of the noise and cheering, which grew and grew, inning by inning, until it was deafening.

That afternoon, in the locker room, DiMaggio teased Rizzuto, who had knocked in two runs. "What are you trying to do, steal my RBIs?" he asked. Rizzuto, who had played with him for almost a decade, had never seen him so playful. Spec Shea went over to him and asked if he was in any pain. "Nothing hurts when you play like this," he answered.

There was one game left. Raschi against Parnell—ace against ace that year: Raschi was 11-2 going in, Parnell was 10-3. If any Boston pitcher could stop DiMaggio in Fenway, it was Mel Parnell.

If there is such a thing as a natural in baseball, it was Parnell. He threw, both teammates and opponents thought, so effortlessly that it was almost unbelievable. He had fully intended to be a first baseman, not a pitcher. As a boy all he had wanted to do was hit. He played on a strong New Orleans high school team, where on occasion he would pitch batting practice to his teammates. "Stop throwing breaking stuff," they would yell, and he would explain that he was throwing fastballs.

One day a Red Sox scout was in town to scout a teammate. Parnell's team was short of pitchers, and his coach had asked him to pitch for the first time in his life. He struck out seventeen. The Boston scout, Ed Montague, reported back that they should go after Parnell. The Cardinals had already begun to make overtures to him and some of his high school teammates. In the thirties, the Cardinals under Branch Rickey had the best farm system in the country, and New Orleans was considered a Cardinal town. The local team, the New Orleans Pelicans, was a Cardinal farm team. Seven players from Parnell's high school team signed professional contracts, six of them with the Cards. A couple of times Parnell pitched batting practice against the Pelicans and that heightened Cardinal interest. Soon Branch Rickey himself began to appear at the Parnell home. He was a dapper figure, very much the gent in derby hat and spats. Patrick Parnell, an engineer on the Illinois Central, loved to talk baseball, and here was one of the most famous men in baseball dropping in on him.

No one ever accused Branch Rickey of not being a wonderful salesman—whether he was selling God or major-league baseball or himself. He mesmerized the senior Parnell with stories of big-league baseball. Patrick Parnell thought Mr. Rickey a wonderful man and a religious man, but Mel Parnell took a harder look. Even though he was desperate to be a big-league ballplayer, he wanted no part of Branch Rickey or the Cardinals. They had a simple philosophy behind their system: Sign every talented kid they could for very little money, put them in a giant farm system, let them fight their way to the top, keep a handful of the best for themselves, and trade or sell a few others. (The penurious quality of the St. Louis organization was well known even within the largely penurious world of baseball. In 1948, the Cardinals had signed their great outfielder, Stan Musial, to a new contract of $28,000, the largest amount of money ever paid to a St. Louis ballplayer.) As their best players became slightly advanced, not so much in years as in salary, they would replace them with younger, less-expensive players. In one period, between 1938 and 1942, the Cardinals sold off a number of their best players for a total of $625,000 while steadily improving their team. "How can I sell so many players and still come up with a winning team?" Rickey said in an interview. "I'll tell you. It's mass production! And by that I mean mass production primarily in tryout camps and mass production primarily of pitchers."

The Cardinals had three AAA teams, two AA teams, and a host of lesser ones. The Cardinal Chain Gang it was called by players caught within it and unable to get out. Mel Parnell at seventeen was smart enough to know he wanted something different. He had heard about Rickey's sales pitch—golden-tongued, yet homey, and was wary of succumbing to it. Therefore, on the frequent occasions that Branch Rickey showed up at the Parnell house, Mel Parnell did not come home until he was sure that their guest had gone.

He signed with Boston, and entered the Boston farm system at the age of twenty. Parnell moved up quickly, and might have made the majors by the time he was twenty-five except for World War II, which took three years out of his career. By 1948 he was ready to pitch in Fenway. That part did not come naturally. He had been purely a power pitcher until then. But power pitchers, he knew, particularly left-handed ones, died young in Fenway. Howie Pollet, a talented young Cardinal pitcher who was a friend in New Orleans and who had pitched in Fenway in 1946, warned Parnell, "Mel, you can't do it with the fastball. You'll go up in big games against the best hitters in baseball and they'll just sit on it and kill you." So Parnell developed a slider by holding the ball differently, off the seams. Also, Joe Dobson, who had the best curve on the team, taught him something about throwing the curve. It was not a lesson that began well. "Dobson," Parnell told Dobson, "why don't you get the hell out of here—I know more about pitching than you'll ever know." Parnell and his friend Mickey Harris, who was also young and talented and left-handed, specialized in being cocky and fresh. They drove Joe Cronin crazy. "The two wise asses," he would call them. Cronin would see them near the bench and he would say, "Out of here, you two wise asses, get out. Get down to the bullpen. Anywhere, but get out of here."

Parnell was determined to figure out Fenway. Most pitchers, particularly left-handers, fearing the Wall, pitched defensively—outside to the right-handers. Parnell refused to buckle under. He would pitch inside and tight, especially to such big, powerful hitters as Lindell, DiMaggio, Keller, and Billy Johnson. He would pin their arms in against them so that they could not gain true leverage. It was later said that Hank Bauer and Mickey Mantle broke so many of their bats against him on sliders coming in to the narrow part of the bat that they felt he should buy them new ones. The hard part of pitching in Fenway, Parnell believed, was not the wall. Rather it was the lack of foul territory. The stands were right on top of the field. It was a fan's delight but a pitcher's nightmare, because a good many foul balls that were caught in other parks went into the stands at Fenway. A nine-inning game at Fenway would have been a ten-inning game anywhere else.

Statistics are not always the best gauge of players, but in Parnell's case they are unusually revealing. In 1949 his earned-run average at home was 2.59, and on the road it was 3.02; for his career, his Fenway earned-run average was just slightly under his road one.

The Yankees were leading 3–2 in the seventh, a narrow margin in Fenway on a day when Raschi was in the process of giving up 12 hits. Again it came down to DiMaggio against the Red Sox pitcher. Stirnweiss had singled. Rizzuto had made the second out of the inning. Then Henrich had singled. Parnell stepped off the mound to think for a minute. He essentially called his own pitches. He did not trust catchers to do it because he did not think they had a feel for pitching; they could not, for example, *feel* the ball and know that the stitches on each ball are different, and as the stitches are different, the pitcher's finger control is different. Parnell liked to take each ball, feel the stitches, and then make his own decision.

On this day his best pitch was his fastball, and he decided to go with it. The one thing he was not going to throw Joe DiMaggio was a change-up. As a rookie he had been in the bullpen during a series in the Stadium, and DiMaggio had come to the plate. Bill Zuber, a veteran pitcher, called Parnell over. "Kid," he said, "whatever you do, don't throw this guy a change. If you do, he'll hit it into the third deck." A few innings later, the Red Sox were in trouble. Zuber went into the game with DiMaggio up and men on base. To Parnell's amazement, Zuber threw a change. DiMaggio hit it into the third tier. It hooked foul at the last moment. Zuber pitched again. Another change. Again DiMaggio jumped on it, and this time it carried into the third tier, fair. That was the game. Afterward, Parnell saw Zuber in the locker room hitting his head against the wall, saying, "Dumb Dutchman! Dumb goddamn Dutchman! I tell the kid not to throw the change and then I do it myself! Dumb goddamn Dutchman!"

DiMaggio was a great hitter on a tear, and if Parnell was going to win, he wanted to win with his best pitch, and if he was going to be beaten, it might as well also be with his best pitch. His first pitch was a fastball just where he wanted it; DiMaggio lifted a high foul to the right side of the infield. Parnell breathed a sigh of relief. Billy Goodman was playing first, and the ball hit the heel of his glove and dropped out. Strike one. Parnell came back with the same pitch. Again DiMaggio fouled it off, this time with a squiggly little ball near the plate. Parnell began to feel very confident because he had DiMaggio 0-and-2. This time he decided to make him go fishing, and threw just off the outside corner. Another batter behind in the count might have gone for it. DiMaggio did not. Ball one. Parnell decided to waste another one, this time on the inside. Again DiMaggio did not bite. Parnell did not want to come in to DiMaggio on a 3-and-2 count and so he threw his best fastball. With a great hitter like DiMaggio, finally you challenged him. DiMaggio, who had been waiting for a fastball, killed it. The ball hit the steel towers in left field. For the next five minutes Parnell was sure that all Joe DiMaggio could hear was the cheers of the crowd, while the only thing *he* could hear was the steel ringing from the impact of the ball. Over Fenway flew a small biplane trailing a banner that said: THE GREAT DIMAGGIO.

It made the score 6–2. Raschi finished the game, and the Yankees swept the series. DiMaggio, in three games, had absolutely demolished the Red Sox: four home runs and nine runs batted in. It was the sweetest of all returns, and after that game, in the madness of the Yankee locker room, DiMaggio walked past Jerry Coleman and grinned, which was unusual; it was as close as he ever came to boasting or gloating. "You can't beat this life, kid," he said.

In the broadcast booth Mel Allen was ecstatic. As he had for more than a decade, he was relaying over the airwaves that day his affection—reverence, even—for DiMaggio. "His fourth home run!" he shouted when DiMaggio hit the last one off Parnell. "What a comeback for Joe!" It was, he noted years later, one of the greatest performances he had ever witnessed, and it was achieved by a player he admired more than any other.

Once when Allen's parents came to New York to visit him, he gave them tickets to a game. Afterward his mother said to him, "Son, I think today I finally understood why I've heard so much about DiMaggio and why he means so much to you." "Why is that?" he asked her. "Well, I just watched the way he trotted onto the field, and he was different from the others—he did it so regally," she answered.

Allen's and DiMaggio's careers were twined; radio as a prime instrument of sports communication, and Mel Allen as one of its foremost practitioners, ascended at the very moment that Joe DiMaggio did. And both were in New York, the city from which much of America's broadcasting originated and where its great advertising firms and communications companies were headquartered. The Yankees were the dominant team, and Mel Allen amplified that dominance. With a soft, almost silky voice, and a natural feel for the microphone, he not only brought the fan into the Stadium but also projected a sense of intimacy with the players; Allen made the fan feel as if he were a part of the greater Yankee family. He would begin by painting a word portrait of the crowd that day, or of the way the players looked. He used the crowd noise with great dexterity, letting it infect the listener at home with excitement. "The big crowd," he would say, "is roaring on every pitch." He used the crowd noise, in his own words, as a chorus. You could not, he warned, ever beat it, so you tried to anticipate it, get the essential call in just ahead of it.

Television would be different in many ways, not least of all for the athletes. In the beginning it seemed to bring them greater fame, but in time it became clear that the fame was not so much greater as quicker. More often than not, it also evaporated sooner. For soon, of course, television would produce overkill: too many seasons of too many sports overlapping, too many athletes whose deeds were played and replayed endlessly on videotape. As radio was an instrument that could heighten the mystique of a player, television eventually demythologized the famous. It is no coincidence that DiMaggio's fame was so lasting, and that he was the last great hero of the radio era.

DiMaggio became something of a television huckster much later in his life. But his fans, looking at this gray-haired figure selling a bank or coffee, did not resent him for doing this. Because when DiMaggio had played, his fans were left with nothing but the deeds. Back then they listened to the deeds and created in their minds a man as heroic off the field as on. Radio, after all, demanded the use of the fan's imagination as television did not.

It was DiMaggio's good fortune to play in an era when his better qualities, both athletic and personal, were amplified, and his lesser qualities simply did not exist. If he did something magnificent on the field, he was not on Johnny Carson the next night, awkward and unsure of himself, mumbling his answers as a modern athlete might. Rather, he had Mel Allen to speak for him. It was the almost perfect combination: his deeds amplified by Mel Allen's voice.

He was raised Melvin Israel in small towns in Alabama, where his parents, with marginal success, ran the local dry-goods stores. Mel Israel's mother wanted him to be a concert violinist, but somewhere along the way he got sidetracked. He was bright and precocious and went to the University of Alabama, where he picked up both an undergraduate degree and a law degree. He also wrote for the school newspaper, and made the public address for the Alabama football team as well as broadcast their games for a Birmingham radio station (the station had asked Frank Thomas, the football coach, for someone who could announce the games, and Thomas, not knowing there was a difference between being the PA announcer and a broadcaster, had suggested Mel Israel).

When he graduated from Alabama in 1936, he went to New York, more on a lark than anything else. But radio was in the back of his mind. He stopped by a new network called CBS for an audition. He had heard stories of these auditions—they were said to be held in a small, dark room without windows. There he would be told to improvise and describe some imaginary scene. (This turned out not to be true.) He was supposed to go back to Alabama and teach speech for $1,800 a year. But the people at CBS were impressed, and they offered him a job at $45 a week—some $500 more a year than Alabama was offering. They also requested he change his name because a Jewish name might become a hindrance to his career.

He accepted the CBS job, much to the annoyance of his father. Julius Allen Israel felt that he had sacrificed for this young man's education, and that a career as a lawyer was more proper. "All you're going to do on radio is talk," his father warned. What was worse was the imminent change of name: "What's so bad with Mel Israel?" To appease him, he took his father's middle name. Thus did he become Mel Allen. He promised his father he was going to do this only for a short time. "You'll never come back," Julius Israel said prophetically.

Allen's first job was doing organ selections on the mighty Wurlitzer on a morning show. There was precious little baseball on radio at the time. In 1937 radio did the Opening Day game and the World Series, but not the regular-season games. Other cities might broadcast their baseball games, but not New York—because there were three teams, and because the owners were all traditionalists who feared that radio would draw fans away from the park. They made a three-way agreement to ban virtually all broadcasting of games.

But by 1939, when the agreement was finished, Larry MacPhail had arrived in Brooklyn, the new owner of what was traditionally the weakest and poorest of the three teams. MacPhail enraged the purists—he put lights in the stadiums and broadcast his games. One of his first acts was to hire the immensely gifted Red Barber as his broadcaster and to do all his home games live. That opened up the broadcasting of baseball in New York.

Mel Allen had always hoped that it would happen. In 1937 and 1938 he had gone regularly to Yankee Stadium, where, seated in the back row, behind first base, as far from other fans as he could get, he transformed himself into Mel Allen, Secret Announcer. He would call the pitches, describe the crowd, talk about the players: "Well, folks, that brings up Lou Gehrig and Lou has one hit today, and his average is right at three-fifty and I know he'd like to push that average up just a little . . ." If someone sat nearby, Allen would stop. But that was not really a problem. One of the first things an outsider realizes about New York, he soon decided, was that there are hundreds and hundreds of people who go around all day long talking to themselves. Sometimes he would watch the game and the crowd and think to himself, God, I would give anything to broadcast from here.

In 1939, the local CBS station secured a contract to do the Yankee and Giant home games, and Mel Allen became the assistant sportscaster for Arch McDonald. The job was open because McDonald's previous assistant had referred to Ivory Soap as *Ovary* Soap. A year later, McDonald, judged too bucolic for New York, was back in Washington and Mel Allen was the principal broadcaster. The Yankees were in the final phase of their transition from the Ruth-Gehrig era to the DiMaggio era. Ruth had last played in 1934, and 1939 was to be Gehrig's last year. In 1938 he seemed to be slowing down, but no one could believe at first that it was illness. Allen remembered being in the dugout the day that Gehrig asked to be taken out. Gehrig sat and cried. Lefty Gomez went over and put his arm around him and said, "Don't feel badly, Lou. It took twenty-one hundred thirty games to get you out, and sometimes it only takes fifteen minutes to get me out of a game."

Sometimes during that season Gehrig would visit the team. On one occasion he came over to Mel Allen and told him how much he liked what Allen was doing. "You know, Mel," he had said, "I never understood the importance of your broadcasts because I never got to listen, but now I've got to tell you that the one thing that keeps me going is hearing your broadcasts." Allen excused himself, walked up the runway, and burst into tears.

The reward for what he was doing was never the money—in the early days he did not make very much, perhaps $15,000 a year. The real reward was in living a dream. This was the best of all possible substitute lives. He was wedded to the mike. That was his love. He never married. His family moved to suburban New York and he lived at home. His mother, a powerful personality, made clear to the young women who went out with him that if they were serious about her son, there was a hard road ahead. He was often seen in the company of stunning young women, but Tom Meany, the sportswriter, would always say, "Here comes Mel Allen with the future Miss Jones."

Gradually he created a signature language. If there was a play that excited him, he would intone, *"How about that?"* A home run was not just a home run, it was a ball that he virtually rode—"Going, going . . . it is gone." Tommy Byrne was not just a pitcher who hit well, he was "one of those gooood hittin' pitchers." "How often is it," he would say when a player led off the inning, "that when a player makes a spectacular play in the field he leads off the next inning." If a pitcher had very little on a given day, Allen did not say that he was pitching poorly, he said instead that the pitcher had plenty of moxie. And he was always selling beer. No one did the transition from the game to commercial better: "Little Phil made a great play on that last ball, and you'll make a great play for yourself if you open up a Ballantine beer." Between innings would come the full commercial: "If you're listening in at your favorite tavern, don't just say 'one up,' but be sure to ask the man for Ballantine. Enjoy the two B's, baseball and Ballantine. As you linger over that sparkling glass of Ballantine beer, as you feel it trickle down your throat, you'll say, 'Ah, man, this is the life!' *Baseball* and Ballantine beer. And while we linger on this pleasant subject, folks, I'd like to remind you that it's a smart idea to keep plenty of Ballantine on ice at home, to serve at mealtimes, to enjoy during leisure hours, so at your dealer's be sure to look for the three rings. Ask him for Ballantine beer." Listening, one could always sense his pleasure in every aspect of what he did.

When Allen switched to television he did not like it nearly as well. His words became extraneous. Such writers as Jack Gould of the *Times* often criticized him for talking too much during a telecast. There was no small measure of truth there, Allen thought. Television, he soon decided, was a medium in which both the broadcaster and the fan became lazy—the broadcaster because he had to let the camera do so much of the work and the fan because he did not have to use his imagination. Allen felt he had a less-intimate relationship with his viewers.

CHAPTER
9

After Joe DiMaggio left Boston's pennant hopes a shambles, the Red Sox lost three in a row to the Athletics, and then went to New York for a July 4 doubleheader. There, in the first game, they played what Bobby Doerr thought was their toughest game of the year.

The Stadium was a hard park for the Red Sox. Among the hitters, only Williams had no problem with its vast spaces. Yankee pitchers traditionally honored him by keeping the ball away, and, more often than not in late innings, by walking him. On this day the Red Sox were hitting Raschi relatively hard (they were to outhit the Yankees 10 to 5, but they went into the ninth inning of the first game trailing 3–2). Dominic DiMaggio, who had homered for one of the Boston runs, struck out to lead off the inning. Then Pesky singled to center, and Williams followed with a single to right. Raschi worked Junior Stephens so carefully that Stephens walked.

That loaded the bases and brought up Al Zarilla, the right-fielder. There was still only one out. Doerr, standing in the on-deck circle, knew that all Zarilla had to do was get the ball in the air, and they had a tie score. Raschi seemed to be tiring. Just then the ball park turned dark. A sudden, violent wind storm blew into the Stadium. Scorecards and debris swirled out of the stands. The game was halted for a moment while the worst blew over. Doerr remembered thinking that wind was a problem in Yankee Stadium because much of it was three-tiered—thus it held in the wind. The storm diminished somewhat, and play resumed, though it was still dark. Forty years later Doerr could still see the events that followed, moment by moment, unfolding as if in slow motion. Zarilla lined a ball sharply to right field, a clean hit for a guaranteed tie score. Cliff Mapes charged the ball, ready to throw. The play was, of course, not about Pesky, who was on third; it was about *Williams*, at second, and whether two runs rather than one would score. Mapes cut loose with the throw, certain even as he let go that he had made an almost perfect play.

Then Doerr looked from right field to third and saw Pesky just beginning to race for the plate. He was shocked. Pesky should have been virtually upon the plate by that time. What had happened was this: Pesky had taken a normal lead—he had broken for the plate when Zarilla hit the ball. But when he was about twenty feet down the line, he had stopped. For in the darkness he could not see clearly enough to tell whether Mapes would catch the ball. As he started for home, he heard the third-base coach, Kiki Cuyler, yelling at him to tag up. So he went back to third. (Both the Yankee shortstop Rizzuto and the third baseman Billy Johnson said that they thought Pesky had played it right. From that angle, it was hard to be sure the ball would fall in.) As Pesky got back to third, he saw Williams roaring toward him, almost on top of him. Williams was screaming at him to go for home. Pesky stumbled momentarily and then raced for home.

Normally Mapes's throw would have been cut off by the first baseman, Dick Kryhoski. But Mapes did not intend this and threw over Kryhoski's head; the ball headed for Yogi Berra on one bounce. On the base paths there was utter confusion. Williams was yelling at Pesky; Stephens had rounded second and was now heading back to it. Zarilla, previously the bearer of a 0 for 14 slump and thrilled with this clutch hit, was watching Mapes as he made his turn past first. When Mapes had gone home with the play, Zarilla started for second, only to see Stephens coming back to the same base. There was only one person who seemed to understand the entire play, Doerr later realized, and that was Yogi Berra. Berra had seen Pesky come down the line and then go back to tag. He waited for Mapes's throw, not crouched down protecting the plate but in front of it, body extended, like a first baseman, stretching for the ball. He took the ball on the first bounce while keeping his left foot on the plate. A fraction of a second later Pesky slid in. Joe Papparella, the home-plate umpire, seeing no tag, called him safe. Berra got ready to charge Papparella. "He's out!" Berra screamed. "You never tagged him," the umpire yelled back. "Look at third base—it's a force play," Berra shouted. Then in an instant Papparella understood: It had been a force play at the plate. "No—you're out!" Papparella yelled at Pesky, reversing himself.

Doerr stood there in utter disbelief. A sure run, perhaps two, had become the second out. Now he was batting with the bases loaded against a tough right-handed pitcher.

At least the wind was with him, for it was blowing out to right. Raschi threw him a ball out over the plate, and when Doerr swung, he was sure that he had gotten all of it, that it was a certain home run. He had hit it toward right, where the grandstand rises in three tiers. He watched Mapes go back to the fence. Then in one terrible glance he watched Mapes, his back almost touching the wall, start to come in one step and then another. Then he caught the ball. Doerr had been cheated by a rare combination of the wind and the contours of the ball park: The wind had swept into the right-field wall and then bounced off, reversing its direction to come back toward the field, carrying the ball back with it.

In the second game the Yankees won again, in part because of DiMaggio's fifth homer against Boston in a week. For Boston it seemed just another missed opportunity in a season that abounded with them. They were twelve games out of first place, and they were emotionally exhausted. Again the spotlight fell on Williams, and again the question of leadership was raised, fair or not.

For the Red Sox, pitching was critical. In the years when their pitching was stabilized, the team was very tough. But when the pitching was weak, the team's other vulnerabilities—

its lack of speed, its weakness away from Fenway Park, the inflated statistics of some of its stars—were emphasized. And then Williams was blamed. It was always more fun to write about him than about the team's real problems.

With the first 50 games completed, the Red Sox had won 25 and lost 25. They were twelve games out of first place. Their pitching rotation was barely set. They had no bullpen. They were not going to win Harold Kaese's 124 games. They were going to be lucky to win 85 games. After the July Fourth weekend, Williams's foremost journalistic nemesis, a Boston columnist named Colonel Dave Egan, said the time had come to trade him. He wrote, "[Williams] has been the doormat over whom others have walked into the halls of fame." His hits, Egan added, always came against the St. Louis Browns "and the other bums of the league."

That he was now the target did not surprise Williams. Years later, he admitted immaturity as a young player, and an inability to deal with some of the Boston press. But he also noted shrewdly that the Red Sox management had not done a particularly good job of protecting him, either. The reason, he noted, was that he was catching much of the heat that ordinarily would have been directed at the front office, which was far from perfect.

No matter that Williams was second in the American League in hitting, with a .319 average; tied for the lead in runs batted in with his teammate Junior Stephens at 55; and second to Stephens in home runs with 14. Some writers claimed the very excellence of his statistics proved their point—Williams was not a team player. Worse, there were more comparisons than ever now with DiMaggio; in those comparisons Williams would never be the winner.

Williams's years in Boston, particularly the early ones, were tempestuous. He was often at war with the Boston writers, and thus, inevitably, the fans. Here the contrast with DiMaggio was most striking. DiMaggio, energized by burning immigrant pride, was always aware of how much he meant to so many people. He could control his anxieties and managed to make them work for him. The New York writers both respected him and feared that he would cut them off. They generously described his aloofness, born of uncertainty and suspicion, as elegance. After all, the Yankees almost always won, and this played no small part in sustaining this unusual covenant.

No such protection was offered Williams. He was arguably the greatest hitter of his era—a skilled, dedicated, and highly intelligent student of the game. He could do many exceptional things as a young man, but he could not conceal his hunger to be the best or his hurt and anger when he fell short—or when others accused him of falling short.

"It is probably my misfortune that I have been and will inevitably be compared with Joe DiMaggio," he wrote in his memoir, *My Turn at Bat*. "We were of the same era. We were the two top players of our league. In my heart I have always felt that I was a better hitter than Joe, which was always my first consideration, but I have to say that he was the greatest baseball player of our time." That was his dilemma. He could never do enough.

If anything, Williams's insecurities were greater than DiMaggio's. DiMaggio, after all, had come from the home of first-generation Americans, but it was a strong home, with an unyielding sense that the future was to be built around a better life for the children. By contrast, Williams's home life in San Diego was a shambles. His mother worked for the Salvation Army, and cared more, he believed, for her constituents there than for her own two children. She was called "The Angel of Tijuana," Williams would note mordantly. His father worked in a photographic shop. The more his wife manifested her religiosity, the less likely he was to come home; and the less often he came home, the more religious she became. As a child, Williams often waited on the steps of his house, hoping for one parent to come home. The house was filthy, and Williams was always ashamed of it; his mother's activities on behalf of her cause did not allow time for housecleaning. When Eddie Collins arrived at Williams's home in 1936 to sign the seventeen-year-old boy, he was bothered by only one thing: The young man never got up to say hello or shake hands. The reason, which Collins couldn't know, was that Williams was sitting in a chair that had a huge hole in the fabric, covered inadequately by a towel. He was too embarrassed to stand up. For his high school graduation, he got only one present—a fountain pen from a friend. The humiliation of those days, his friends thought, never left him. Later, when sportswriters wrote critically of him, he reacted as if they were stripping away a hard-won veneer of respectability, reducing him from the star he had become to the neglected boy he had been.

Upon graduation from high school Williams was brought out to practice with the old minor-league San Diego Padres. The other players simply stopped and watched; for here was this tall, thin young boy, easily six feet three—could he weigh even 140 pounds?—and yet he could whip the bat. In fact, he weighed 148 pounds, which he remembered because a story in the local paper said he weighed 155, and he recalled wishing that he weighed that much. The veterans were saying he would be signed before the week was out.

Even then, Williams had time only for baseball. A restaurant was a pit stop. He would slap the counter with his hands and tell the waitress to hurry, he was in a rush, he had to catch a train. Ossie Vitt, who had been the manager in Doerr's rookie year, before Williams joined the team, was a former big-leaguer, so he taught Doerr, who in turn taught Williams, how to order and how to tip. They had $2.50 a day meal money. Vitt told Doerr it was important to act like a big-leaguer and leave a fifteen-cent tip. Of that year Williams remembered being constantly hungry, and desperately wanting to put on more weight so that he would become stronger. On the Padres' first road trip, they pulled into Oakland on their third stop. Williams walked into the hotel lobby and saw Bill Lane, the team owner, sitting in a big armchair. "Kid," Lane said in a gravelly tough voice, "you're leading the list." "What list?" the surprised and nervous young Williams answered. "The overeaters' list," Lane said. Williams was constantly signing for more than the daily allowance. "You'll have to take it out of my pay," he said.

Williams was a perfect target for the veteran players, who were not above hassling him when he tried to go to bed. On occasion he simply gathered up his blankets, went to the ladies' room on the train, locked himself in, and slept there. When the team was at home in San Diego, he would go to Frank Shellenback, the manager, and ask for any used baseballs. Then, loaded down with scuffed-up balls, he would go back to the neighborhood park where he had grown up and get the local kids to pitch to him until it was too dark to see.

The one thing Williams always had was a quick bat. That was the first thing Eddie Collins noticed. Collins had made a scouting trip to San Diego to look at Doerr and another prospect. But he soon began to talk about San Diego's young left-handed hitting outfielder. At first Lane, the San Diego owner, couldn't figure out who he was talking about, for Williams was barely playing. "Oh, you mean *Williams*," he said. "Hell, he's just a kid out of high school. He's only seventeen. Give him a few years." But Collins took an option on him anyway.

Like so many other young players, Williams had trouble with breaking pitches. He was never ready for them. Once a pitcher got him out on a curve. Williams, furious with himself, still cursing, trotted back to his position in the outfield. One of the San Diego pitchers, a former major-leaguer, yelled over to him, "Hey kid, what'd he get you out on?" "A goddamn slow curve," Williams answered. "Can you hit his fastball?" the pitcher continued. "You bet," Williams answered. "What do you think he'll be looking to put past you the next time?" the pitcher asked. There was a brief pause. Ted Williams had never thought about pitching to Ted Williams—that was something pitchers did. "A curve," he answered. "Hey kid," the pitcher said, "why don't you go up there and wait on it the next time." Williams did, and hit the ball out for a home run. Thus began a twenty-five-year study of the mind of the pitcher.

When he finally came up to his first major-league camp, Doerr traveled east with him. On the train, Williams practiced his swing in the aisles, not with bats but with the only thing available—pillows from the sleeping car. He was a boy living his dreams: All he could talk about on that trip was how exciting this was, arriving at the very precipice of the major leagues, and how he hoped to be not just a major-leaguer but a great hitter. "Bobby," he kept telling Doerr, "I'm going to be the greatest hitter that ever lived." To Doerr, there was something touching about his eagerness and his innocence. But to the veterans that spring, he seemed unbearably brash. He did not understand his own lowly position in the pecking order of a major-league team. As a result, veteran outfielders

Doc Cramer, Joe Vosmik, and Ben Chapman ragged him hard. A story that made the rounds of the Red Sox camp that spring was that Doerr had told him, "Wait until you see Jimmie Foxx hit," and Williams had answered, "Wait until Foxx sees me hit." Williams said later that the story was not true, but given his attitude at the time, it might as well have been. The first thing he said to Joe Cronin, the manager, was, "Hi, sport." That, thought Doerr, guarantees him a ticket to the farm team in Minneapolis.

In his letters home that spring there was no brashness, only childlike wonder—he described the beauty of watching Grove pitch, the purity of his motion, and the explosive crack of the bat when Jimmie Foxx hit a ball, a sharper sound than he had ever before heard. He heard something similar later in his career when Mickey Mantle came along, Mantle being built along the same lines as Foxx. But he was not, somewhat to his surprise, destined to stay with the Boston club that season. Williams liked to tell of how he was at last sent back to the minors. Johnny Orlando, the clubhouse boy, escorted him to the bus station. As he prepared to board the bus, Williams turned to Orlando and told him to tell Cramer, Vosmik, and Chapman that he'd be back, and that he'd make more money playing baseball than all three of them put together. Then Orlando lent him five dollars to get to Daytona.

When he finally arrived in the major leagues a year later, Williams was only twenty years old. He became the first rookie ever to lead the league in runs batted in, with 145; and he hit .327, with 31 home runs. It was a breathtaking debut, and it was overshadowed only by DiMaggio, who, in his fourth year, hit .381. Williams was absolutely fearless. On one of his first trips to St. Louis with the Red Sox, he and Doerr ran into Fred Haney, the new Browns manager, whom they both knew from the Pacific League. Haney said to Williams, "Hey kid, we'll see how you hit today sitting on your ass." Williams and Doerr both laughed because they thought of Haney as a friend. But the first time Williams came up, the ball whizzed in right at his head. Williams dropped to the ground. His very career, he knew, was at stake. He picked himself up and very deliberately dug his left foot even deeper into the ground. Then he hit the next pitch against the right center-field fence for a double. The next time up, the pitcher knocked him down once more. Again, very slowly, he got up and planted his back foot deep into the dirt. Focusing fiercely on the pitcher, he hit the next pitch into the right-field seats. With that the knockdowns stopped. It was, thought Doerr, as if some tribal drumbeat went through the entire league: Whatever you do, don't throw at this kid; if you do, he'll kill you.

The first time Lefty Gomez pitched against him in Yankee Stadium, it was said that Williams hit a tremendous home run that landed about a third of the way into the deep right center-field seats. Gomez went back to the dugout, where Red Ruffing accosted him. "What'd you throw him?" he asked. "My fastball," said the deflated Gomez. "I'll be damned if he'll hit my fastball that hard," Ruffing said.

The next day Ruffing pitched Williams a fastball, and it landed *two* thirds of the way up into the right center-field seats. "Just as long as it wasn't a fastball," Gomez needled him when they got back to the dugout.

Williams was emotional, and his mood on any given day was directly keyed to how well he was hitting. Lou Stringer, the backup second baseman in 1949, felt he could gauge Williams's attitude during batting practice. If he was hitting poorly, he would be down, and he would take extra batting practice. Pitch by pitch, as he found his groove, his body and his spirits would lift, like a man climbing stairs, Stringer thought. Once when he had finished hitting, Stringer turned to him and said, "Ted, you look great." Williams replied, "You're goddamned right! Did you see that wrist action? Did you see that swing? You see that power? I'm the best goddamn hitter in the world, kid, and you better believe it, the best goddamn hitter who ever lived!"

In 1941, the year he hit .406, he constantly took batting practice with Joe Dobson. Williams wanted not just to hit every pitch but to call it as well. Often they would argue over whether a pitch was in the strike zone, and if Williams hit one to right field, they would argue whether it was an out, a single, or a double. Williams would never give an inch. He wanted nothing less than the best batting-practice average in the history of the game. Even in the locker room he competed. There was a small spittoon filled with sand there, and he liked to bet that he could cast a fly into it eight times out of ten. "Just eight out of ten," he would say, "any bets?"

Richard Ben Cramer noted with great shrewdness in *Esquire* that Williams sought fame but could not deal with its fellow traveler, celebrity. Even worse, he had unfortunately picked the most difficult city in America in which to grow up in public. Boston's newspapering in the late forties and into the late fifties was probably the worst of any major city in America. It specialized in sensationalism, parochialism, prejudice, and ignorance. The Boston tabloid headline in the event of World War III, the standard joke went, would be HUB MAN WITNESSES/ATOMIC BLAST/IS LIGHTLY BURNED/20 MILLION DEAD. The competition was venomous, and to visiting players, there seemed to be twice as many writers in Boston as anywhere else. "They ought to put numbers on their backs," Williams once said. "There's so many of them it's the only way you could figure out who they were."

Williams, a young brash kid with rabbit ears, was raw meat to the Boston writers, and in terms of press relations his behavior was often wildly self-destructive. The makings of a war were there. Soon the papers divided between the reporters who liked Williams and those who pursued him relentlessly. The latter might not have practiced good journalism, but it was a living.

In a culture of journalistic scoundrels, the greatest scoundrel of them all was Dave Egan, a columnist for the Hearst tabloid the *Record*. Egan was known as the Colonel, though it was not known whether he had ever actually been a colonel in anything, least of all the United States armed forces. He was a man of immense talents, considered by many to be the most gifted sports columnist in Boston, but he was also locked in a terrible battle with alcohol, a battle he never won. Gentle and kind when sober, he became, when drinking, a monster, a man with the foulest tongue imaginable. He was nothing if not shrewd, and he soon hit upon the perfect formula, which enabled him to be distinctive: He became, in an age when most sportswriters were fans, the provocateur. What everyone else was for, he was against. Did Boston celebrate the triumphs of its young undefeated heavyweight champion Rocky Marciano? Well, then Egan ripped him.

What he did, especially to Williams, was not pleasant for anyone who cares about the American press. His coverage amounted to a vendetta. He knew exactly which buttons to push with this sensitive young man. He loved to claim that Williams was not a clutch hitter, and was, in Egan's cruel phrase, "the inventor of the automatic choke." There was little real evidence of this, but Egan cleverly picked what *he* considered the ten most important games of Williams's life (play-off games, World Series games, etc.) to show that Williams hit only .232 at such critical moments. Though no two games had been more important than the two final regular-season games against the Yankees in 1948, in which Williams had been on base eight of ten times, Egan declined to include them in his stress test. That Williams carried his team for weeks against pitchers who never gave him a decent pitch, that pitchers vastly preferred to walk Williams and pitch to Junior Stephens, did not matter.

What Dave Egan did was brutal and relentless. But it worked. Each day New Englanders *had* to read what the Colonel had written about Williams. "I knew New England well," Birdie Tebbetts once reminisced. "I didn't just grow up there, but I lived there off-season and I knew what happened in New England—I knew that in every small town throughout the region there would be people waiting in the early morning for the delivery of the *Record* so they could read the Colonel."

Part of it was sheer talent: At his best he was the most outrageous and talented writer in Boston. He had a nickname for everyone. Fiorello La Guardia was "The Little Flower with the Big Pot"; a local fight promoter named Sam Silverman, who used a variety of small local arenas, was "Subway Sam." He kept up a running feud with Jim Britt, who for a long time broadcast the Red Sox games. "Meathead Britt," he called him on occasion. In honor of Britt's valiant but doomed efforts to maximize the thinning hair at the front of his head, Egan also called him "The Tuft." On one occasion he wrote of Britt, "He's putting in his car what he should be drinking, and he's drinking what he should be putting in his car."

As Egan and a few other writers provoked, so Williams responded. Soon the fans understood, at least subconsciously, that it was fun to ride Williams because he would react to their taunts. If they went to Fenway, sat in the left-field stands, and diligently baited him, they became momentarily his equals. This was a forerunner to the more complicated relationships of the seventies and eighties among young, talented, and highly paid superstars, the press, and their fans.

The senior executives at the *Record* were warned by their lawyers that Egan's writings were so vitriolic and personal that Williams had, with the tighter libel laws of those days, cause for a libel action. "I wouldn't give those bastards the satisfaction of a lawsuit," Williams told friends.

Egan was often too drunk to write his column, and had to be taken to his favorite drying-out home, Dropkick Murphy's (where he was known to smuggle in his own bottles). A group of younger men at the *Record* would cover for him. Egan would call one of them and begin, "Ted Williams today outdid himself . . ." Then there would be a pause, and Egan would say, "Ah, the hell with it, Bill, you fill in the rest." Soon management became suspicious, and the job of faking it became more complicated. Sammy Cohen, the sports editor, would order the others to make it seem like they were taking dictation from Egan over the telephone while an executive of the paper stood nearby. This called for high theatrics. The writer actually had to write the column while faking a conversation with Egan: "Yes, Dave . . . Wait a second, Dave, you're ahead of me. . . . Oh, great, Dave, that's great stuff. . . . Wait 'til Ted reads this one. . . ."

Egan had graduated from Harvard College and Harvard Law School. He first took a job as a lawyer in one of Boston's grand firms for ten dollars a week. When he was told that he was not entitled to a paid vacation, he walked out of the world of law and into the world of sportswriting. Egan worked at several Boston papers, and his reputation always preceded him. Editors hired him hoping that they could somehow live with his darker side—the whiskey-fed rages, the disappearances, the hiding of forbidden whiskey bottles in the men's room—because of his talent. But eventually they would decide reluctantly that they could not.

The *Record* was Egan's last stop. Hardly Boston's most prestigious paper, its formula was simple: sex scandals, racing results, and baseball. Its extraordinary efforts, channeled almost exclusively into these areas, brought the paper a circulation of around 500,000, but it did not bring it peer respect. George Frazier, a Boston writer who worked for the *Globe* for much of his career, once noted of the *Record* and its successor, the *Record American,* "When I went to the *Record-American* as a columnist I was aware that its devotees moved their lips while they read. What I did not realize was that its editors did too." It was engaged in a never-ending circulation war with other, richer papers. Once Mel Parnell, the Boston pitcher, cornered Egan after a game and asked why he had to be so *personal* in his criticism. Egan replied, "Kid, it isn't personal—I'm just selling newspapers." When another Boston writer criticized Egan, the Colonel asked, "How much mail do you get?" A few letters a week, the writer answered. "I get a barrelful every week," Egan said, "most of them telling me what a bastard I am. But they write. Maybe they're right—but I'm the bastard they write to."

There were those who thought things easily might have gone the other way: that had Williams taken Egan in, made him his insider, then Egan would have celebrated Williams. Williams's failure to play that game cost him dearly.

That spring, with Boston losing but Williams hitting well, Egan came down on him regularly. He was, Egan wrote in a late-April column, hitting but not the way he used to—his power had disappeared. Soon that was followed by a column attacking Williams for his alleged jealousy toward Junior Stephens. Williams, it appeared to Egan, did not congratulate Stephens enthusiastically enough upon the occasion of Junior's home runs. Williams would walk, Egan wrote, "stonily" to the bench, "looking more displeased than otherwise, and it must be obvious that victory in itself, however melodramatically won by others, is not important; that his personal role in the victory is the all-important consideration, and that defeat with him starring is preferable to victory when he must stand in the shadow of another." (If anything, Stephens was somewhat envious of Williams, or more particularly of his salary, which was double his own. From time to time he would complain to teammates. "Junior," Joe Dobson once asked him, "there are thirty-five thousand people out there today. How many are here only because Junior Stephens is playing?")

There was another column attacking Williams for hits that were not timely, home runs that were not needed, when the Red Sox already had a healthy lead. "Here are seven runs which he batted in after the battle was over and the issue decided and for my money they're just frosting on the cake." By mid-May Williams was hitting around .320 and near the lead in both home runs and runs batted in, but there was no doubt to readers of Dave Egan that he was responsible for the slow start of the Red Sox.

There was a game here, the journalist as cynic. The role of the player was to be equally cynical. But Ted Williams did not play the game. Other athletes who cared not a bit more for the needs of the press were good at pretending that they did. But Williams would not accept writers as peers; he could hit a fastball, they could not. Even for those Boston writers prepared to write generously of him, he did not make it any easier. For he did not disguise his feelings. He scornfully called the writers "the knights of the keyboard." He would get on the Boston team bus, spot a writer, and say, "Ugh, I smell something rotten. It smells like shit. There must be writers on this bus—you write such shit."

He made a few exceptions. Though Joe Cashman worked for the *Record,* which was Egan's paper, Williams liked Cashman. In late winter, if the *Record* wanted a long piece on Williams as he prepared for the upcoming season, it would assign Cashman. Cashman would call Williams in Florida. "Joe, if it's for you and you can make some money off a magazine piece, I'll do it," he said. "You come down here, stay with me, we'll fish, and I'll give you all the time you want. But if it's for that damn paper, just forget it. Don't come down. I'm sorry. You know why."

The writers paid him back for his disdain in many ways. Some of them withheld their votes for the Most Valuable Player Award; in 1947, a season in which Williams led DiMaggio in every single category, he lost the MVP to the Yankee star by one point. One Boston writer had not even listed him in the top ten players. If he had listed him as even the tenth most-valuable player, Williams would have won the award.

Neither was Williams diplomatic with the fans. He refused the most basic courtesy of the era—to tip his cap after a home run. DiMaggio had the hat-tip down perfectly: He did it lightly and deftly, without looking up, as he moved past home plate toward the dugout. He never broke stride, thus satisfying the fans without showing up an opposing pitcher.

In time Williams's refusal to tip his hat became a major civic issue. Management and teammates pleaded with him to do it—this was, after all, a small gesture. But he refused. He was nothing if not stubborn. Birdie Tebbetts, the catcher, suggested a compromise: Williams could tip his hat and at the same time say, under his breath, "Go to hell, you SOBs." The fans, Tebbetts pointed out, would be happy and would not know what he was saying. The idea pleased Williams, but he never followed through on it. Instead, he fought back. If a fan was particularly obnoxious, he would stand at bat and deliberately try to line baseballs at him. On occasion he'd reward obscenities with an obscene gesture of his own. In all, he gave the tabloids just what they wanted: a great hitter, and a great side show as well.

In a way it was too bad because it distracted people from concentrating on his talents, which were spectacular. His eyesight was legendary. Some said that he could see the ball at the exact instant he hit it. Others swore that he could see the signature of Will Harridge, the president of the American League, as the pitcher released the ball; or that he could read the label on a record playing at 78 rpm. He himself thought that the talk about his eyesight was silly. Yes, he had exceptional eyesight—20/10. But his right eye had been damaged when his brother hit it with a walnut in a childhood fight. There were days when he woke up and could not see very well out of that eye.

Then there were his marvelous reflexes. He could wait until the last split second on a pitch and hit it, in the baseball vernacular, right out of the catcher's mitt, and still pull it. He loved to drive cars because he saw it as a test of eyesight and reflexes. His friends considered him a brilliant driver, a man with a feathery touch who could easily have been a race-car champion. Once he drove with Matt Batts on a long trip through Florida. Williams was obviously impressed by Batts's driving. "You know, Batts," he said, "you're not bad. In fact, you're the second-best driver in baseball." "Ted," said the young catcher, "I'm the best." "No, Batts," said Williams. "You use the brake too much. I never use the brake. I'm the best." Case closed.

But eyesight and reflexes were only the beginning. It was what he did with them that was important. "God gets you to the plate," Williams would say, referring to the fact that he had great eyesight and physical size, "but once you're there you're on your own." No one ever worked harder to build himself up, and no one took better care of himself in order to play ball. He did not pal around with the other ballplayers because he could not bear late hours, and he did not want to drink whiskey at night. He did not smoke, and he hated the smell of other people's tobacco. His favorite beverage was malted milk.

When he went to the movies he would take a rubber ball with him and squeeze it constantly to strengthen his hands. He also had a metal contraption with a built-in spring, which he squeezed to build up his hands, wrists, and forearms. When a game was over, no matter what the weather, he would do one hundred push-ups, his feet elevated on a chair in order to make the exercise harder. He supported his body on his fingers instead of his palms to strengthen not just his upper body but his hands as well. Sometimes he would lie down on the locker-room floor, under two chairs on top of one another and raise and lower the chairs slowly. Gradually he transformed himself into a powerful, muscular man.

Nothing was left to chance. If he was batting and a cloud passed over, he would step out of the batter's box and fidget until the light was just a little better. He honed his bats at night, working a bone against them to make the fibers harder. He was the first to combine olive oil and rosin in order to get a better grip on the bat. He learned to gradually decrease the weight of his bats as the summer wore on and fatigue set in. That practice began one day when he had gone to the bat rack and picked up a bat belonging to Stan Spence, one of his teammates. It felt like a toothpick made out of banana wood, in his words. He asked Spence if he could use it, and in his first at-bat he went after an outside pitch. It was not even a full swing, more a light flick of the bat, but the ball seemed to jump out of there—a home run to the opposite field. That taught him something: Bat speed, not bat weight, was critical.

In those days the big hitters traditionally used heavy bats—36, 37, 38 ounces. Williams had been using a thirty-six. He soon met with John Hillerich of Hillerich and Bradsby, the bat manufacturers, and asked for bats styled more on the Spence model, at 33 ounces. "Ted," Hillerich argued, "that's too light—you can't get good wood on the ball with them." But Williams argued that torque, the whip of the bat, was more important than mere weight, and he was right. Besides, he was losing roughly 10 percent of the weight of the bat; he measured it against the pitcher, who, in Williams's mind was now losing 10 percent off his fastball. Shortly after his conversation with Hillerich, Williams visited Louisville and talked with an old-timer named Fritz Bickel, who actually took the raw wooden cylinders and meticulously fashioned bats out of them. "Ted, here's a wonderful piece of wood for you," Bickel said, holding up a cylinder. "See, it has two knots, and that's good; it hardens the wooden." Pleased, Williams gave Bickel twenty-five dollars, and from then on Bickel carefully looked for just the right piece of wood for Williams, and Williams sent him occasional small gratuities. He was glad he had done that; it meant he had light bats that remained strong.

He was also aware that on damp or muggy days, bats picked up extra moisture and became heavier. He would warn his teammates not to put their bats down on the damp grass at night. When some of them argued with him, Williams immediately set off for the post office, where he had a variety of bats weighed. Sure enough, he was right: They had picked up a critical half-ounce from the dampness, an increase of about 1.5 percent. It was important to him, even if no one else cared.

Every advantage helped. In those early days of night baseball, Williams was more successful than most hitters at adjusting to playing under the lights. One reason, he was sure, was the regimen he put himself through. The other players stayed out later, got up later, ate a heavier meal, and then took brief naps. By contrast, Williams woke up early, ate an early light lunch, went for a long walk, and then took a long nap. He was always fresh at the ball park at night.

Fielding did not intrigue him quite as much as hitting did. Only later in his career did he begin to take this aspect of the game more seriously. Once he turned to Dominic DiMaggio and asked him how he managed to charge ground balls hit to the outfield with such aggressiveness. DiMaggio was startled by the question: It was, he thought, so long in coming.

But Williams loved hitting, especially against fastball pitchers. "No one can throw a fastball past me. God could come down from Heaven, and He couldn't throw it past me," he liked to say. He loved playing against certain teams: the Tigers because they had great power pitchers—Trucks, New-houser, Trout, and Benton—who came right at him, and who rarely walked him; and Cleveland because the Indians had Bob Feller, the standard by which other pitchers were mea-sured. When baseball players were talking about another pitcher, they would say, "His fastball is almost as fast as Fel-ler's," or, "His curveball is almost as good as Feller's." It was Feller, after all, who had caused Lefty Gomez to say, after tak-ing his third straight strike without moving the bat off his shoulder, "That last one sounded a little low."

"That was the test," Williams reminisced years later. "He was the best and I wanted to be the best, and three days be-fore he pitched I would start thinking Robert Feller, Bob Fel-ler. I'd sit in my room thinking and seeing him, thinking about him all that time. God, I loved it. That was a personal challenge. I'd always get my rest and I'd weigh my bat that day. I did pretty well off Robert Feller. I hit sinking line drives off him, a lot of top spin on them. Allie Reynolds of the Yan-kees was tough and I might think about him for twenty-four hours before a game, but Robert Feller, I'd think about him for three days."

Williams had complete confidence in himself. He was once called out on strikes at a home game in Fenway, and he came into the dugout ranting and raving that home plate was out of line—that was why the umpire had called the strike. Mel Parnell, Tex Hughson, and some of the other pitchers teased him about it, said he was blaming a strikeout on the plate. But he persisted. A great injustice had been done. The

next day, just to humor him, Joe Cronin went out and mea-
sured the plate, and, of course, Williams had been right. It *was*
out of line. Eleven pitchers on the team, Parnell had thought,
and only Williams picked up on it. Somewhere in the record
book there is a mistake: He is credited with 709 career strikeouts, but one of those is because of a faulty alignment in Fenway Park. It should read 708.

It was often written that he was disliked by his teammates.
That was a canard. He was invariably generous and
thoughtful, especially to young players coming up behind
him. His colleagues regarded him with an unusual affection
long after his playing days were over. There was a feeling on
their part that he was devoid of meanness or narrowness;
whatever faults he had were simply the inevitable, lesser side
of someone so gifted and so passionate. He forged especially
long-lasting friendships with three teammates: Doerr, Dom
DiMaggio, and Pesky. He and Doerr shared their love of the
outdoors; with DiMaggio, the friendship was based on Williams's great affection and immense respect for his intelligence; and with Pesky, it was the affection of an older brother
and little brother—a fifty-year marathon of playful insults. In
1985 he and Pesky were still needling each other. Pesky would
say to him, "You know, Ted, you've got a high school diploma,
and *I've* got a high school diploma. How come you're so much
smarter than me?" "Because you're dumb, Needle, you're just
goddamn dumb is why," Williams would answer.

What such teammates as Boo Ferriss remembered about
him more than anything else was the excitement Williams
brought to the game—his energy and vitality, and the belief
that in any baseball game something marvelous was going to
happen. He was, Ferriss thought, always studying the game.
Ferriss had one clear memory of Williams: Williams sitting in
the dugout on the second step, his head propped on his arms,
his elbows resting on the top step. From there he would study
the pitcher as clinically as a scientist looks through a micro-
scope. "Hey, look at that. Did you see what he just threw?"
Ferriss would hear him say. "He never threw that before."

Having Williams on the team was like having an additional hitting instructor. "Needle," he once told Pesky when
they were playing New York at the Stadium, "that pitcher on

the mound is named Spud Chandler. He throws a sinker. A damn good sinker. A very heavy ball. You keep trying to pull him and you can't. You're not big enough or strong enough. I am forty pounds heavier, damn near a foot taller than you, and a hell of a lot stronger, and I can't pull him, in case you didn't notice. You're zero for fourteen against Mr. Chandler this year. Just go with the ball. They are not going to walk you to get to me, believe me. You're going to get a good pitch. So just slap it by them." Pesky did. Enraged, Chandler stood on the mound cursing him, so upset that he lost his concentration. Thereupon Williams hit a home run. When Williams reached the dugout he yelled, "Where is our horned-nose little shortstop?" Pesky shook his hand. "Did I tell you how to hit him?" said Williams. "Did I?"

If there was anything wrong with Williams's advice as a hitter, it was his assumption that everyone would get the same pitches he got. Once in a series with Detroit, Mickey McDermott, who was a very good hitter, was sent up to pinch-hit against Virgil Trucks. "Bush," Williams told McDermott, "just sit there and wait on the slider." So McDermott did, but Trucks fed him three fastballs in a row. He struck out on three pitches. "Ted," McDermott told Williams, "there are no Trucks sliders for me—only for you."

Pitchers were, of course, the enemy, but those who understood the challenge immediately gained Williams's respect. Eddie Lopat was one, because he threw so many different pitches with such varying speed and because his sequence was never predictable. He and Williams became friends, and they would stand around before games talking about hitting and pitching. Williams even lent Lopat some of his bats. To those pitchers on his own team who paid attention and wanted to learn, he gave brilliant advice. He would explain during a game what a given hitter was expecting, and then, based on his knowledge of the pitcher, project whether or not he was going to get it. He was invariably right.

Parnell, a left-hander, believed that Williams, as much as any man, forced him to become a better pitcher. Williams felt that he never saw enough left-handers when the Red Sox were at home, since most visiting managers were unwilling to let their lefties pitch in a park constructed for right-handed hitters. So he talked Parnell into coming out to the park early to throw special batting practice to him. Williams demanded that Parnell throw his best stuff. If it was helpful for Williams, then it was great for Parnell too, for if he could pitch against Ted Williams, move the ball around on him and surprise him, then he could do it against anyone. There were, Parnell soon learned, no blind spots. If he made a perfect pitch, Williams still managed to get some of the bat on it, and if he was off just a little, then Williams was likely to kill it. But there was some reassurance in all this—if Williams could barely touch a pitch, then the chances were that a mere mortal batter would not be able to touch it at all.

He was forever giving tips to visiting players as well. When Detroit played Boston he would talk endlessly with young Al Kaline about hitting, giving him pointers. Finally Tom Yawkey, the Boston owner, asked him to stop because he was helping the opposition. "Come on, T.A.," Williams answered, "the more hitters we have in this game, the better it is for the game. Listen, when you're coming towards the park and you're two blocks away, and you hear a tremendous cheer, that isn't because someone has thrown a strike. That's because someone has hit the ball." In the end, Yawkey conceded that Williams was right and permitted him to continue his seminars with the opposition.

He was, thought his friend Curt Gowdy, the least bigoted man of his time. He could not comprehend judging a player by his color or background. Baseball, he thought, was a universe of its own—a better one, where talent was the only thing that mattered. Gowdy remembered him as the first person in baseball to predict the coming importance of black athletes in American sports. "Curt," Williams had once said to him, "they're the only kids in America who work that hard anymore. White kids drive cars, black kids walk or ride bikes. White kids go off to drive-ins or play tennis, and the black kids spend all their time on sandlots trying to get their fifty at-bats. You'll see it show up in the majors soon enough—their bodies are stronger." His speech in Cooperstown in July 1966, when he was elected to the Hall of Fame, is notable for its generosity to Willie Mays: "The other day Willie Mays hit his five hundred twenty-second home run. He has gone past me and he's pushing, and I say to him, 'Go get 'em, Willie.' Baseball gives every American boy a chance to excel. Not just to be as good as anyone else, but to be better. This is the nature of man, and the name of the game. I hope someday Satchell Paige and Josh Gibson will be voted into the Hall of Fame as symbols of the great Negro players who are not here only because they were not given the chance . . ."

Williams intellectualized the game far more than DiMaggio did. This is not to diminish DiMaggio's own considerable powers of analysis, but a moment would come when he simply *played*. Williams never stopped thinking, analyzing. This methodological difference led to some practical differences—for instance, over the issue of whether to take certain pitches. Williams would never, no matter what the situation, go for a pitch that was even a shade outside the strike zone. DiMaggio was different: He believed that, as a power hitter on the team, he sometimes had an obligation to swing at imperfect pitches. On certain occasions a walk was not enough; it was a victory for the pitcher. Williams understood DiMaggio's point, but felt that if, even under duress, he swung at what he thought was a bad ball, then it might cause deterioration of his batting eye. It was all or nothing. For him, to swing at any bad ball was a victory for the pitcher.

Williams's brain was like a computer. What a pitcher threw in a given situation would be entered permanently into his memory, to be recalled in comparable situations against the same pitcher. His teammates loved watching him take his revenge. In the early fifties he played in an exhibition game with the White Sox. A pitcher named Bob Keegan, pitching against Williams for the first time, got him to hit a giant pop-up off a slider. The Red Sox players watching the scene were amused. They knew that Keegan thought he could now handle Williams with a slider, and that Williams would be waiting for it. Sure enough, a few weeks later in Chicago, Williams faced Keegan again. That day Williams hit three home runs off him. Even as Keegan let go of the ball the last time, he realized he had grooved it and yelled out, "Oh, shit!"

Williams hated for a pitcher to show him up. It was one thing to get him out, but another to embarrass him. Once when Bobby Shantz, the great relief pitcher, was playing for

Kansas City, he struck Williams out on a big, fat slow curve. That had happened with the score tied in the ninth inning. Williams did not like being fooled by a slow curve, and he came back to the dugout in a rage. "Hold them until the eleventh," he told his teammates. "I want one more at bat." The score remained tied, and when he did get up again, Williams hit a ball off Shantz so hard that as it whistled past the mound it seemed likely to kill the pitcher.

On another occasion he was batting against Hal Newhouser of Detroit. Newhouser, who liked to come over the top, had two strikes on him. He came in sidearm with a cheap curve for strike three. Williams was enraged. Newhouser was a great power pitcher, but Williams felt that this time he had struck him out by cheating. It was a matter of pride, as if he had ruined a no-hitter of Newhouser's by bunting. "A dinky nickel curve," he said coming back to the bench. "I'll bet any son of a bitch on this bench I hit one off him today." It was a bet that no one cared to take. Inevitably, his next time up he hit a home run.

Williams wanted no interruptions to his concentration on hitting. His marriages always suffered because his real love was baseball. He preferred living in hotels in Boston because it was simpler, and less time was wasted. He never stopped talking about being the best. "Tex," he would say one day to his friend Tex Hughson, "don't you think I'm the greatest hitter in baseball?" "Damn right, you are, Ted," Hughson would answer. But the next day the question would be asked again, this time to Parnell. "Mel, who's the greatest hitter in baseball?" There was, Parnell knew, only one answer.

In those years there was a photographer in Boston whom Williams liked named Fred Kaplan. Once Kaplan's two-year-old son said he wanted to go to the ball park. "Why?" his father asked. "I want to see Teddy," the little boy said. "Teddy who?" the father asked. "Teddy Ballgame," the little boy said. That was it, the perfect nickname, just how Williams thought of himself, and he adopted it for his own—Teddy Ballgame.

CHAPTER 10

Gradually the veteran Yankee players were coming to know Stengel. He was shrewd, talkative, and theatrical. He could be arbitrary, and sometimes he seemed a bit odd. When a player swung too hard on a given pitch and missed, he would suddenly jump up, swing an imaginary bat, and yell, "Not too hard, and not too easy. Just butcher boy." But there was a growing, somewhat reluctant admiration for his instincts. It was not long before the sportswriters started to notice in print how well Casey Stengel handled his team in the face of constant injuries, and how brilliantly he platooned his players, changing the nature of contemporary baseball by ending the set lineup, in which every day the same eight players played and batted in the same order.

In the outfield Stengel platooned Bauer and Woodling, close friends. Both were constantly at war with the manager because each wanted to play every day. Bauer smashed water coolers when Stengel pulled him for a pinch hitter. Woodling on occasion muttered darkly that you had to wear a cross on a chain to play regularly, an allusion to the idea that Stengel favored Catholics. Woodling, a marvelous natural hitter, was sure that if he played more often he would hit even better. He called Stengel "that crooked-legged old bastard."

In 1949 Woodling and Bauer, between them, batted .271 with 15 home runs and 99 runs batted in; in effect they gave the Yankees, in an injury-filled season, a composite all-star outfielder. Theirs was a constant competition, however. One time a right-hander was pitching, and Woodling, the left-handed hitter, was sure he was going to play. But Stengel went with Bauer, which enraged Woodling. "Hey Gene, you caddy for me today," Bauer said. Bauer got three hits, but late in the game the other team went to a left-hander. At that point Stengel pulled Bauer and went with Woodling, which enraged Bauer. He returned to the dugout, throwing his bats and screaming at the goddamn old man who would do this kind of thing. When the game was over Stengel said that he wanted to see Bauer and Woodling. Both of them were still steaming when they filed into his office. He turned first to Bauer. "I don't give a good goddamn what you call me—you can call me a crazy old man, and maybe I am. But it's my team and I'm going to run it my way. Now I'm going to tell you why I pulled you. You got your three hits, right? So let me tell you something, Mr. Bauer. You're not a one-thousand hitter. And you're not a five-hundred hitter. In fact, Mr. Bauer, you're not even a three-thirty-three hitter. So you had your three hits for the day and that's all it was going to be. That was your quota. I didn't think you had any more hits in you. And you," turning to Woodling, "the same goes for you. So forget all this old-man crap and play your position and do whatever the hell I tell you." For Bauer, part of the frustration with Stengel's platooning was his desire to play every day, and part of it was the fact that George Weiss and Roy Hamey, his deputy at contract time, exploited the way Stengel was using him. As Bauer's career progressed, he found himself constantly engaged in battles with Weiss. Bauer would ask for a sizable raise, and Weiss would tell him that no, he could not really give him a major raise, because, sad to say, *Bauer was not a regular.* Bauer would then cite his considerable contributions to the Yankee success and Weiss would answer, Yes, Hank, I know, but you're not a regular.

For only part of the team's success was due to Stengel; more than anything it had to do with George Weiss. The Keller-Henrich-DiMaggio team had represented the first flowering of the new farm system, which Weiss had built steadily even during the war, when most baseball executives had turned away from the long-range planning. By 1949 the team reflected Weiss's careful stockpiling of talent. Coleman had emerged as a graceful second baseman; at third Bobby Brown was clearly a remarkable hitter. Berra, as a catcher, was showing signs that he could provide acceptable fielding skills to go with his hitting ability. Already the trademark of the Weiss era was emerging: The team was never to be allowed to grow old; sentiment was never to interfere with judgment. Each year there were to be three or four new players spliced into the team's fabric.

George Weiss was almost completely devoid of charm. But, along with Branch Rickey, Bill Veeck, and Larry Mac-Phail, he was one of the ablest baseball executives of his era. He might have loved baseball, but for him it was first and foremost a business. There was never any confusion over his objectives. He was ruthless and cold-blooded in contract negotiations; he had a God-given knack at contract time, one Yankee said, of turning healthy relationships into cold and bitter ones. Weiss firmly believed that a well-paid ballplayer was a lazy one. That gave him the philosophical justification to be penurious, but unbeknownst to the players he had a more basic motive: The lower the sum of all the players' salaries, the greater the additional bonus he received from the owners. The owners gave Weiss a budget, say, $1 million a year. If Weiss kept the salaries down to, say, a total of $600,000 a year, he took home 10 percent of the remaining $400,000. It was not surprising, therefore, that in the fall of 1948 he strongly opposed paying DiMaggio $100,000. He did not want the base for the team's best player to be that high, for it would become the goal that the other players would use. A few years later some of the players, including Lopat, discovered his side deal. Most of them hated him anyway. To discover that he had been secretly profiting by his own miserliness was almost too much.

Weiss was immensely skillful at selling off players the Yankees did not need. A good minor-league ballplayer, he liked to say, was worth $40,000, and in most trades, since he was usually dealing from strength, he kept the pressure on until an extra ballplayer was thrown in by the other party. Then he would sell the player to some third club, keeping a significant percentage of the sale for himself.

If the players resented Weiss, so did the writers, in part because they did not like the way he treated the players, and in part because they sensed his contempt for them. "I can buy any of these sons of bitches for a five-dollar steak," he once told a friend, looking around a room filled with writers who were helping themselves to sandwiches and drinks in the Yankee clubhouse. He was, however, unusually sensitive to criticism, and he did not like it when Jimmy Cannon started calling him "Lonesome George" in print. When those columns appeared in the *Post,* Weiss came into Shor's, put a bunch of them on the table, and started to complain about Cannon to Shor. "But what the hell, Toots," he concluded, "who reads that guy anyway?" "You do, George," Shor answered.

His strength was attention to detail. Once during a Sunday doubleheader against the Indians with 60,000 people in the stands, Red Patterson was in the press box, and the phone rang. It was Weiss. He was checking the free-ticket list, and there was a name he did not recognize. It was, explained Patterson, the elevator operator from the Yankee office building. *"The elevator operator from the office!!"* Weiss exploded. He began an angry lecture about which games free tickets should be given to, and which they should not. Elevator operators went to day games against the Browns during the week. Patterson, overwhelmed with other work, blew up and quit on the spot.

It was the way he always thought. At the team party celebrating the Yankees' four-game sweep of the Phillies in the 1950 World Series, he managed to dampen the joyous occasion significantly by getting up and making a speech. He reminded the players that because the Series had lasted only four games, the owners had not made as much money as they should have; therefore, salaries would have to be held down in the coming year.

Every day, Weiss liked to check in with the people who worked for him, usually by calling them on the phone just

before quitting time. He watched expense accounts like a
hawk. He was convinced that his scouts were padding them,
which they probably were because they were wretchedly paid.
"Look," he once said to Lee MacPhail, whose job it was to go
over scouting expense accounts, "here he claims he drove
three hundred miles and still saw a game that day. How can
you do that?" MacPhail was new on the job, but he immediately knew that Weiss was telling him both that the scouts
were not to be trusted, and that Weiss was watching *him* to see
if he was tough enough to stay on. Years later Weiss was out in
California going across the Golden Gate Bridge with one of
his scouts. The toll was twenty-five cents. As they reached the
other side, Weiss turned to the scout and said, "I just want you
to know that you've been billing me fifty cents for each trip all
these years."

No one was ever perfect; everyone, it was clear, always let
him down a little, and therefore everyone else should be on
the defensive. Once Weiss visited the Newark ball park. Parke
Carroll, the general manager, knew Weiss was a perfectionist
and decided that this time the park would be in perfect shape.
Even Weiss would not be able to complain. Never had the field
looked so good, never had the seats, freshly painted, seemed
to shine so. When the visit was over Carroll was beaming, until
Weiss took him aside. "Parke," he said, "I have to tell you that
on the way down the ramp I stopped in a pay phone and
the windows on it were dusty. I have to tell you that I'm disappointed, very disappointed." On another occasion when
Lee MacPhail was running the Kansas City farm team, Weiss
had driven over during spring training to the minor-league
park at Lake Wales, Florida. For MacPhail it was a big day
because he was finally going to learn which players the parent club was going to give him for the season. It was also a
beautiful day, although attendance at Lake Wales was never
very high. MacPhail sat in the stands watching the game, listening to Weiss, when suddenly Weiss noticed two young kids
climbing over a fence in right field. *These kids were going to
watch a Yankee farm team play in spring training for free!* All
other business stopped. "Lee, this sort of thing really must
stop at once! We've got to stop kids from doing things like
that," he said.

His obsessiveness was very difficult for those around him. When in 1960 the Yankees let him go, for a brief time he was unemployed. He was not at all easy for his wife, Hazel, to deal with then. "I married George," she said of those days, "for better and for worse, but not for lunch."

But no one could question the success of Weiss's scouting system. It made his reputation in the early thirties. Colonel Ruppert was tired of paying a lot of money for older ball-players, and he brought in Weiss to create a farm system, modeled on what Rickey had done in St. Louis. Weiss put together a network of great scouts. He did not pay them well, but he left them alone. He accepted the idea that scouts were, as a breed, eccentric. He might hear from them only when they felt like it, and if they went off on a tear once in a while, he learned to live with that. But he listened to those scouts, and if they said to take a chance, he took that chance.

He wanted, he made it clear, a Yankee type. A Yankee type was first of all a good ballplayer, but he should also be a gent and look like a Yankee. Yogi Berra or no, there was a Yankee look. If at all possible, he was physically big. At one meeting Paul Krichell started to describe a prospect: "You're going to love him—good hitter, good fielder, great jaw—he really looks like a Yankee." Weiss also wanted players who did not cause problems. Vic Power might have been the most talented first-base prospect in the Yankee organization, an almost sure bet to be the team's first black player. In 1952 Power had hit .331 and driven in 109 runs at Kansas City. But he was flashy on the field and flashy off the field. ("I'm the original showboat hotdog," he once noted.) He was said to be fond of white women. But there was no denying his talent, or the fact that the Yankees were slower than almost any other major-league club in bringing up a black. Fan expectations had been building, in no small part because of Power's minor-league credentials. The first thing management had to do was discredit Power. It moved, of course, through the writers. Typically, they planted a story with Dan Daniel, who was, as ever, accommodating. "Power is major-league material right up to his Adam's apple," Daniel wrote. "North of that location he is not extraordinary. He is said to be not too quick on the trigger mentally." That was it for Power, who was returned to Kansas City in 1953, and soon traded out of the organization. He was not a Yankee type.

It was generally made clear, anyway, that a black player was not a Yankee type. The prejudice that existed in the nation at large extended to sports. Prejudice was merely perceived as the norm: Segregation existed but it did not exist, because it was not seen and not written about. That generation of players was white, and the Yankees and the Red Sox were to remain the whitest in professional baseball, among the last to integrate black players—the Yankees brought Elston Howard up in 1955 and Boston brought Pumpsie Green up in 1959. The top people in both organizations were, despite Jackie Robinson's wildly successful debut in 1947, disdainful of black talent.

The Yankees thought of themselves as the elite team of baseball. They felt they did not need black players (as the Dodgers, a poorer cousin in Brooklyn, did) because their teams were already so good, their farm system so well stocked, and their overall operation so profitable. The whites-only policy reflected the attitudes of men, born around or before the turn of the century, who felt the use of black players tainted their operation. They were the snobs of baseball. Once during the thirties, Ed Barrow had noticed a well-dressed young woman in the grandstand smoking a cigarette. He sent an assistant to tell her to put it out. This kind of behavior—a woman smoking—was not tolerated at Yankee games. The same attitude existed about black players. They would, management believed, draw black fans, who would in turn scare away the good middle-class white fans. When the question of blacks, or Negroes, as they were then called, arose, the Yankee answer was that they would sign one when they found one worthy of being a Yankee.

With the Red Sox, it was a less-refined sort of racism. The top management of the Red Sox was mostly Irish, the most powerful group in Boston. They had established their own ethnic pecking order, which in essence regarded Wasps with respect and grudging admiration for being where they already were; Jews with both admiration and suspicion for being

smart, perhaps a little too smart; and Italians by and large
with disdain for being immigrants and Catholic and yet failing
to be Irish. Blacks were well below the Italians.

In 1949, both the Red Sox and the Yankees, despite the
recommendations of their scouts, failed to sign one of the
ablest if not the ablest black player of the coming era: Willie
Mays, who was playing for the Birmingham Black Barons.

The Yankees sent Bill McCorry, who was a Southerner,
to scout him. As the head office obviously knew, McCorry
did not want any blacks to play for the Yankees. He reported
back that Mays could not hit the curveball. For years afterward John Drebinger of the *Times* would tease McCorry, who
was also a Yankee road secretary, whenever Mays hit a home
run. "Do you think it was by any chance a curve, Bill?" he
would ask. "I don't care what he did today or any other day,"
McCorry would say, as quoted by Peter Golenbock. "I got no
use for him or any of them. I wouldn't want any of them on
the club I was with. I wouldn't arrange a berth on the train
for any of them."

Boston's lapse regarding Mays was even worse. Since the
white Birmingham Barons were a Red Sox farm club, it was
assumed Boston had an edge on picking up black players in
the Birmingham area. Eddie Glennon, the white Barons' general manager, had seen Mays play and called Joe Cronin. But
at first Cronin failed even to send a scout to see Mays.

George Digby, the Red Sox scout in the area, heard about
Mays from Glennon, and the next time he was in Birmingham
he stayed over when the white Barons left to watch Mays play
a Sunday doubleheader. Digby was thirty-one, a former
minor-league player. He saw immediately that Mays was going
to be a great player. Not just a good player, but a great player.
Mays was still in high school, but the speed was already there,
and his arm was better than most major leaguers'. But the
most surprising thing was that he hit the ball with such in-
credible power for so skinny a kid. Mays seemed to be joyous,
full of enthusiasm for the game. Everyone who knew him said
he was sweet, and God knows he was poor, which further ap-
pealed to Digby.

If Digby as a scout had a prejudice, it was not about
color, it was about economics. He always looked for poor

boys, kids who were from the cotton fields or the melon fields or the tobacco fields and who never wanted to go back to them. That guaranteed a good attitude. Scouts, Digby knew, were supposed to project, to look at the bodies of boys and see the bodies of men, and he did that with Mays and was impressed.

"Is he as good as I said?" asked Glennon. Digby said he was right, that Mays was every bit as good as he claimed. Glennon suggested they call Joe Cronin at his home that afternoon. When the Red Sox general manager came on the phone, it was clear to Digby that Glennon had talked often and enthusiastically to him about Mays in the past. Glennon spoke first and told Cronin, "Here's Digby—he'll tell you whether I'm right or not and whether this kid is a great prospect." Digby took the phone. "He's the best-looking kid I've seen all year," Digby began. He knew from Glennon that he could buy the rights to Mays for $5,000 from Tom Hayes, the black Memphis undertaker who owned the Black Barons. But Digby sensed an immediate coolness in place of the usual enthusiasm he got from Cronin. The more he talked, the more he could feel Cronin pulling back. "Do you want me to follow up on him and watch him some more?" Digby asked. It was, after all, his territory, and this was a great prospect. "No," Cronin answered, "no need for that. We'll send someone in."

So Cronin sent in Larry Woodall, their pitching coach, a former major-league catcher and a Southerner. Woodall, not surprisingly, reported that Mays was not the Red Sox type. They signed instead a much older player, Lorenzo (Piper) Davis, the player-manager of the team. Davis was thirty-three, though his baseball age, to buy him some more playing time, was thirty-one.

Racism, in fact, ran rampant through the Red Sox organization. Clif Keane was stunned once when, as a sportswriter covering the Red Sox, he watched the great Minnie Minoso, a black Cuban ballplayer, work out in pregame drills during the fifties. He said almost innocently to Mike Higgins, the Red Sox manager at the time, "You know, that's probably the best all-around player in the league." Higgins turned angrily on him. "You're nothing but a fucking nigger lover," Higgins said.

For the moment the failure to sign black players did not hurt either the Yankees or the Red Sox. Both were strong teams with strong farm systems. But the Red Sox had lost the chance to have Willie Mays play alongside Ted Williams for a decade; and the Yankees, although Mickey Mantle brought them a decade of excellence, came on hard times in the mid-sixties because they had missed out on the great black players of the time.

CHAPTER
11

The Red Sox were in desperate shape. The losses in the doubleheader put them twelve games back. There were rumors in the Boston press that McCarthy would be fired before the week was out. But on July 5, still playing in Yankee Stadium, they began to turn things around—thanks to a rookie. The rookie was Maurice McDermott. With 60,000 fans in the Stadium, he held the Yankees to 4 hits and 2 runs, while striking out 7, and beat them 4–2. It was his third victory with the Red Sox.

In June McCarthy had asked for and gotten Mickey McDermott from Louisville. McDermott was six feet two and seemed even taller because he was so skinny. Blessed with remarkable natural talent, he had a whip for an arm, the scouting reports said, and had shown his talent at such a young age that Boston had originally signed him when he was fourteen. He was too young, so the contract was invalid. Boston resigned him two years later. In 1946 he posted a record of 16-6 in Louisville. Every year he showed up at spring training and dazzled management and veterans with his talent, his wildness, and his capacity for flakiness.

McDermott was nothing if not cocky. He had hoped to

make the club in 1948, and had been furious when he was sent down to the minors. At Scranton he simply overpowered the hitters he faced. Soon Johnny Murphy, the head of the Red Sox farm system, dropped by to see him in Scranton. "Kid," he said, "I hear you're getting that control. Keep it up and you'll be back in the big leagues soon for good." Most rookies would have been thrilled with that prophecy. Not McDermott. He reached for Murphy's tie. "Kid," he said, "your tie is too small. I thought I gave you the word once already. Here, let me fix it for you." He untied the tie of the farm director, and retied it in a Windsor knot. Murphy soon departed. "You know," McDermott told a group of sportswriters, "that Murphy, he'll never learn."

In 1949, he struck out 117 men in only 77 innings in Louisville. He had been sure he was going to the big club and had told reporters, "Last year I wasn't ready. I was so nervous that I couldn't find the plate. I realized I needed time in the minors. I'm ready now. I've quit trying to throw too hard. Control is the thing, and I think I have it." Not everyone agreed, particularly those who batted against him. In Louisville, for the first time, he seemed to master his wildness. In one game he struck out twenty men. When he came up from the minors he was only twenty years old and probably had more natural talent than any pitcher on the staff, including Parnell.

In June, with Boston playing its worst baseball of the year, McDermott became a member of the regular rotation. He was all ears and elbows; years later he would look at his photo in *Life* magazine and say, "There, there it is, see for yourself, no wonder I could never get laid." He drove McCarthy crazy. "Maurice," the old man had told him in spring training, "all you have to do is aim for the middle of the plate and they'll all jump in the barrel for you." But he took no advice. "Maurice, can I tell you a few things?" Mel Parnell once said to him that year. "Not a few things, just one thing," McDermott answered. "Maurice," Parnell said, "I don't think the world is ready for you yet." McDermott wanted to throw the ball past anyone he faced, in his own words, "Hard, harder, hardest."

He did not try to be a flake. He *was* a flake. The Boston sportswriters were calling him Mickey, and he announced that he wanted to be called Lefty because he thought and felt like a Lefty. He sang at local nightclubs and told writers he would rather be a singer than a pitcher. Having been poor all his life, he loved to throw money around now that he was making a big-league salary, albeit a very small one. Everywhere he went he bought new suits and new shoes. "I led the league," he once said of that rookie year, "in stolen hotel towels and buying suits." He bought shirts and wore them only once. He often left clothes behind in hotels. "Mickey," said his roommate Mel Parnell, "half the bellhops in the hotels in the American League are going around wearing your clothes." "That's just fine, Mel," he answered, "let's go out and buy a new suit." He also seemed on his way to setting records in food consumption. He would go into the dining car on the train, eat one dinner, then order another. One day Tom Dowd, the road secretary, caught him doing it. "All right, McDermott, that meal's on you," Dowd said. "Why, because Tom Yawkey can't afford it?" McDermott said. "No, kid, because you just had the biggest dinner of anyone on the team an hour ago," Dowd replied.

His first few starts were impressive. Early in the season he had talked with the great Hal Newhouser. "Harold," he had asked, "when am I going to learn?" "Someday you're going to walk out on that mound and it's going to feel like you own it," Newhouser had answered. That seemed to be happening now. Suddenly a team that had been surviving with two pitchers had a third starter, one that batters feared. He dominated almost every game he was in. His control was better than expected. On July 5, at the lowest point in the season for the Red Sox, now twelve games out, McDermott started for Boston. He allowed the Yankees only four hits, struck out seven, and won 4–2. It was his third victory in four decisions (the defeat being the game in which DiMaggio had beaten him in Boston), and his power seemed to promise more for the future. On the last day of July, he shut out Cleveland 3–0. It was his fifth victory in seven starts. The Boston writers were ecstatic. BEST BOSTON ROOKIE SINCE DAVE FERRISS, said one headline. There were comparisons with other great pitchers of the past and how they had fared at a comparable moment in their careers (Lefty Gomez at nineteen had been 2-5, Hal

Newhouser at nineteen had been 9-9, Bob Feller at seventeen, 5-4). But even with McDermott's victory, the Boston players left New York with a feeling that any vestige of luck had deserted them.

Dominic DiMaggio thought that, given the way the Yankees were playing, it would take 98 games to win the pennant. That meant that the Red Sox for the rest of the season would have to be 63-20, a record of over .750, as close to perfection as one could imagine for baseball. Actually, The Little Professor, as DiMaggio was called by sportswriters because he wore glasses, was slightly off—it would not require 98 games to win the pennant; it required only 97.

In those darkest days Ted Williams kept saying they were a hot-weather team and he was right: Boston was a team of good hitters, and by the middle of the summer the other teams' pitchers had worn down. In the vernacular, they lost a yard or two on their fastballs. That helped the hitters, but it was a condition to which the Boston pitchers were not immune. Catching the Yankees appeared at that moment an impossible task.

It was Dominic DiMaggio, as much as anyone, who started the Red Sox comeback. He was probably the most underrated baseball player of his day, in part because of his size—he was smaller than most outfielders, and he hit with less power—in part because he wore glasses, and mostly because he played in the shadow of his brother Joe, and also that of Ted Williams. But he became one of the premier center fielders of his day. He was chosen in eight All-Star Games and played in seven (missing one because of injuries). In the American League only his brother Joe was as good a defensive outfielder, for Dominic DiMaggio played center field like an infielder. He charged balls fearlessly, holding runners back from extra bases. He had speed and range and the special DiMaggio knack of anticipating the play, to get an exceptional jump on a ball. He was a good hitter, perhaps not a great one, but he studied pitchers almost as closely as Williams did. He knew that his job was to get on base, and he was probably the best lead-off hitter in the American League. He was an unusually intelligent man who could easily have run a baseball team, and he went on to become a remarkable financial success after his playing days were over. He did this not, as often happens, by cashing in on his name, but rather by starting a second career as the owner of a plastics manufacturing company in New England.

There was about Dominic a sense that he was different, more serious than other players. It was not just the glasses, which made him look different, almost scholarly, it was his demeanor, his language, his comportment. Once he was called out on strikes on what he clearly thought was a bad pitch. He turned to the umpire in rage, stared at him, walked angrily back to the bench, and then, poised on the top step, yelled, "I have never witnessed such incompetence in all my life."

The Yankees were aware of Dominic's value to the Red Sox. They believed they had to keep him off the bases. Not only was he a good contact hitter and a good base runner, but Johnny Pesky hit right behind him in the number-two slot. Pesky was a much better hitter with men on base, and was one of the best hit-and-run men in the league. If Dominic got on, the Yankee pitchers believed, it guaranteed that Ted Williams would come up with men in scoring position. Then they would face the choice of having to walk him and risk an even bigger inning, or pitching to him and risking several runs.

Even while the Red Sox were losing in June, Dominic DiMaggio had already hit in 8 straight games. He was to hit in 26 more games, for a total of 34, before his streak ended on August 9. That remains a Red Sox record. More important, it helped turn a sagging team around. He would get on base, Pesky would move him around, and Williams, Junior Stephens, and Doerr would bring them home.

Dominic was the youngest and smallest of the DiMaggios. By the time he passed adolescence, it had become acceptable within the DiMaggio family to be a professional baseball player. Both Joe and Vince were playing professional ball, and Giuseppe DiMaggio had not only changed his mind about a career in baseball, he positively basked in Joe's fame. "And when are you going to play baseball?" Giuseppe asked Dominic when he was still in high school. The old world had finally accepted the mores of the new one.

The boys' mother, Rosalie DiMaggio, her youngest son was sure, was the real engine in the family's drive for success and a better life. Giuseppe DiMaggio was a good man, a hard worker, but he would have been content with his life in the Old World. He was a man who accepted what was around him. She did not. She was the one who pushed her husband, first to move to the small fishing village of Martinez in the Bay area, and then to San Francisco; once in San Francisco, she pushed to find better houses in better neighborhoods with access to better schools. Schools were important, for she had been a schoolteacher in the old country. It was understood that the DiMaggio men of the next generation were to be more than fishermen. That was what all the sacrifice was for.

However, the fame that came to engulf her children somewhat perplexed Rosalie DiMaggio. She was pleased that they did well, but it was more important to her that they were respected as men, not just as players. She was, thought Dominic DiMaggio, a wonderful old-fashioned woman of immense strength, yet she never raised her voice. She was guided by an unshakable religious faith. She told her children stories from the Bible, all with a proverb, all with a purpose. She constantly set standards of behavior that they were to live up to.

When Dominic was a newsboy, he once found a roll of crisp new bills worth thirty-five dollars. There was no wallet, and no way to return it. Dominic brought it home, somewhat pleased with himself. But his mother did not share in his pleasure. "Dominic, I feel badly about this," she said. Dominic asked why. "I feel badly for the man who lost it—it is surely his week's pay." The lesson was clear: There was nothing else they could do, no way to return the money to the rightful owner, but there was to be no pleasure in this small windfall.

Dominic was the runt of the family. He was always eager to prove that he was as strong as his older brothers. He worked hard on the fishing boat, claiming that he liked it in order to show that his size was not a problem. Joe, by contrast, hated the boat, hated even the smell of fish, and he made no secret about it. At Galileo High School, Dominic did not play until his last year, and he batted ninth. He hit .400, but had not even played enough to get his full varsity black "G"; instead, he got the lesser "G" in a scroll, which he did not choose to wear. He was still small—five feet seven and 135 pounds— and a professional career seemed unlikely. But he liked the

game and there were the footsteps of his two brothers in
which to follow. So after graduation he kept playing, for the
Presidio–Monterey Army team. He played shortstop and
qualified for his availability by working as a lifeguard for the
army.

He began to grow bigger and stronger and took a job with
the Simmons Bed Company as a laborer. There he clamped
springs onto mattresses. He was paid 40 cents an hour—which
meant he was drawing a check of $19.20 for 48 hours of work.
He also played for the Simmons semipro team on Sunday. He
often thought about a professional-baseball career, and decided that what he wanted was just one season in the major
leagues. That would be enough to prove he could do whatever
he wanted. In those days the Cincinnati Reds and the San
Francisco Seals, an independently owned unaffiliated Pacific
Coast team, held an annual joint tryout for local boys. They
alternated which team got first pick each year, and in 1937,
when Dominic was just twenty, he decided to go to the camp.
Being a dutiful son, he talked it over with both parents, and
they gave him their blessing. He did not want to lose his job so
he went to his boss and explained about the tryout: The camp
would last about two weeks. His boss said that his job would be
waiting if he did not get a contract.

There were 143 kids at the tryout, but Dom DiMaggio
was the best player there. The Seals decided to sign him. Dom
thought of himself as an infielder, but Charley Graham, who
was the principal owner of the Seals, took one look at him and
said, "With those glasses we better get him in the outfield."
Graham's fear, Dominic realized, was that a sharp infield hit
might take a bad bounce and break his glasses.

Because neither of his parents spoke English, his older
brother Tom negotiated the contract. Tom DiMaggio wanted
to protect his younger brother, and was very tough with the
Seals. Above all he did not want him playing in Tucson in the
terrible Arizona heat, as Vince had done. "You can't send him
out to Tucson," Tom said. "He's so small and it's so hot there,
you'll have to wipe him up with a blotter."

The real burden was not so much Dom's size, but the fact
that he wore glasses. In that pre–contact lens era, wearing
glasses was unthinkable. Hitters had to see, and they had to

have great vision; if a player wore glasses, it was a sign that something more than just eyesight was missing. "Four-eyes" the schoolyard taunt went. It was about manhood as well; perhaps he was not really tough enough to play in a man's game. Occasionally a pitcher—pitchers did not hit—was allowed to wear glasses. Dominic DiMaggio could not, however, remember any other regular ballplayer who wore glasses at the time he broke in.

But Dominic had great confidence in himself; he knew he could see the ball and make contact. He was fortunate in his first season because Lefty O'Doul, who had managed his brother, was still managing the Seals. He was the best hitting instructor that Dominic ever saw. O'Doul recognized both the talent and the flaws in this young player. He saw power in the chest and arms, and he worked hard in spring training to improve Dominic's swing, above all to keep him from lunging at the ball. DiMaggio, self-conscious about his lack of size, lunged because it seemed to promise greater power. O'Doul showed him that power was dissipated that way. He was to wait for the pitch and then swing, turning his hips into the ball, not lunge with his body. O'Doul was a patient teacher with a good eye. He would stand for hours behind the tiny batting cage they used in those days, armed with only a fungo stick, which was an unusually long bat. When DiMaggio moved his body, O'Doul would jab the fungo stick in his butt as sharply as he could.

One day Joe DiMaggio, who was already a star with the Yankees, dropped by the Seals camp and took some batting practice. Someone had an early movie camera and photographed both Joe and Dominic at bat. It was, thought Dominic years later, quite possibly the first use of the camera as a teaching vehicle in baseball, and it was an unusually dramatic one. When Joe was at bat, there was everything O'Doul had been preaching: The bat was cocked, and his entire body was still, as if frozen. The ball arrived, and Joe swung at it. His head did not move more than an inch, and the rest of his body did not move at all—except for his hips as they went into the ball. Thus his whole body was channeled into the swing.

Then there was the movie sequence with Dominic: As he waited for the pitch, his shoulders moved, the trunk of his body moved, and, worst of all, his head moved forward twelve inches. All the things O'Doul had said were true: It was a body unfocused. So Dominic paid attention. For a time his hitting got worse, because he was undoing what he knew and trying something different. But a few weeks later they were playing in a small mining town near Monterey, and Dominic was taking batting practice. Suddenly he was hitting balls over the fence, and he knew it had finally worked for him. Without the help from O'Doul, he would probably not have made the major leagues, he later decided.

Dominic DiMaggio hit .306 in his first season. But very early on the comparisons with Joe began. A sportswriter named Tom Laird, who wrote for the *San Francisco Daily News,* often praised Joe DiMaggio as the greatest player he had ever seen, and wrote that Dominic DiMaggio was a poor player cashing in on Joe's name. Nothing had ever stung Dominic more, and nothing made him more determined to make the major leagues. (Among those who concurred with Laird was Joe DiMaggio. He told the Boston sportswriters in Dominic's rookie year that at first he had thought the same thing. Only when he saw his younger brother play was he converted.)

By his third year, 1939, Dominic hit .361 and became the league's most-valuable hitter. The next year, 1940, he was in the major leagues and hit .301.

For a long time the comparisons with his brother remained difficult. He met every challenge, overcame the problem of his size, showed that glasses were not a problem. Dom was a consistent .300 hitter, yet he was always somehow made to seem lacking in comparison with Joe DiMaggio. For a time, when he was in the minor leagues, it spurred him and made him work harder. Then, when he arrived in the major leagues and still did not get the recognition he felt he deserved, he became bitter. But gradually he overcame it. The war years helped. In the service he learned that there was a great deal more to life than baseball, and slowly he learned to ignore other people's expectations. That was his greatest victory—to accept his own talents and limitations and to live happily with them.

In July 1949 his hitting streak did not surprise Dominic DiMaggio. He knew that he was, above all else, consistent. He had two other streaks, both of 27 games, and he knew that his final batting average was usually between .285 and .305. (One reason he lost about ten points a year on his average was that the Red Sox catchers were unusually slow and batted in front of him. When one of them was on base, it cost him an infield hit from time to time.) He knew that he needed his hits earlier in the season because the length of the season and the heat wore him out. He might be hitting .330 in mid-July, but slowly his weight would drop, and then so did his batting average. In those long hot summers, his batting average always came down 20 or 30 points.

That summer he had been hitting about .325 when the streak began. He was on base in every game at a time when many Red Sox players had lost their concentration and come apart. He brought back the excitement that helped bring them alive. When it was over he was hitting .340 and Boston was no longer twelve games out of first place. The Red Sox were playing well; the pitching was improving; and they were sneaking back into the pennant race.

Then in August, Boston became a hot team. Parnell was pitching his best baseball of the year. Kinder was in the midst of a prolonged winning streak. Kramer, virtually useless until then, was beginning to pitch well, and Stobbs pitched regularly and started winning.

Ted Williams was enormously confident. He studied the box scores every day, and he noted that the Yankee pitchers were struggling just a little. Raschi was on a losing streak. Reynolds was not finishing his games. They were worn thin, Williams thought. He was not surprised. Even when the Red Sox had been ten games out, Williams was sure that they would make a run at the Yankees. There was just too much talent on the Boston team not to. Boston was a hitter's team, not a pitcher's team, and July and August belonged to the hitters. Playing constantly in hot, muggy weather became a test of the mind over an unwilling, sluggish body. Sometimes on those suffocating days Williams would feel worn down. After all, he was not relaxing in the dugout—he was on base more than half the time, and that was tiring. Then he would look at the opposing pitcher. It is hard on me, he thought, but he's the one really paying for it. The heat, he knew, would disappear for him in the sheer pleasure of baseball.

On August 8, the Yankees went into Fenway for a three-game series. Boston was six and a half out. The Red Sox badly needed to win at least two: That would make it five and a half out, instead of seven and a half out if the Yankees won two. In the first game it was Kinder against Raschi. Dominic DiMaggio, who had hit in 34 games going in, was stopped by Raschi in the first game. He made five trips to the plate and the last time up he was sure he had a hit. He lined a pitch hard, right past Raschi's ear, and as he broke out of the batter's box he thought, I've got it. But the ball kept carrying until finally it reached his brother in center field. He had hit it too hard. After the game one of the New York writers suggested to Joe DiMaggio that he had made a good catch, but he dissented. "If I hadn't caught it, the ball would have hit me right between the eyes." Dominic DiMaggio's streak was over.

But the Red Sox won the game 6–3, and Ellis Kinder's record was now 13-5. The defeat was Raschi's fourth in a row, and made his record 15-7. Then Parnell beat Reynolds for his seventeenth win that season. Williams had seven hits in three games. He felt exhilarated. The Red Sox had won two out of three; they were closing the gap.

The Yankees were worried about Raschi. On July 21 his record had been 15-3, the best in the American League, but he was struggling now. The heat was wearing him out. He had lost his last four starts in a row. It was a long season. Yogi Berra hated catching doubleheaders, particularly in the heat. He complained so often that finally Eddie Lopat asked him, "Hey, Yogi, what do you think Birdie Tebbetts is going to do today? Catch one game or two?" It had no effect. In mid-July Berra came to the park one Sunday and turned to Charlie Silvera. "Silvera, you're catching the second game today." "No, I'm not," Silvera answered. "The only way I catch is if you're home sick." Silvera suspected he might have planted an idea because a few weeks later Berra called and said that he was staying home because he had a bad cold. "You call Mr. Berra right back," Stengel told the trainer, Gus Mauch, "and tell him to come to the ball park anyway—I might want him as a pinch hitter."

The strain of the heat on the pitchers was even more obvious. They kept a jug of orange juice mixed with honey to drink as a pick-me-up and also a bucket filled with ice and ammonia. Gus Mauch would dip a towel in the bucket and drape it over the pitcher's neck between innings. "Florida water," they called it. It was believed that water, any amount of it, would bloat you up, make you heavy, and slow you down. So none of the pitchers took even the smallest drink of water during the game. Allie Reynolds, as a special reward to himself if he made it to the seventh inning in the hot weather, would go over to the cooler, take a mouthful, wash it around in his mouth for a moment or two, then spit it out.

Two years later, when Johnny Sain, a masterful veteran pitcher, joined them, he brought an even more remarkable secret. In the late innings on hot days Johnny Sain would go to the bucket of ice, grab a handful, and stuff it into his jock. The others were appalled—here was the worst kind of cold shower imaginable. But Sain swore that it helped him fight off fatigue and dizziness. Soon some of the others tried it and came to swear by it.

There were days when a pitcher simply didn't have it, and the opposing players would virtually take batting practice. The manager was loath to go to the bullpen and sacrifice a good relief pitcher in a game already hopelessly lost. When this happened it was the duty of the starting pitcher to stay out there and let the hitters club him and his earned-run average to death. The Yankee pitchers had a phrase for it: "Your turn in the barrel," for it was like being the target in an arcade.

During a season, Vic Raschi thought, a pitcher won some games that he shouldn't win, but then during that long July-August stretch, he would lose some he should have won. Raschi would lose thirteen or fourteen pounds a game and change uniforms as many as three times—wearing a heavy wool uniform with five or six pounds of sweat in it made things worse. Unlike Raschi and Reynolds, Lopat was not a power pitcher and he lost less weight. Sometimes he would pitch the first game of a doubleheader on an oppressive day, then come into the dugout at the end of the seventh inning and show that he had no stains under his armpits. "It's not that hot," he would say.

Raschi used his full power on every pitch, and had to drive off the mound as hard as he could. The heavier he was, the more powerfully he could drive off the mound. But in August 1949 he was slumping, and he was sure that it was from loss of weight. He had started the season at 224 pounds, which was a good weight for him; he was tall and big-boned. Gradually, as June and July passed, his weight began to slip, below 220 and then down to 215. An additional problem, Raschi thought, was that the weight loss put more pressure on him mentally. He had to think more, and concentrate more; lacking optimum physical power, his placement of pitches had to be more precise. He became more of a finesse pitcher.

The day after Kinder beat Raschi, Eddie Lopat beat Joe Dobson. Before the game Ted Williams and Walt Masterson had been talking about Lopat. "I think he's the best pitcher in the American League," Masterson said. "No way," said Williams, "no way." "Come on, Ted, think about it. What other pitcher gets by throwing with so little." There was a long silence.

Stengel did not like to pitch Lopat in Fenway, but on this day he had no choice, and Lopat was brilliant. The 101-degree heat did not bother him. He walked four men in seven innings and gave up only four hits. After the seventh, before Lopat could tire, Stengel went to Page, and Page also dominated the Red Sox, giving up only one hit. Afterward Williams wanted only to talk about Page. He was, claimed the Boston hitter, the difference in the teams. "I wish we had someone like him who could just go out there and fire the ball. If we had someone like that we'd be ten games ahead. Pitching is the reason the Yankees are ahead, make no mistake about that."

The next day Parnell beat Reynolds, who did not last past the third inning. It was Parnell's seventeenth victory. Boston, with a third of August gone, was five and a half games out. It had become a pennant race after all.

Williams felt particularly good. He was seeing more and better pitches than he normally did. The reason, he was sure, was Junior Stephens hitting right behind him. Later, after his career was over, he decided that Junior had offered him more protection than anyone else in his career. He was aware of

Junior's weaknesses: He was not a supple hitter. Good pitchers working in big ball parks could almost always handle him with the right pitches. He knew that Junior's strike zone was far too big. "That man," Hal Newhouser once said, "goes after pitches way out of the strike zone, and hits home runs with them." Junior was a good hitter, Williams decided, but an imperfect one. When Williams had first come up, others had hit behind him—Jimmie Foxx and Joe Cronin at times. But their skills were beginning to decline. Junior was at the top of his game in 1948, 1949, and 1950.

Junior Stephens was an amazing physical specimen. He played hard all day, and he played just as hard all night. He was not so much a drinker as a carouser. William Mead, in his book *Even the Browns,* described him as a young man "with a baby face and an insatiable appetite for female compan- ionship." "I roomed mostly with his suitcase," Don Gutteridge, his teammate, once said. In 1944, Charley DeWitt, one of the Browns owners, asked Junior to quit running around at night and get some rest—because the Browns had a chance at the pennant. Stephens agreed. Thereupon he went for three weeks without a hit. DeWitt then told him, "Go out [at night] and stay out." How did he do it, Gutteridge once asked rhe- torically—stay out all night and then play so well? "He was a superman," Gutteridge said. On the Red Sox he continued his demanding schedule. But during the 1948 season he was com- pletely worn out in the last month. In 1949 he was somewhat better, but his teammates thought they could sense fatigue coming on toward the end. No one on the Red Sox, however, was going to tell Junior what time to go to bed, and certainly not Ted Williams. By August, as the team continued to win, everyone seemed more relaxed. Bobby Doerr, who was play- ing in considerable pain and whose legs were being carefully wrapped every day, was now called Johnson and Johnson. There was more teasing and clowning around. Once before a night game on an evening when he was not going to pitch, Jack Kramer asked Matt Batts to warm him up. He did it along the first baseline bench as the fans were pouring into the box seats. There was no doubt in Batts's mind from Kramer's exaggerated motions that he was preening for the crowd just a little. Kramer was good-looking and was generally thought incapable of passing a mirror without admiring himself. As Kramer delivered the next pitch, Batts dropped his catcher's mitt and caught the ball bare-handed. Kramer turned immediately and walked to the outfield. He never asked Batts to warm him up before a game again.

Birdie Tebbetts, the prime needler on the Red Sox, took pleasure in provoking Williams. Tebbetts was the leading bench jockey on the team, and no one was immune from his sharp tongue. He picked his spots, of course. He knew when to do it to Williams—when Williams was hitting and feeling good. Then Tebbetts would carefully scan the Boston papers and pick out something that Egan or one of the other writers had written that day. "God, Ted, did you see what they wrote about you today? About your being jealous of Junior over here? I wouldn't put up with that crap if I were you." Sometimes he needled Williams about his power: "You know, Ted, when you were a rookie I was sure you would get the Ruth record of sixty home runs, but now all you hit are thirty or forty." Sometimes it was about his hitting in general: "Ted, you know I've been thinking and I think you've slipped a bit as a hitter from when you first came up. I think you were a better hitter then than you are now."

Williams, of course, would always bite. "What the hell do you mean?" he would ask, dead serious now.

"Well, when you first came up back when I was in Detroit you would come up to the plate and stand there and say, 'Throw the goddamn ball—I'm going to knock it out whatever it is.' You didn't give a damn about who was pitching or what he was throwing. Now it's always, 'Dommy, what's he throwing today? . . . Is he sharp, is he off? . . . Is he sneaky?'"

Williams would go on the offensive: "Do you know what our fleet-footed catcher used to do when he was at Detroit?" he would say to the others. "He would ask me when I came to the plate what kind of pitch I wanted. 'How about a fastball, Ted? Would you like one on the inside corner?' So of course it threw me off, I didn't know what to expect—was he setting me up?—and so I didn't say anything and he kept on it, and one time he asked me if I wanted a slow curve and I said yes, and I waited and he got me a slow curve, Mr. Tebbetts did, just like I asked, and I hit it out and he never let me order a pitch again."

The sportswriters *always* gathered around Birdie's locker after the game for a daily debriefing—Birdie was a voluble and articulate source. Williams, if he was not too angry at the writers at the moment, would say, "Well, guys, there's no need to buy the papers tomorrow. We know what's going to be written. Just what this man says. There might as well be a byline on all those stories. By Mr. George Tebbetts." The others loved the sound of such give-and-take: It was the sound of baseball players who were winning.

CHAPTER 12

As the pennant race became tighter, the writers and the players began to notice something fascinating: For the first time there was a sense of importance of television. Red Smith, who was the first to write about it, observed it, oddly enough, not in the behavior of the players but in the behavior of the umpires and the fans.

"Today, conscious of the great unseen audience, they [the umpires] play every decision out like the balcony scene from *Romeo and Juliet*. On a strike they gesticulate, they brandish a fist aloft, they spin almost as shot through the heart, they bellow all four parts of the quartette from *Rigoletto*. On a pitch that misses the plate, they stiffen with loathing, ostentatiously avert the gaze, and render a bit from *Götterdämmerung*. In parlor and pub you see the umpire today. And hear him." Then Smith added, prophetically, "The virus is infecting the fans, too. When a foul is hit in the stands, the camera usually is trained on the fan who recovers the ball. Used to be that a guy catching a foul would pocket his loot almost furtively and go on watching the game. Today he wheels towards the camera, holds his prize aloft, shouts, and makes faces. Television is making us a nation of hams."

Television was still very primitive. In 1947 the World Series had been broadcast for the first time, on the old DuMont network to five cities. Gillette sponsored the game, and an estimated 3 million people watched. The company intended to introduce a new Gillette razor, which came in a flashy plastic package. The selling point of the new razor was how easy it was to feed the blades into it. There was to be a live demonstration on TV, but the Gillette people had forgotten to bring an associate to do the feed, so Otis Freeman, the DuMont engineer, had to wash his hands quickly and double as the blade feeder. Freeman loved being in on something as novel as television. Like many in the industry at that time, he was young, had been in World War II as an engineer, and was eager to experiment with this marvelous new toy.

There had been, he thought, looking back years later, three stages to modern television. In the beginning it was engineer-driven, for the questions that hung over every broadcast were: Could this actually be accomplished?; Are the technical facilities good enough? Then, in the late fifties, after a decade of remarkable technological achievements, it became director-driven. The technological skills were a given; now it took creative skills to complement what the engineers had wrought. After that it became, like so many other successful enterprises in America, accountant-driven. In this final stage, the new generation of well-educated accountants limited the freedom of the directors and minimized the risk in order to maximize the profits.

But in those early years, something new could be tried every day, it seemed. Otis Freeman had started with an experimental station in New York, W2XWV, which in time became WABD after its owner, Allen B. DuMont. It was then the third station in New York—WNBC and WCBS were first. The early television sets were extremely temperamental and apt to go out of focus for no discernible reason. When that happened the tavern owner (for the sets were invariably in bars) would call the station to complain. Freeman told the DuMont telephone operators to intercept those calls and relay them to him at home. Then, like a doctor on a house call, he would rush out, grab a cab, and repair the afflicted set himself for fifty dollars. The fees added up to almost half his salary, and he

gratefully cut the telephone operators in with a five-dollar tip
per call. In 1948, when WPIX, owned by the *Daily News,* went
on the air, Freeman became its chief engineer. It was relatively
easy for WPIX to get the Yankees—the other fledgling net-
works did not like baseball, because it did not end exactly on
the half hour and was therefore hard to schedule.

WPIX used Mel Allen and Curt Gowdy as its television
team; there was no difference between what they said on radio
and what they said on television. Setting up the technical facilities, Freeman found himself in a perpetual struggle with the
Stadium groundskeepers and officials, and, of course, George
Weiss. Whatever he tried to do, someone would object and tell
him no, it had never been done before.

Nor were Freeman's responsibilities restricted to the Stadium. He had to serve as the personal television repairman of
Yankee owner Dan Topping as well. Several times a season
Topping would send his seaplane to pick up Freeman and fly
him out to his Southampton home. As the plane made its ap-
proach, it would buzz the house, and a driver in a Rolls would
be sent to meet Freeman. At the house he would work on either the set or the 125-foot antenna—it was so tall, it had to be
taken down at the end of the season because of the danger
from high winds and ice, which would form on it.

If the announcers, trained in radio, were somewhat uneasy with television, the early sponsors were not. The commercial possibilities of televised games were immediately obvious.
The Gillette people had been stunned by the success of their
first TV ad campaign, and for many years after would unveil
its new shaving devices on the occasion of the World Series. In
1949 Gillette paid $175,000 for the TV rights; it was also
ruthless in keeping costs down, paying such preeminent announcers as Allen and Red Barber, both of whom were eager
to get the prestigious assignments, $200 a game. But Gillette
was just skimming off the biggest games.

In the coverage of regular-season games, the beer companies were there first. In 1949 Leonard Faupel was a young
salesman for the Ballantine Brewing Company, which sponsored the Yankee games. Faupel understood the pull of the
new medium immediately, mainly because of the enthusiasm

of the city's tavern owners. That was where television was having its first, big impact. Fred Allen, then one of the leading comedians on radio, noted that there were still a few New Yorkers who had not watched television yet—little children, he noted, too young to go into saloons.

In 1949, there was a belief among American tavern owners that theirs was an endangered business. Ordinary Americans were becoming better educated, going from blue-collar jobs to white-collar jobs. No longer, the tavern owners feared, would they automatically stop off at the neighborhood bar on the way home from work for a beer or two. Worst of all, Americans were moving to the suburbs. That was the real threat. There, aided by better refrigeration and new beer packaging—for the first time beer came in cans—potential customers could now drink at home. The old-fashioned tavern might well go the way of the blacksmith shop.

Therefore, the city's tavern owners saw a considerable lure in the early television sets, which they displayed prominently over their bars, and tuned almost exclusively to the sports shows: the Friday night fights, the occasional football game, and, above all, the big baseball games. In their windows they displayed huge signs with the Ballantine (or a competing beer's) logo which announced the games and fights to be televised. Business prospered; for a big baseball game, the crowds in the bars were enormous—regular customers had regular seats, and newcomers had to stand in the back.

For Ballantine, a relatively small Newark-based company that was trying to gain a more significant share of the New York market, the radio and television sponsorship of the Yankee games was a gift from the gods. The package was unbelievably inexpensive. It gave the Ballantine salesman immediate identity in his area. He did not merely sell beer; he was the man who brought you the Yankees. Faupel, though, had a sense that an entirely new era was beginning, and that television sets were not going to be almost exclusively in taverns for long. The price of sets, he was sure, would continue to drop, and their technological capacities would increase. What was coming was nothing less than a great new American theater in the home where the best live entertainment would most likely be sports.

Not everyone shared his enthusiasm. Such traditionalists as George Weiss were wary. Weiss had never liked radio broadcasting. It struck him as being perilously close to giving away the product, and he resisted it as much as he could. If he made a connection between the staggering jump in postwar attendance and the coming of live radio broadcasts, he never admitted it. As far as he was concerned, the attendance came from the superiority of his product, not from this new cumbersome amplification system that was stealing it.

There was constant pressure for increased broadcasting rights, but Weiss was going to make the broadcasters do it his way. He lost no opportunity to remind everyone who held the power and who was the supplicant. Every meeting with the WPIX people was a battle, every increment of expansion a small war.

Slowly, Otis Freeman of WPIX realized that there was a ritual to dealing with Weiss. The broadcast people were not to congratulate themselves in front of him on how much their ratings had increased, or how many letters they were getting from fans. Quite the reverse. They were to go in and listen to a litany of their failures. Weiss would berate Freeman and Ben Larsen, the station manager—their coverage was clumsy, they promoted the games poorly, and they did not have a proper respect for the Yankee mystique. Then, when Weiss was finished, he would turn to Arthur Patterson and say, "Okay, Red, now you tell 'em." Patterson would continue the assault. It was, Freeman soon realized, really about money. It was a negotiating strategy.

Weiss did not see television as expanding the market for baseball; rather he saw it the same way he saw radio—as competition with Stadium attendance. He fought a constant rearguard action, trying to limit TV's presence. That very first year there were prolonged struggles over camera angles. In the beginning there were only two or three cameras—one behind the plate, one at first, and occasionally one at third. But Mel Allen came up with the idea of placing a camera in center field. The engineers experimented with it, and they were impressed with the results; it provided an entirely different view of the game, and fans could see things they had never seen before. It made the game infinitely more immediate. But

Weiss refused to let them use it all. "Why not, George?" Len
Faupel asked. "It'll give away the catcher's signals," Weiss answered. They argued and finally Faupel won permission to
place the camera there, but Weiss immediately set a ceiling on
how many shots from it they could use per game. Three.
Then four. Then five.

Frank Scott was the road secretary for the Yankees in
1949, a job that was part wagon master, part secretary, part
nursemaid. During that season Weiss asked Scott, as was his
custom, for information on the players' private lives. To do
that, Scott thought, made him nothing less than a spy. He felt
Weiss was placing him in an untenable position. He refused to
produce the information, and Weiss did not forgive him.
After the 1950 season Scott and Weiss had an angry meeting
in which Weiss accused Scott of disloyalty. Scott protested that
he had been loyal to both the Yankees and the management.
"You don't get paid to be on the players' side," Weiss said,
"and you took the players' side." Weiss won the argument—he
fired Scott.

Shortly thereafter Scott spent a day with Yogi Berra in his
New Jersey house. Near the end of the day he asked Berra
what time it was. "Here," said Berra, and opened a drawer
and flipped him a watch. "Where did this come from?" Scott
asked, and Berra opened the drawer again. There were about
thirty watches. "That's what they give me when I make
speeches," Berra explained. Scott understood immediately
that there was room for a new role here; that if he represented a player like Berra and negotiated his appearances,
Berra might do better than getting a watch. He made an offer
to Berra on the spot. Thus in 1950 did Yogi Berra, by Scott's
and his teammates' reckoning, become the first player in baseball to have an agent. Aided by Scott, Berra probably made
about $2,500 from speeches in his first year, instead of adding
to his watch collection. Soon most of the rest of the Yankees
and many Dodgers signed up with Scott.

George Weiss was not pleased. It was a threat in many
ways. It was an outside source of income, which limited management's ability to regulate the players' hunger. It might also
signal that players would soon want agents to *represent* them.

Weiss was convinced that Scott was acting out of spite. He told Scott that if he was going to represent Berra and others, he could not do it inside the Stadium. In addition he made it clear that there was to be no representation in contract dealings.

A few years later during spring training, Weiss was having trouble signing Berra, and the catcher was threatening to hold out. Red Patterson offered to help out. Patterson walked into Berra's motel room, feeling confident that he was a friend of Yogi's and that they could settle this quickly. There, sitting with Berra, was Scott. That still did not bother Patterson; after all, the three of them were friends.

The first words out of Berra's mouth were, "All right, Patterson, none of your shit." "Yeah," added Scott, "Yogi's right." I don't need this, thought Patterson, and immediately removed himself from the negotiating team.

Slowly the old order was changing: Television was making everyone richer and it was turning the players into personalities. They began appearing on *The Ed Sullivan Show* and making $500 for it. Soon they began to establish identities that removed them somewhat from the reach of management.

CHAPTER
13

That August, as the Red Sox made a run at the Yankees, going to work was a pure pleasure for Birdie Tebbetts, the Boston catcher. There was nothing more satisfying than seeing a team achieve its true potential and begin to believe in itself. Tebbetts had come to Boston from the Detroit Tigers in a trade early in the 1947 season. He had been thrilled about the move to New England because he was born in Vermont and raised in Nashua, New Hampshire. He knew that the Red Sox were not so much a Boston team as a New England team. They were also stronger and younger than the Tigers. Now he was sure he was going to catch every day.

Tebbetts had enjoyed playing in Detroit before the war, for Detroit was an ideal baseball city, a blue-collar town that sometimes seemed to revolve around the Tigers. But things changed in 1945. When he and other veterans returned, and slowly made the adjustment back to baseball, they were welcomed by neither fans nor teammates. It was not pleasant, and for the first time in his life Birdie Tebbetts did not enjoy going to work in the morning.

In 1946 he thought they were booing Hank Greenberg out of town, and then in 1947, when Greenberg went to Pittsburgh, it struck Tebbetts that he was next. The problem was, he thought, that he was not a good ballplayer in 1946 and much of 1947. His hands had gotten hard in the four years away. The one thing a catcher had to have was soft hands— that is, hands that were quick and flexible, and could make last-second adjustments as a pitcher's ball broke down. Only slowly after the war did the touch come back to his hands. The Boston pitchers agreed. Birdie, they thought, was a good defensive catcher who managed to compensate for a below-average arm by the use of very quick hands—he was as quick on the release of the ball as anyone in baseball.

More than anyone else, Tebbetts became the leader on the Boston team. He was thirty-seven in 1949, feisty and combative by nature. His nickname came from his constant needling and chirping at other ballplayers. Young pitchers learned to let him call his game, and they shook him off at their risk. In the early part of the 1949 season, Tebbetts did not think that the Yankees were a better team than the Red Sox. Their only real advantage, he thought, was Joe Page. He gave them the best bullpen in the league. But for much of the summer, the Red Sox were getting by with only two pitchers— Parnell and Kinder. Dobson and Kramer were struggling. Stobbs was young. McDermott's control was a problem. Could a team make it on two pitchers? That was the question at first. But Parnell and Kinder began to pitch even better, and some of the other pitchers began to help. On August 20, with Boston only three and a half games out, Tebbetts told reporters that in the last 47 games, the starters had finished 32 times. Since McDermott had beaten the Yankees on July 5, the Red Sox had gone 36-10. Tebbetts was sure there was going to be a real pennant race. He was right: In August, Parnell was 6-0, Kinder was 6-0, Stobbs was 3-0, and Kramer was 3-0. Suddenly Boston's pitching seemed to be more solid than the Yankees'.

Tebbetts himself was having a very good year. He was hitting well, and he was, to everyone's astonishment, leading the team in stolen bases—not bad for one of the slowest men on the team. Pesky and Dom DiMaggio were, of course, faster, but their job, with Williams hitting third, was to get on base and not take any risks. Once, when Pesky was a rookie, he had gone to Joe Cronin and asked for permission to run. "I can steal twenty-five bases a season," he said. "Jesus Christ, Pesky, they told me you were raised in a ball park and now I find out you've got a hole in your head. You've got the best hitter in baseball coming up right behind you, and he hits the ball and you're going to score," Cronin said. "You damn well won't run."

Late in the season Dom DiMaggio went to Tebbetts and noted that the catcher was leading the team in stolen bases. "Birdie, that's embarrassing to the rest of us, especially if you end up the season leading the team," he said. "I wonder if you'd mind not stealing for a while. I'd hate to go through the winter being razzed about it." Tebbetts said that was okay, and so Dom DiMaggio quite determinedly set out to correct the record. He was trailing 8–6 when he started out, but he soon had his seventh, eighth, and ninth steals. "Okay," he said to Tebbetts, "that's it for now." He ended up leading Birdie Tebbetts and Johnny Pesky 9–8–8 in stolen bases that year.

Jim Turner, the Yankees' pitching coach, faulted himself for Raschi's August slump. Short-handed on starting pitchers, he had pitched Raschi on three days of rest in the first half of the season. It had worked initially, but then Turner realized he had asked too much of his pitcher.

The Yankees' problem was that they were still short a fifth starting pitcher. In the spring they had seemed blessed: They had Frank Shea, who had pitched brilliantly in 1947; Bob Porterfield, seemingly the most talented young pitcher in the minor-league organization in 1948, and obviously destined for stardom; and Fred Sanford, whom the Yankees had gotten in December 1948 in a major trade with St. Louis, giving up three players and $100,000.

But Shea had been bothered by a sore arm, and Porterfield, a star performer in the minor leagues, had not blossomed as a Yankee—in three years he won only eight games for them and was traded to Washington. But the biggest disappointment turned out to be Sanford. In 1948 he had won twelve and lost twenty-one for St. Louis. Twenty-one defeats was the high mark for the American League, but Sanford's team had lost 94 games. That qualified him as, so to speak, the

ace of the staff. He had been happy playing for a team where
everyone was relaxed, where no one really expected to win. So
what if it was unbearably hot and the infield was like concrete.
So what if the franchise was dying right underneath them and
every year they lost their best players to the Red Sox or the
Yankees in an ongoing fire sale. Still, like any player, he
longed to play for a contender. When Sanford heard he was
going to New York a few weeks before Christmas, he said that
Christmas had come early.

Sanford was a small-town boy from Garfield, Utah. He
was thirty years old that year, already a veteran player. Never
had George Weiss checked out a deal so carefully—he even
questioned the St. Louis clubhouse boys and the St. Louis
reporters about Sanford's personal habits. An exorbitant price
was paid for him—$100,000. Much was expected. There was
talk in the papers that he would be a 20-game winner. The
Yankees seemed to demand high performance from Sanford
even in spring training. The first day, Pete Sheehy, the clubhouse attendant, handed him a uniform. "You know who wore
that number?" he asked. Sanford admitted that he did not.
"Spud Chandler," Sheehy said in a voice that implied very
clearly that Sanford better be worthy of it. Spud Chandler's
number, Sanford thought—all I wanted was a uniform.
Spring-training games with the Yankees seemed to Sanford to
bring more pressure than regular-season games with the
Browns. Writers, quick to criticize the deal, were everywhere.
They were, he soon decided, merely an extension of the
fans. But he quickly sensed management's disappointment
with him. Both Jim Turner and Frank Crosetti began to tin-
ker with Sanford's delivery, trying to make him change it.
"You're throwing against the weight of your body," Crosetti
told him. "But that's the way I've always pitched," he said. "It
feels right to me." They wanted him to have a smooth motion and objected to what they thought was a herky-jerky
motion. He tried to change, and ended up satisfying neither
them nor himself.

Sanford started the season poorly, and the pressure grew
worse. The writers were very hard on him. Joe Trimble wrote
in the *Daily News* that he was "the one-hundred-thousand-dol-
lar lemon." He was stunned by that. The *Daily News* was a

newspaper with more than 2 million readers. Two million people think I'm an expensive lemon, he thought. Soon he heard fans yelling angrily at him, always the same chant: Sanford, you hundred-thousand-dollar bum; Sanford, you hundred-thousand-dollar lemon. He knew that Turner and Stengel were unhappy with him. New York was unlike anything he had ever seen before—it was dog-eat-dog here. It was, he told his wife after it was all over, the worst two years of his life—he had been near a nervous breakdown. The final ignominy came when George Weiss told people that trading for Fred Sanford was the worst deal he had ever made.

With Sanford a disappointment, the Yankees got help from an unexpected source on their team—Tommy Byrne. Byrne was a power pitcher with an exploding fastball, which Eddie Lopat thought must have been around ninety miles an hour; a curve almost as good as Reynolds's or Feller's; and such exceptional all-around athletic ability that he was frequently used as a pinch hitter. He had only one weakness—an almost complete lack of control. His games were masterpieces of a sort, a lot of two-hitters and three-hitters, but usually with about eight or nine walks as well. "And the hit batsmen," Byrne reminisced years later, "don't forget the hit batsmen. I always hit two or three men as well. I *was* wild, wasn't I? I'd have walked my own mother if she had come up to the plate and looked half sorry."

During the war, he played on a pickup team on an aircraft carrier in the Mediterranean. He sent a postcard to Joe McCarthy noting that he had pitched a shutout, struck out ten, and walked no one. McCarthy held the postcard up in the dugout when it arrived and showed it to reporters. "Wouldn't you know," he said, "Mr. Tommy Byrne has finally found the plate and he's only five thousand miles from Yankee Stadium." "My Wild Irish Tommy," McCarthy called him.

In 1947 in the minor leagues, Byrne's wildness had exhausted both teammates and manager. Once in Minneapolis he had pitched a typical Byrne game, walking two and three men an inning and then managing to strike out three men in an inning. The bases always seemed to be loaded, but no one could hit him. In the seventh inning Kansas City had an 11–0 lead. At that point Billy Meyer, the manager, sent in a relief pitcher to take over for him. Byrne was enraged. "Jesus, Skip, how can you do that to me—with an eleven-nothing lead?" he complained. "Tom, it wasn't personal," Meyer answered. "We have a train to catch in two hours and if I keep you in there we miss it and we spend the night here."

For three consecutive years, 1949–1951, Byrne had the dubious distinction of leading the league in walks. Batters, unable to touch his best stuff, learned that the way to beat him was to wait him out. Games with him went on and on. Infielders and outfielders alike complained about playing behind him. Of his catcher, Yogi Berra, Byrne said later, "I did more to keep Yogi's weight down than anyone around—when he caught me, he caught a game and a half." Finally, because Dan Topping, the owner, could no longer bear watching him pitch, he was abruptly and unceremoniously traded to St. Louis.

Everyone had tried to help him with his control problem. Bill Dickey and Johnny Schulte, the bullpen catcher, put in extra hours in the bullpen, and Charlie Silvera, the backup catcher, worked with him. Even Charlie Keller would put on a catcher's mitt hoping to help him develop a better sense of the target. They tried to get him to pitch with no windup, in the belief that he didn't need the extra power. They told him he was overthrowing and overgripping, and there was even talk of sending him to a psychiatrist. Nothing helped.

The problem was that he truly believed in his natural ability to overpower hitters. Power pitchers did not need lessons on how to pitch, he thought. They just went out and did it. "I hated for the hitters even to foul the ball off me," he reminisced years later. "I wanted to get all twenty-seven men on strikes." In his heart he did not believe he was wild. Once he came into the dugout in the fifth inning of a game in which he was having his usual control problems. "How do you think I'm doing?" he asked Eddie Lopat. "You're doing fine, Tommy," Lopat answered. "Pretty good control too, right?" Byrne said. "Absolutely, Tommy, don't pay any attention to the five guys you've walked." Somehow in those years he was sure it was not his fault. He would be enraged when Stengel pulled him for a pinch hitter. He was sure it cost him $1,500 each time it happened. A twenty-game winner, he figured, made $30,000. A twelve-game winner made $18,000. That made it $1,500 a game. So he hated to be lifted.

Much of the problem, Byrne was convinced, was the umpires, who simply, because of his somewhat unjustified reputation for a little wildness, never gave him a break. He dated part of the problem to his rookie year, when he was on the bench needling some players on the Athletics. Bill McGowan, who was calling balls and strikes, finally turned to him. "Shut up and get back in the dugout, Bush." That did not deter Byrne, who kept up his jockeying. Finally McCarthy went over to him and said, "Tommy, that's Bill McGowan, and he's the best ball-and-strike man in this league, and he can make your life absolutely miserable if he wants. If I were you I'd go over to the far end of the bench and I'd shut my mouth." He had gone to the end of the bench, but after that McGowan seemed to want to bait him, even when he was at bat. A ball would come in far wide of the plate and McGowan would look at it and call it strike three. "How do you like that, you left-handed son of a bitch?" he would say.

Byrne's starts were memorable: long drawn-out games when no one hit the ball. Forty years later, he could remember a game in which he walked 16 and lost 3–2 in thirteen innings; he threw 248 pitches, which he thought might be a record of some sort. He believes he never started a major-league game in which he did not walk someone. In 1948, his career was on the line. The Yankees brought him up with the major-league club but did not know what to do with him. He was too wild to use and too talented to let go of. Finally Bucky Harris, in desperation, decided to give him a shot. He beat Detroit 7–0. With that he had finally made the majors.

Stengel liked him and understood his talent. He soon decided that there was only one way for the manager to deal with Byrne. "Look," he once counseled Ralph Houk, who would eventually be his successor, "don't watch him pitch. You'll die too young. Just turn away, and listen to the crowd. You know he'll walk in a run or two in some situations, but then you'll hear the cheer when he strikes someone out. Listen to the noise. It's easier on your stomach. If you watch him you won't last long." Stengel knew that Byrne was eccentric. (The

first time he returned to pitch against his old teammates after
he was traded to St. Louis in 1951, his catcher, Matt Batts,
himself traded to the Browns from Boston, was stunned to
find that before every pitch Byrne would shout out what was
coming to the Yankee batters. Curveball, Batts would signal.
"Curveball!" Byrne would shout out to the Yankee batter. Fastball, Batts signaled. "Fastball!" Byrne shouted. Batts called
time. "Tommy, what in hell are you doing?" he asked. "Well,
hell, Matt, they couldn't hit me in batting practice when they
called out the pitch when I was with them, so there's no reason
to think they can hit me now when they know what's coming,"
Byrne answered.) Stengel saw that Byrne was an asset, particularly as a number-four pitcher; he might not be the pitcher
you wanted in a winner-take-all playoff, but he was perfect to
pitch the second game of a Sunday doubleheader in the Stadium—Lopat pitching the first game, keeping the hitters off-
balance with his shrewdness, and then Byrne coming in and
using his power as the shadows lengthened in the Stadium.

In the beginning of the season, Byrne had struggled. In
the middle of July, when Raschi was 15-3, his record was 6-6.
Then on July 22, Byrne beat Detroit 8–2 on a 5-hitter, although he walked 7. Starting with that game, he was 9-1 for
the rest of the season. His next game was a 6-hit victory over
Chicago, in a game in which he walked 6. Then he beat the
Browns on a 6-hitter. Then Philly with 6 hits and 8 walks. For
the Yankees he was a desperately needed booster shot: He
plugged the gap created when Raschi and Reynolds both faltered. He led the league in walks, but it didn't seem to matter.
No one could hit him. His teammates were pleased; they
thought he was concentrating better than ever. Byrne thought
nothing had changed, that he had always concentrated this
well.

The Yankees seemed to be wearing down by a combination of the heat, their age, and injuries. In mid-August the
Athletics had gone into Boston, and two of the Philadelphia
players, Wally Moses and Sam Chapman, talked to the Boston
players and writers before the game. The Yankees, they said,
were not as powerful as they might seem on paper. One reason, they said, was DiMaggio. He was no longer the player

they remembered. You had to see it over a period of a couple of days, but he had definitely slowed down. "He's lost something on that swing of his," Chapman told one Boston writer. "He isn't getting around on the fastball the way he used to. He was cutting late on balls he used to send out of the park." Moses agreed: "I could see it from the bench. When he was hitting, he was hitting curves, not fastballs." Almost every player in the Yankee lineup had been injured in some way or another. They had started the season with the injury to DiMaggio's foot, and that had cost them the services of their greatest star for two months. Henrich had been hurt several times and by mid-season was playing in constant pain. Keller's back problems continued to bother him. Soon the Yankee management was keeping an official record of how many players were injured. It got so bad that when Bobby Doerr of the Red Sox was knocked down in a play at second and was slow to get up, Joe McCarthy rushed out on the field. "Come on, Bobby, get up," he said. "People will think you're a Yankee."

One of the most serious injuries occurred on August 7 when Yogi Berra was hit on the left thumb during a game against St. Louis, and the thumb was fractured. With the Red Sox coming on, the most important of their young power hitters was sidelined—a real blow. Nor was Berra a quick healer. Finally, on August 25, Dr. Sydney Gaynor, the team doctor, visited him and said that the cast was ready to come off and he could play. But just when Stengel was ready to play him, the Yankees went to St. Louis, and Yogi visited with his family. His mother took one look at the thumb, cut open a lemon and placed it on the thumb, and told him not to take it off for a certain number of days. This was the way injuries had been healed in her family in the past, and this was the way they would be healed now. When Berra joined the team later in the day, the lemon was still there. Stengel wanted to put him back in the lineup immediately. Berra refused. He was not playing until the allotted number of days had passed and it was time to take off the lemon. Folk medicine triumphed over modern medicine. He followed his mother's instructions, not those of Sydney Gaynor. "My catcher, Mr. Berra," Stengel told the writers, "is wearing a lemon instead of a mitt."

By the time Berra came back in September, the Yankees

badly needed him. For by then the Yankees had lost another player they could not afford: Tommy Henrich. On August 28, in Chicago, in the first inning, with Fred Sanford pitching, a batter named Charlie Kress had been up, a left-handed hitter. Kress was not a power hitter, and Henrich was not playing him deep. But Kress hit the ball over Henrich's head, which annoyed him at first. Henrich had a sense as he went back that he had room, but that he wasn't going to get back in time. He put on all his speed, and just as he reached for the ball, he crashed into the wall. The pain was crushing. He lay in the outfield knowing that it was a serious injury. Casey Stengel rushed out to right field and hovered over him like a mother hen. "Lie down," he commanded. "Don't get up. Take it very easy." He really cares about me, Henrich thought through the gasps of pain, that coldness I felt in the past wasn't real. This man cares. I was wrong. "Lie down and give me a little more time to get someone warmed up and get this clown out of here," Stengel added.

Henrich had fractured the second and third lumbar vertebrae processes. The injury seemed a final cruel blow from the gods. Along with DiMaggio, Henrich was considered to have the highest threshold of pain on the team. Earlier in the season he had broken a toe and the team doctor said he would be out for at least a week. He played the next day. But this pain was different. The doctors put him in a cast at Lenox Hill. Henrich prided himself on never taking pain killers, but this time he relented. Then he begged for an additional pill. Henrich was sure that they had put the cast on wrong, trapping his body at the wrong angle. The next morning the doctors, without ever admitting a mistake, redid the cast. The pain decreased significantly. The immediate prognosis, they told him, was that he was out for the season. "Can't be," he said, "there's a pennant race on." He decided that no matter what the doctors thought, he would return in three weeks. From then on he hoped for rainy days, especially when the Yankees played the Red Sox. Each rained out Red Sox game meant one more time he might play against them.

The Yankees returned from a long road trip to play three games against Boston in the Stadium. Their lead had dwindled to a game and a half, and for the first time in a month Berra was ready to play. Before the game the Boston writers gravitated toward Stengel. "I've never seen anything like this for injuries," Stengel was telling them. "Bauer just tore a stomach muscle warming up."

"You've still got more players than us," Harold Kaese of the *Globe* said. "With the players you've called up from the minors, you've got thirty and we only have twenty-five."

"I don't have the one I want," Stengel said.

"Mize?" asked Kaese, referring to Johnny Mize, a veteran National League power hitter whom the Yankees had picked up in August from the obliging Giants.

"Henrich," said Stengel.

The matchup in the first game was Reynolds against Kramer. Reynolds was wild, and eleven of his first twelve pitches were balls. He walked the first three men he faced— Dom DiMaggio, Pesky, and Williams. Then he struck out Junior Stephens with a ball that almost bounced in the dirt. Doerr hit a ground ball through the middle, and two runs scored. But Reynolds settled down and kept them from scoring any more. By the eighth the Yankees were ahead 3–2. With one out, Doerr tripled into the alley in left. Stengel immediately went to the mound. That was it for Reynolds. In came Page. He struck out four of the five men he faced. Only Al Zarilla touched the ball, a weak pop-up to Coleman. The game was over. The Yankee lead was back to two and a half again.

Afterward, Tebbetts, one of the men Page had struck out, told reporters that the last two pitches were the fastest he had ever seen. If Zarilla hadn't popped up, Page might have struck out all five men, he said. "Zeke didn't get a good piece of the ball," one of the reporters said to Tebbetts. "No, but he got a better piece than the rest of us," Tebbetts answered.

Joe Cronin was almost ill over the failure of the Red Sox to drive Reynolds out in the first. "If we knock him out we win, because they can't go to Page so early and they have to go to their humpty-dumpties and we would have flattened them," he said. Joe DiMaggio, talking with reporters, agreed. "When you have a chance like Boston had in the first and don't make the best of it, you don't win. I think that's one of the big differences between the Yankees and the Red Sox. We don't flub chances like that."

On September 9 Kinder beat the Yankees again—7–1 in the Stadium. He gave up only four hits for his nineteenth victory against only five defeats, the last of which was in early June; it was his fifteenth win in a row. The win pulled Boston to within a game and a half of the Yankees.

Kinder was pitching, the Yankees thought, like a man who had studied and mastered all of their weaknesses. His ball was always on the corners of the plate. He never seemed to give a batter a good pitch. He masked his delivery brilliantly, and his change-up was simply the best in baseball. He threw not just one change-up but several—there seemed to be no limit to the variations in speed. He had a good curve, which was really an early slider (a slurve, Birdie Tebbetts called it); what made it so dangerous and kept the hitters off-balance was that it broke at the very last instant without warning—it simply happened. Unlike many other pitchers with great change-ups, Kinder could throw reasonably hard.

He was also exceptionally skillful at creating doubt in the hitter. If the count was 2-and-2, and the logical next pitch was a curve, Kinder would shake off Tebbetts's sign. Birdie would signal again. Again Kinder would shake him off. By this time the batter would be wondering what exotic pitch was coming in. Birdie would signal yet again—the pitch he had called for the first time. Kinder would nod. The batter did not know what was going on. It almost always worked.

Kinder, thought Tebbetts, was one very tough man. Birdie believed that all those years in the minors had created a different kind of ballplayer than most of the other players he knew. Kinder neither wanted nor needed anything from anyone else. There was a fierce independence to him. He boasted that he still had his union card from the railroad engineers. It was his way of saying he could always walk away from baseball. No one, he seemed to be saying, told Ellis Kinder what to do.

As the pennant race wore on, it took on a relentless quality. There was no room for mistakes. "Keep your eyes off the scoreboard," Stengel told his team. "Keep them on your own game. Pay attention to your own game."

Though not as affected by injuries as the Yankees, the Red Sox regulars were simply exhausted, Bobby Doerr thought. McCarthy was using fewer men than Stengel. Doerr was having a very good second half of the season, but he could feel some of the other players wearing out, notably Junior Stephens. Junior was a power hitter who played the infield, and he was on base a lot. He was playing every day—against second-division teams as well as first-division teams. He also stayed out on the town at night a lot. Doerr thought Stephens needed a rest, but in those days it was a sign of weakness to take a day off. Junior would have been seen as a sissy. It was funny about the prejudices of those days, Doerr later thought. There was an odd definition to manliness. Often Doerr himself had desperately wanted some kind of a pick-me-up during a game—a candy bar, for instance. But that too would have been seen as a sign of weakness.

As the Red Sox continued their pursuit, a mini-disaster struck them: They played a doubleheader against the Athletics and lost both games. That, the Boston writers noted, virtually ended the American League pennant race. Boston had fourteen games left, and was five games behind in the losing column. The Yankees remained a tough team, with a deeper pitching staff. Nothing less than an extraordinary winning streak would save Boston.

McCarthy told Kinder and Parnell that they would have to carry the team the rest of the way: They would start with three days' rest and possibly less, and when they weren't starting he wanted them both in the bullpen. They were his starters, and they were his bullpen. Of the Red Sox's final 19 games, the two of them started 10 and relieved 7 times. Even on the rare occasions when they didn't actually go into the game, they warmed up. Both were already tired, but the burden was harder on Parnell, who was skinnier than Kinder and whose weight was down sharply, from 185 to 160. Parnell was already, in this, his second full season, feeling constant pain or a light tenderness in his left elbow and shoulder. Nothing so sharp that he could not pitch, particularly in this pennant race, but certainly enough to make him uneasy. Early in the season he had started using different methods to protect his shoulder and lessen the tenderness. Before each game he would stick it in the whirlpool bath for ten minutes. That improved circulation and helped relieve the tenderness. Before a game in which he was going to pitch, he would rub a fierce red salve into the shoulder. It was so hot that it seemed to burn right through the skin. He recommended it to Kinder, who tried it, but then wanted no part of it. Another technique, which he heard about later, was a specialty of the great Satchell Paige. After a game, if there was pain, he would go to the shower, turn the water on as hot as he could bear it, and then let it cascade down his arm.

The new schedule of starting and relieving was easier for Kinder; he seemed able to pitch one day and go to the bullpen the next. "I'll just go out there and snooze a bit," he told the other pitchers. "But make sure they wake me up in time to throw four warm-up pitches." So, with their backs to the wall, the Red Sox engineered the winning streak they needed—going on for ten games.

On September 24, the Yankees went back to Fenway for a two-game series. They brought with them a two-game lead, but it was not as good as the one-and-a-half-game lead they had come with last time. The reason was that they had been four games up on Boston on the losing side then, and now they were only two games up. Boston had in reality cut two games off their lead. The heroes were, of course, Kinder and Parnell. In the month of August, when the pennant race began, they had both been 6-0. Now, in September, Kinder was 5-0 and Parnell 4-1. That meant that since the beginning of August they were a total of 21-1.

In the first of the two games Kinder went against Lopat. The Yankee third-string catcher, Ralph Houk, had known Kinder well at Binghamton—they had roomed together there. The night before the game, Houk ran into Kinder. Ellis had a certain ritual to his nights; he would hit certain bars, often starting at the Kenmore. There he found Houk, his old minor-league buddy. Off they went, defying normal levels of alcoholic intake as well as the commissioner's rules against fraternization with opposing ballplayers. Well after midnight, changing locales but not drinks, it became clear to Houk that this was nothing short of a marathon. But it was a good thing, Houk decided, because even if he was sacrificing himself, a

Left to right: Johnny Pesky, Junior Stephens, Bobby Doerr, and Bill Goodman

Left to right: Chuck Stobbs, Maurice McDermott, and Mel Parnell

Dominic DiMaggio

Ellis Kinder

Birdie Tebbetts

Maurice McDermott

Ted Williams

Casey Stengel, new manager of the
New York Yankees, leaves Pennsylvania
Station for St. Petersburg, Florida, and
his first spring training with the
Yankees.

Tom Yawkey

Jimmy Cannon

Mel Allen

October 1, 1949: In the fifth inning of the 153rd game of the season, Doerr's smash was fielded by Yankee second baseman Coleman (left), who relayed the ball to shortstop Rizzuto (right), catching Boston's Vern Stephens on second base. Rizzuto's throw to first (note ball at Coleman's heel) will wipe out Doerr, making it a double play.

October 1, 1949: Johnny Lindell is shown being congratulated by a bat boy as he crosses home plate after hitting his eighth-inning home run, which gave the Yankees a 5–4 win. Boston's Birdie Tebbetts is looking on dejectedly.

UPI/Bettmann Newsphotos

October 1, 1949: While Yankee fans throw up their arms in jubilation after Lindell's home run, Ted Williams reflects Boston's pain.

UPI/Bettmann Newsphotos

October 2, 1949: The Yankees' Tommy Henrich is shown being congratulated by his teammates as he scores his eighth-inning home run. It gave the Yankees a 2–0 lead.

October 2, 1949: Stengel (seated center) and his triumphant Yankees celebrate in their locker room after defeating Boston 5–3 to win the pennant.

Joe McCarthy, manager of the Red Sox, walks alone through the corridor under the stands in Yankee Stadium after visiting the victorious Yankees in their locker room.

The Dodgers' Jackie Robinson scores Brooklyn's first run in the second game of the World Series. Gil Hodges has just singled for the Dodgers. Vic Raschi, the Yankee pitcher, later credited Robinson for breaking his concentration—and thus allowing Snider to get a hit.

The end of a great pitchers' duel: Tommy Henrich crosses home plate after his ninth-inning home run off Don Newcombe in the first game of the World Series.

reserve catcher, he was taking out the star pitcher of the Red
Sox. Ever more willingly he accepted Kinder's suggestions that
they try yet another place. Their evening ended in daylight.
Later, Houk arrived at the ball park sluggish and the worse
for wear. He detailed the previous evening's debaucheries and
assured his teammates that they would have no trouble with
Kinder. Houk was wrong. Kinder shut out the Yankees on a
six-hitter, his third victory over them that season, his eigh-
teenth win in a row as a starting pitcher. Jim Turner, the Yankee pitching coach, kept notes on both his and the opposition's
pitcher in every game. About Kinder he noted in his diary:
"Good fastball at times. Good fast and slow curve. Very good
let-up fastball. Good control and good with men on bases.
Made most hitters hit breaking ball or let-up fastball. Then
would sneak fastball. Very good pitcher."

That victory in the 147th game brought Boston back to
within a game of the Yankees. The 148th game, Parnell
thought, was crucial. It would take place in Fenway. If Boston
won, the two teams would be even. If the Yankees won, they
would be two games up. With so few games left, the difference
would probably be decisive.

That day Parnell felt comfortable. He was pleased with
his speed and with the movement of the ball. He did not need
to overthrow. He stayed in front of the hitters all day long.
Four hits and three walks—that was all he gave up. Jim
Turner graded him high: "Good fastball and curve. Very
good control. Keeps curve low. Good in clutch. Outstanding
pitcher this year." It was his twenty-fifth win of the season.

There were 6 games to play for both teams, and after 148
games they were dead even.

Never was Phil Rizzuto more important to the Yankees.
McCarthy had been known to say, "We don't win on power,
we win on defense." The key to that defense was Rizzuto.
"You want to know the key to our team," Billy Johnson, the
third baseman, once told Ted Williams, "it's that little guy
there. Without him we're just another team. You have to be
with us to know, because what you see once in a while we see
every day." To Johnny Pesky, his opposite number on the Red
Sox, he was in those years "the best shortstop I'd ever seen.

He was so quick, with extraordinarily quick feet, he could always make the plays. He was the best shortstop of the era—he
held that team together the way Pee Wee Reese held the
Dodgers together."

The Yankee regulars were very much aware of Rizzuto's
value. It was understood that since he was small and physically
vulnerable, Rizzuto had to be protected. If any opposing
player went into second hard at him, the Yankee players
would immediately retaliate against the opposing infielders
and the Yankee pitchers would throw at the offending player.
Earlier that year, Pesky had taken Rizzuto out in a play at second. The next time DiMaggio was up he singled. DiMaggio
turned at first, never hesitating, and raced for second, though
it was obvious he had no chance. He laid a savage block on
Doerr as revenge.

To the Yankee pitchers there was something special about
Rizzuto's ability to anticipate the ball and make the play. He
had come up to the majors eight years earlier, and he was in
his prime in 1949. Those who watched the Yankees and
Boston every day thought him the most-valuable player in the
American League. (He came in second in the voting. Ted Williams won while he and Joe Page split the ostensible Yankee
vote and came in second and third. The next year he did win
the award.) No one valued Rizzuto more than the Yankee
pitchers, off whose earned-run averages he was saving a half-
run or more. "I remember when I first came up for the Yankees and in my first inning someone hit a shot which went
right by me which was going out over second like a rocket,"
said Frank Shea. "I thought 'base hit,' and never even followed the ball. Then I heard the crowd roar and I looked
around and saw that Rizzuto had made the play quite easily,
and I thought to myself, 'Welcome to the big leagues, Spec.'"
Vic Raschi admired the suppleness with which Rizzuto seemed
to make every play. His arm was not very strong—in fact, it
was almost weak—so he had to play in rather than deep,
which meant giving up the angles. Even so, his throws to first
had a unique softness. A typical Rizzuto play, Raschi thought,
was always close at first, the ball reaching the first baseman's
glove just a split second before the runner touched the bag.
This was true not just on hard plays, but on the easy ones as

well. Raschi could usually hear the pop of the ball entering the glove, and then a split second later the slightly softer sound of the runner hitting the bag. Always a cliff-hanger, Raschi thought, and yet he always makes the play. For Whitey Ford, the ball going to first seemed to travel so slowly that it looked like a parachute opening.

Some of the first basemen, of course, hated that style; they were sure they were going to be spiked. They were always complaining about the lateness of the throws. That was about his only liability, other than the fact that he could not jump very well.

"Phil, you've got to jump," Coleman would tell him after a close play at second.

Rizzuto would answer, "Jerry, I *did* jump."

When Rizzuto finished high school in Brooklyn he had been a good enough all-around athlete to earn college scholarships at both Columbia and Fordham. These were not just for baseball but for football as well. Rizzuto, a high school quarterback who weighed 135 pounds, took one look at the Fordham linemen and decided to end his football career. There were three baseball tryouts in New York: Bill Terry of the Giants took one look at his size and didn't even let him go up to bat; Casey Stengel of the Dodgers told him to go get a shoe-shine box, a remark neither forgotten nor forgiven; then the Yankees, with Paul Krichell, the famous scout, in attendance, offered him a minor-league contract for $65 a month. Rizzuto, never much given to holdouts, asked for a little more. The Yankees held a meeting and decided to sweeten it to $75. With that he chose baseball.

Throughout his career Rizzuto loved to play the ingenue. When he had played in the minors in Kansas City, his teammates took him, in the great Southern tradition, on a snipe hunt. They went into a field at night and left him there with a giant sack. He was to hold it open and catch the snipes that they would drive into the field. Then, of course, they took off. It was the oldest gag in the book.

He was the primary victim of the Yankees' locker-room jokes. The pranks on Rizzuto were not unlike those played at a prep school, and indeed Rizzuto knew what was expected of him by his teammates, and he played to it. Because he was afraid of practically anything that moved, gags often involved some live animal being hidden in his clothes or belongings. It could be simple: Frank Shea putting a live snake in a handsome gift-wrapped box that looked like it contained jewelry and was addressed, "To my sports idol, from Jenny"; or Shea chasing him on the field with a live lobster. Or it could be more complicated: a group of players filling his bunk on the train with live crabs. The entire team would wait up for his screams as he came tearing down the aisle in his pajamas. Once Lindell, knowing that Rizzuto was particularly afraid of birds, got hold of a live bird and tied it to the inside of a drawer where Rizzuto put his valuables every day when he dressed for the game. When Rizzuto put his hand in the drawer, the bird moved and Rizzuto not only fled the room but refused to put his things in the drawer for three days.

Once the Yankees were in Detroit and it rained heavily, forcing a delay. Finally the sun came out and the game was played. During the fifth inning, as the Yankees came in from the outfield, Lindell beckoned to Bobby Brown, the third baseman. "You won't believe what I've got here." He pulled some thirty nightcrawlers out of his back pocket. They had been coming to the surface after the rain, and he had dutifully collected them. In those days, when the players left the field to bat, they left their gloves on the field. Lindell managed to get Rizzuto's glove and stuffed the fingers with his enormous worm collection. The other players were onto the gag and held Rizzuto up for a minute as the Yankees went back out on the field. That way he would be a little late getting back to his position and the explosion would come in full view of the crowd. Everyone was ready as Rizzuto got to shortstop. On came the glove. It was like someone had given him an electric shock. He threw the glove high into the air and did what looked like an Indian war dance. Both teams were incapacitated with laughter.

This role in some part was a protective device; he played along with their gags because they symbolized not just his role but also his acceptance. When he had first joined the Yankees he had been called Little Dago to DiMaggio's Dago or Big Dago. The only time he resented being called Dago was when Leo Durocher used the phrase in a harsh way. Rizzuto knew

that baseball was the first great American opportunity for the
Italian immigrants. He had been an eighteen-year-old high
school kid when DiMaggio had become the first Italian superstar. Rizzuto could remember going to the Stadium and sitting
in the bleachers, which were filled with Italian immigrants.
Most of them could not speak English and barely understood
the rules of baseball. But they would wave flags and unfurl
banners they had smuggled in.

When Rizzuto joined the Yankees himself, he thought
that the Italian-American players were still feeling their way.
The tone of a baseball locker room was still set by rural Southern boys who had their own language, and habits. It did not
occur to them that *they* might be different, or that other Americans had different habits. But in that atmosphere, the Italians
were different—they did not hunt or fish or chew tobacco.
Most had grown up in homes where their parents did not
speak English. In a generation or two that would change, but
for the moment the Italian players mostly kept to themselves
and spoke on the one subject about which they were sure—
baseball. That was one reason why Rizzuto enjoyed the teasing. It meant that he was not just a baseball player but a full-
fledged American.

Rizzuto played in all but one game that season. He became the leader, and yet he was also the kid. If a few of the
players went out to speak on behalf of the Yankees and they
were given $50 apiece, he would say (for part of his role was
that he was scared of Cora, his wife), "Now, I'm not going to
tell Cora about this."

They also continued to tease him about his glove. It was
practically a museum piece. He had bought it for ten dollars
when he first broke in. By 1949 it was perilously close to having terminal rot. Every year Harry Latina, who was the Rawl-
ings glove man, repaired it. In addition, a shoemaker near the
Stadium worked on it two or three times a year. It was a relic
from an era when ballplayers used much smaller gloves,
barely bigger than their hands. It had not only been filled with
worms, but also bugs and chewing tobacco, the last mostly by
Pete Suder and Nellie Fox, prominent Rizzuto tormentors
from other teams. The clubhouse gag was that it should have
gone to Cooperstown in 1918, the year Rizzuto was born. But

Rizzuto loved it. Part of its appeal was superstition, because he had gotten it when he came to the major leagues. But also the glove felt right. Because it was so small, he could dig the ball out quickly. Once Bobby Brown lent him a newer and bigger glove, and, to the applause of his teammates, he even tried it. But then someone hit a grounder right to him and he could not get the glove down in time. He immediately called time, walked back to the dugout, and got his own glove.

With only six games left for each team, they met again in the Stadium. It was a sloppy game, and there were two critical plays that decided it. Boston drove Tommy Byrne out before he got a man out in the first. Then the Yankees came back and rallied for six runs. They went into the eighth leading 6–3. Stengel had brought Page in during the fifth inning. But then in the eighth, he faltered. Tebbetts singled to right. Lou Stringer walked. With runners on first and second and no outs, and the count 3-and-2, Dominic DiMaggio hit a sharp line drive right at Rizzuto. Both runners were off and running, and the ball was hit like a bullet. *Triple play!* Rizzuto thought, timing his jump perfectly. He speared the ball and got ready to make the throw to second, warning himself not to rush it. But he looked over and the runners were still moving, not scurrying backward to their bases. That's really dumb baserunning, he thought. He reached for the ball and it was not there. It had torn through the webbing of his glove. Boston tied the score at 6–6. Now, with only one out, Pesky was on third and Williams was on first with Doerr at bat. Doerr suddenly dropped an almost perfect squeeze bunt. Tommy Henrich, back in the lineup but playing with a corset, seemed to anticipate it. He made a perfect play, firing home to Ralph Houk, who was catching. The throw appeared to beat Pesky by several yards. But Bill Grieve, the plate umpire, called Pesky safe. Houk charged Grieve, Stengel charged him, and the Yankee bench charged him. But safe Pesky remained. At first Pesky thought he might have slipped by the tag, but later, when he saw a sequence of photos, there was no doubt in his mind that he was out. (Much later, when Houk was managing Boston, and Pesky was one of his coaches, one of the Red Sox players found the old sequence of photos. He pinned them up in the locker room with a note saying, "Ralph, was he really out?") But the play counted, and Cliff Mapes was fined for yelling at Grieve, "How much did you have bet on the game?" Henrich was disgusted. After the game a reporter asked him if Pesky had scored. "Only a mole could have scored on that play," he answered. The Red Sox won 7–6. Ellis Kinder had pitched the last two innings of shut-out relief to secure the victory. With five games left, the Red Sox were in first place. No one joked about Phil Rizzuto's glove in the locker room that night.

The win gave the Red Sox their first lead of the season. Of the five games left for the Red Sox, three were against Washington in Washington and two were in the Stadium. If they were nearly invincible at home, then going on the road was another story; they might be 61-16 in Fenway, but as they set out for Washington, their record on the road was 33-39. Still, Boston had a chance to lock the pennant up in Washington, for the Senators were not just a bad team, they were practically patsies for the Red Sox, having won only three of the previous nineteen matchups. Boston won the first game 6–4. Then came what many of the Red Sox would remember for years to come—the one they called the Scarborough game.

Ray Scarborough was a very good Washington pitcher, perhaps their best, and also Boston's nemesis. He had beaten Boston three times in the 1948 season, including a critical game at the end of the season. Scarborough was a right-handed pitcher, and he was nothing if not smart and crafty. Not only did he give the Boston right-handers a difficult time, but he was poison to their best left-handed hitter, Ted Williams. Scarborough could decoy Williams better than any other pitcher in the league. It was not just a matter of his selection of pitches, it was his motion as well. He would show fastball and then at the last minute go to his curve. Forty years later Williams paid Scarborough the ultimate accolade: He said that he probably chased more balls out of the strike zone with Ray Scarborough than with any other pitcher in the American League.

On this day Scarborough was going for his thirteenth victory against only eleven defeats, a considerable achievement on so weak a team. He was at his best that day, holding the Red Sox to only four hits. But Chuck Stobbs was equally sharp, and he took a one-run Boston lead into the ninth. McCarthy had both Parnell and Kinder throwing in the bullpen. In the bottom of the ninth, with Boston leading 1–0, Roberto Ortiz led off for the Senators with a short single to left. Gil Coan, an exceptional base runner, ran for him. Ed Stewart sacrificed Coan to second. Ed Robinson hit a slow roller to Doerr, which Doerr fielded cleanly, but which Robinson beat out. Now there were runners on first and third with one out. Al Kozar then singled between third and short to score Coan and tie the game. Robinson went to second base. In came Kinder to pitch to Sam Dente. Dente singled cleanly to right field. In right Al Zarilla charged the ball, holding Robinson at third. That loaded the bases. Buddy Lewis was sent up to pinch-hit. McCarthy waved Parnell in from the bullpen. Some of the Boston players were ready for a squeeze attempt. On Parnell's third pitch Robinson broke for the plate. But Tebbetts picked up the play, moved over to make the tag, and Parnell threw a perfect pitch for him to handle. Robinson was easily out. Two outs. But Kozar moved to third. Parnell had Lewis 1-and-2, and on his next pitch he simply put too much on it. It might have been a great pitch, but it broke too much. It was low and bounced wide of the plate. Tebbetts stabbed at it, but it was past him. Washington won 2–1. Ted Williams had gone hitless. A year later, largely at the urging of Ted Williams, it was said, the Red Sox traded for Ray Scarborough, by then thirty-five. But it was too late for him, and too late for them. He lasted a little more than one season before moving on.

CHAPTER
14

While the Red Sox played with the Senators, the Yankees took on the Athletics, winning two of three. The Red Sox came into the Stadium with a one-game lead, with two games left to play. All they had to do was to win one of two against the Yankees. Had the Red Sox won the Scarborough game, they would have had a virtual lock on the pennant, a two-game lead. The Yankees would have been forced to win both games, and then there would have been a one-game playoff—meaning the Yankees would have had to win three in a row. Most of the Yankee players had waited in the Yankee locker room to listen to Mel Allen's re-creation of that key Boston-Washington game, and the tension had been enormous. Jerry Coleman was too nervous to listen with the others, so he had gone to his apartment a few blocks away on Gerard Avenue. The moment the game was over, his friend Charlie Silvera called him. "Did you hear?" Silvera asked. "Yes," Coleman said. "We're still alive, Jerry," Silvera said.

Now the door was open just a little again. The Yankee veterans were confident that they would win. Fred Sanford, new to the team, new to the idea of winning, asked a few of his teammates whether, if the Yankees won the pennant, they got any money even if they lost in the World Series. The moment the words were out of his mouth, he realized he had made a terrible mistake. No one said anything to him, but the looks he got were very cold. These were the Yankees, he realized, and if you were a Yankee you never thought of losing, and you certainly did not talk about it. You expected to win and you won.

The Boston writers coming to the Stadium early before the next-to-last game found out the same thing. Joe Cashman of the *Record* stopped to talk to Tommy Henrich. "Tommy, how do you feel—it must be hard to be behind after leading for most of the season?" What struck Cashman was how confident Henrich was. "Well, Joe," he said, "we would have liked to have wrapped it up earlier, and maybe we should have, but we're glad to be in this situation," Henrich said. "We don't have to depend on anyone winning it for us—we can do it ourselves. All we have to do is win two games. That's fair enough." These guys, Cashman thought, have played in so many games like this that they really do have an advantage.

Tom Yawkey was equally confident. Wives had not accompanied the Boston players to New York, but Yawkey sent out word that every wife was to have her things packed. The moment the Red Sox clinched the pennant, a special train would leave for New York for a great celebration.

Ted Williams, though, thought the Yankees had the advantage. It was their ball park, and it tilted away from most of the Red Sox lineup. The Yankee pitchers were not going to give him, the one left-handed power hitter, anything good to hit. He was right. The Yankees were convinced that they could handle Junior Stephens in the Stadium. His Fenway homers would become easy outs. But not so with Williams. Years later Allie Reynolds was at an All-Star Game when he suddenly felt a pair of immensely powerful arms wrap around him. He thought he was in a vise. "When are you going to give me a decent pitch to hit, you Indian SOB?" the voice belonging to the arms of Ted Williams asked. "Not as long as Junior's hitting behind you," laughed Reynolds. Williams normally liked to hit in the Stadium, but he hated it near the end of the season when the shadows were long. That made hitting much tougher. He thought the Yankee management should turn the

lights on during day games at this time of the year, but he
knew why they didn't—it was an advantage to the Yankee
pitchers, and New York's strength was its pitchers, not its hitters. The Yankee hitters were accustomed to the shadows. But
Williams, purist that he was, thought that anything that diminished a hitter's ability subtracted from the game.

It was a sports promoter's dream: the two great rivals
playing two games at the very end of the season with the pennant in the balance. The pitching matchups were perfect—
Reynolds against Parnell, and Raschi against Kinder. The
great question was: Would DiMaggio be able to get back into
the lineup? He had been sick with viral pneumonia for almost
two weeks, during which time he had lost eighteen pounds.
But he was determined to play. The first of those two games
in the Stadium was, by chance, Joe DiMaggio Day. The Yankee star, drawn and emaciated, husbanding his energy, had
been forced to stand in front of the huge crowd of 69,551
while receiving endless gifts. His mother had come east for the
games (his father had died earlier in the year), and she was
introduced to the crowd. She came on the field and, much to
the amusement of the huge crowd, raced past Joe to greet
Dominic in the Red Sox dugout—she had seen Joe the day
before but had not yet seen Dom. Dominic came out of the
Red Sox dugout to be a part of the ceremonies, and he could
feel his brother leaning heavily on him. Dominic was wary of
staying too long in Joe's spotlight, and he quietly asked his
brother if he should leave. Joe quickly said, "No, don't go!"
and Dominic understood that Joe needed him to lean on.

Parnell was sure it was going to be a great game; he
thought Allie Reynolds a magnificent competitor. This was a
great Yankee team, Parnell thought, far better than most people realized, with an exceptional blend of the old and the new:
DiMaggio, Henrich, Berra, Bauer, and Woodling, and that
great pitching staff; also a late-season pickup—Johnny Mize.
No one should underrate a team that had Johnny Lindell and
Johnny Mize on its bench. Maybe the 1927 Yankees had been
as good, but Parnell was by no means sure.

When he got up that morning Allie Reynolds felt strong
and ready; it was one of those glorious days when he felt he
could throw a ball through a battleship. Then he went out to

the mound and his control simply evaporated. It was, he later decided, probably a case of overpitching, of trying too hard. The game started as a disaster for the Yankees. The Red Sox scored one run in the first—Dom DiMaggio singled, Williams singled, Reynolds threw a wild pitch that moved DiMaggio to third. Then Junior Stephens lined to left and Dom DiMaggio scored.

In the Boston third Reynolds did himself in. It was clear to his infielders that he was unable to find his true rhythm. He got Dom DiMaggio out on a well-hit ball to right. But then he walked Pesky, Williams, and Stephens. Doerr sliced a ball just past Coleman, and Pesky scored. The Red Sox led 2–0 with the bases filled and only one out. Stengel immediately brought in Joe Page. It might be only the third inning, but there was no time to waste. If Stengel needed a relief pitcher the next day, he could always use Reynolds. But Page started disastrously. He walked Zarilla, forcing in a run. Then he walked Billy Goodman on four pitches. That made it 4–0. The Yankee bench was completely silent. Two runs walked in, and Birdie Tebbetts was at bat. On the bench, Gus Niarhos kept thinking to himself, The one hope we have with Page is his rising fastball. Probably no pitcher in the league, he thought, forced hitters to chase as many bad balls as Page. The ball left Page's hand looking like it was going to be in the zone, but it kept rising, and the hitter could not control himself. Now, with one out and the bases loaded, Niarhos sensed that Page, wild though he was, might work himself out of it. Tebbetts seemed to want to end the game right then and there. Birdie swung away, trying to kill the ball; He jumped on three pitches, all of them, Niarhos thought, well out of the strike zone. Then Page struck out Parnell, a good hitter, again with pitches outside the strike zone. Maybe now Joe will settle down, Niarhos thought. But Boston had a 4–0 lead.

That looked like a very big lead for a team as good as Boston. Some of the Yankees thought a critical moment had taken place in the third inning. In the bottom of the third, when Rizzuto came up, Tebbetts began to needle him. With Rizzuto, Tebbetts usually concentrated on his Italian origins, his size, and his hitting ability: "You goddamn little Dago, you know you can't hit the ball out of the infield. You know you should be out behind the Stadium playing in some kids' game," he would say. This time he went further. With Boston's big lead, he couldn't resist. Rizzuto fouled off a pitch, and while they were waiting to get a new ball, Tebbetts started in. "Hey Rizzuto," he said, "tomorrow at this time we'll be drinking champagne, and we'll pitch the Yale kid against you guys. Think you can hit a kid from Yale, Rizzuto?" He was referring to Frank Quinn, the bonus-baby pitcher out of Yale who had pitched a total of twenty-two innings and had never started a game. (Tebbetts denies saying this, but the memory of it and Rizzuto's reaction remain fresh with almost all the Yankees.)

Rizzuto was stunned and then angered. He grounded out, and on the way back to the dugout he hurled his bat. Then he kicked the water cooler. "Do you know what that goddamn Tebbetts just said," he shouted. "They're going to pitch the kid from Yale against us tomorrow!" Rizzuto was normally mild-mannered and slow to anger. No one on the team had ever seen him like this before. The Yankee dugout, which had been silenced by Reynolds's failure and the four-run Boston lead, began to come alive. Henrich remembered it as if the entire team had been slapped in the face. But Vic Raschi had a terrible feeling that the season was slipping away from them. He sat in the dugout squeezing a baseball with his right hand to control his nervous tension.

By the fourth it was obvious to everyone in the Yankee dugout that Page was overpowering on this day. His ball was fast, and he had great movement on it. Vic Raschi, watching from the bench, decided that the Red Sox were not going to add to their lead, that now it was a matter of trying to chip away at it. On the Red Sox bench, Johnny Pesky, watching Page, was awed. This was a great pitcher at his best. This was pure power. Page was pitching without deception on this day. There were no curves, no change-ups. Every pitch was a challenge. It was as if he were taunting the Red Sox hitters: Hit me if you can. God, what a pitcher, Pesky thought. This game was not over.

In the fourth Joe DiMaggio came up. He had told Stengel earlier that he would try and play three innings, but at the end of the third he held up five fingers, meaning he would go at least five innings. He had struck out in the first inning, but now in the fourth he lined a double to right field. Billy Johnson struck out, but Bauer singled DiMaggio home with a hard shot to left. Lindell hit another hard single to left, sending Bauer to third. Then Coleman hit a fly to Dom DiMaggio and Bauer scored. It was 4–2.

As the Yankees began to come back, Raschi squeezed the ball harder and harder. In the fifth, Rizzuto singled. Henrich hit a ball past first base, sending Rizzuto to third. Then Berra singled and Rizzuto scored, with Henrich stopping at second. With DiMaggio up, McCarthy pulled Parnell and brought in Joe Dobson. DiMaggio hit a vicious line drive low and to the right of the pitcher. With perfect fielding it might have been a double play. But Dobson did not get around on it quickly; the ball bounced off his glove and rolled fifteen feet behind the mound. By the time Dobson recovered it the bases were loaded. Billy Johnson hit into a double play, but Henrich scored. It was 4–4 now.

The game continued 4–4 through the sixth and seventh innings. On the Yankee bench there was a sense of growing confidence. Page seemed untouchable. In the bottom of the eighth Stengel sent up both Bobby Brown and Cliff Mapes, left-handed pinch hitters, to face the right-handed Dobson. But Dobson handled them. The next man up was Lindell, a right-handed hitter. Stengel had the left-handed Charlie Keller on the bench. But Lindell already had two hits, and he had driven Williams back to the fence his first time up against Dobson. Stengel decided to stick with Lindell. Lindell was the team rogue. He was exuberant, generous, and crude, and his humor seemed to dominate the locker room. In order to avoid being snared by one of his gags, the others always checked to see where he was before they entered. Even the trainer's table was not safe. A player lying down for treatment would often get whacked on the forehead by Lindell's phallus, which was considered one of the wonders of the Yankee locker room. His favorite victims were Page and Rizzuto, but no one was spared. Coleman was christened "Sweets" because he was so good-looking and because once at a restaurant he had ordered crabmeat in an avocado instead of steak, which was preferred by the other ballplayers. "Isn't that sweet," said Lindell, and the nickname stuck.

Even DiMaggio was vulnerable. Once DiMaggio walked into the locker room in a beautiful and obviously expensive new Hawaiian sports shirt. Lindell immediately shouted out, "Hey, beautiful, where'd you get that sports shirt? You look pretty in it." DiMaggio froze, his face reddened, and he never wore the shirt again. "We've got to keep the Dago honest," said Lindell when the others looked at him quizzically.

His teasing was generally good-natured, however, and he was generous with the younger players. When the team arrived in New York, he would take them to his favorite hangouts near the Stadium, including one where the specialty of the house was something called "The Lindell Bomber." "Try one, you're going to love it," he told the young Charlie Silvera earlier that season. It turned out to be the biggest martini anyone had ever seen—as big as a birdbath. He was the bane of management because his off-field activities were so outrageous. He liked to boast about how much money George Weiss had spent putting private detectives on him.

Lindell was a low-ball hitter, so Dobson and Tebbetts decided to feed him high fastballs. The first pitch was a ball. Again Dobson came in with a fastball. The ball was both high and inside. Lindell knew he was not going to see anything low. But he got ready, and he crushed the next ball. The moment he hit it, everyone knew it was a home run. We went to the well once too often, Dobson thought to himself. I had probably lost just enough off my fastball, and he was ready for it.

Vic Raschi was thrilled; it meant that he was going to get a chance the next day at the biggest game of his life. The celebration in the clubhouse was almost out of control. Finally Joe DiMaggio decided to calm his teammates down. "Hey, we've got to win tomorrow," he kept saying, "just don't forget that. It's not done yet." But they had escaped a bullet, and it seemed inconceivable to them that they could come that close to defeat and not win the pennant. DiMaggio, they thought, was amazing. They knew he was desperately ill, but he had played the entire game and gotten two hits.

                         *   *   *

John Lindell III was ten years old that summer and he did not like living in New York. As far as he was concerned, home was Arcadia, California. Arcadia was where his friends were. In New York there were thousands and thousands of little boys who would have given anything to have a father playing for the Yankees, but young John Lindell was not one of them. He had no interest in baseball, and when on occasion he went with his father to the locker room, he did so grudgingly.

Near the end of the season his parents had explained the immediate future to him: If the Yankees did not win the pennant, the family would return to Arcadia immediately, but if they did, then the family would stay on in New York for two more weeks. So it was on October 1 that when Johnny Lindell hit his dramatic home run, everyone in their Bronx neighborhood was happy and excited but little John Lindell. Hearing the news, he burst into tears because he was sure it meant staying in New York for an additional two weeks.

On October 2 the Yankees and Red Sox faced each other in the last game of the season with identical records. On that morning John Morley, a student at Manhattan College, rose at the unbearably early hour of five-thirty and dressed quickly for work. Morley, then eighteen, considered himself exceptionally lucky. He worked for Harry Stevens, the company that did the catering at Yankee Stadium. In the eyes of his neighborhood buddies and college friends, he was a privileged insider in a magic world. If he did not actually know Joe DiMaggio, he often saw him beautifully dressed in civilian clothes, and to Morley's friends in the Bronx, the ability to spot a player in civilian clothes was the same as intimacy. Morley was able to report on how he treated the fans who waited after the game, and in the minds of Morley's friends this also was something like true intimacy. Morley sometimes worked in the press box, so he was also able to tell his friends about serving such prominent sportswriters as Joe Trimble, Bob Considine, and Dan Parker. They were spiffy, well dressed, and wore straw hats (though they were not necessarily great tippers).

Morley had worked for Stevens for three years and had slowly advanced to a privileged position: He was a gateman/beerman, first working at the outside gates before the game selling scorecards, and then, the moment the game started, switching to a roving beer salesman. On a normal day during the season, he made, with his 10 percent commission, about $50 or $60 a game. On a big game like this, with every seat in the Stadium sold, he might make as much as $150. It was a long day of hard, backbreaking work, because refrigeration within the Stadium was primitive in those days. Therefore, almost all preparation had to be done on the day of the game. Because it was the weekend, someone had already gone to the Corn Exchange Bank at 170th and Jerome Avenue for the thousands of dollars in coins that would be needed for change during the weekend.

An old-timer named Tom Carmody ran the Stevens operation at the Stadium. He had been there for twenty-six years, since the day the Stadium opened, and he ruled with an iron hand. He was always the first one there, and the first thing he did was to make a large vat of coffee, the strongest and most vile Morley ever tasted, then or since. Then Carmody would turn into a nineteenth-century drill sergeant. The rules for the boys were exactly the same as they had been in 1923, when Carmody first came. They were simple: You were to show up exactly on time, never a minute late, never be flip, and always, *always* say "sir." To Carmody the failure of even the lowliest Stevens worker was his own failure.

The hardest part of the day was the morning delivery of ice to the big cooler tubs throughout the Stadium. The young men had to cart three-hundred-pound blocks of ice. Then they would break up these giant slabs and place them over beds of beer bottles, which were lying on the bottom of the giant tubs. After the game they would run hoses from the tubs so that the water from the melted ice could run out through the drainage system. The only thing that cheered Morley while doing such exhausting work was the knowledge that for every bottle of beer sold (at 35 cents), 3.5 cents would go toward his college education.

Like the other Stevens workers he hoped for a long game, because that meant more hot dogs, soda, and beer sold, and more money earned. But he was also a Yankee fan, and on this day he was as nervous as anyone else. This was the big game. They expected crowds so large that Stevens had sent over extra help from Ebbets Field. The regulars viewed them not as colleagues but as intruders. Obviously, the Dodgers were not as good a team as the Yankees, nor was their ball park as elegant.

That morning as he worked, Morley stole glances at the players coming out of the dugout for their early workouts. He was struck by how casual they seemed, as if this were just another day. Then, suddenly, the long slow morning was over. It was time to go out and sell programs.

It was a huge crowd, and it was arriving early. Many people had come the night before and camped out in their cars in the parking lot in order to buy bleacher tickets, which went on sale early in the morning. It was as large as a World Series crowd, but not as fancy, Morley immediately decided. The World Series drew a reserved-ticket crowd, the kind of people who were called swells in those days; the men wore sport jackets, and often came with women instead of other men. But today it was a baseball crowd, knowing and hard-edged; these people would be quick to complain if a vendor blocked their view, even momentarily. As the crowd crushed forward to get into the Stadium, Morley was struck most of all by the noise, and then by the excitement in the air.

Vic Raschi was confident that he was ready to pitch. His last few starts had been good, and he felt as if he had worked through his dry spot. He had won for the Yankees in the 152nd game, a game they absolutely had to win against the Athletics.

After the Yankees came from behind to beat Boston, Raschi was determined to stay calm. He never had trouble sleeping before a big game, and this one was no exception. He was up at eight, and he, Reynolds, and Lopat drove to the ball park early together. Their wives would come later. He was not nervous. The previous day he had been nervous because events were beyond his control. Now he was not bothered by the crowd and the thunderous noise. Even as the players were dressing in the locker room before noon, they could hear the crowd's excitement. The key to pitching in this game, Raschi thought, was to concentrate, to cut out the crowd and noise, to think of only one thing: what to do on each pitch. Jim Turner, now his pitching coach, a few years earlier his manager in Portland, had taught him that at a critical juncture of his professional life.

Turner was a marvelous teacher, Raschi thought. He knew when to teach and when not to. If a pitcher threw the wrong pitch and lost a game, Turner did not intrude at the height of the pitcher's pain and anguish. Rather, he waited a day or two. Then he would make the pitcher himself talk his way through the situation—what had happened and why. Every game, Turner said, could be broken down, hitter by hitter, pitch by pitch. Each pitch was connected to the next pitch, Turner thought, for the strength of a pitcher lay partly in his ability to set up a batter for the next pitch.

Raschi had come to him desperate to learn—he was proud of his skills, and deeply wounded by the failure of Yankee management in the spring of 1947 to see his career as he did. Turner immediately saw Raschi's talent. But there were too many lapses—moments when he was pitching but not thinking. In an early Portland game, Raschi had a lead in the third inning. With two outs, two men on base, and the pitcher up, Raschi had allowed the pitcher to get a hit, and that had cost him the game. Turner waited a day and then took Raschi aside. "When you have a situation like a weak hitter up, you *crucify* him. You never let a pitcher beat you, Vic. Never!" Raschi's ability to concentrate improved immediately.

Turner taught him not just to study the hitters but also to prevail over them. "Vic—those hitters are your enemy. If they get their way, you're out of baseball," he would say. "I've seen pitchers with talent who might have made the major leagues, but they didn't hate hitters enough." Raschi proceeded to do well with Portland, winning 9 and losing 2, and in mid-season the Yankees brought him back to New York. He won two games during their extraordinary 19-game winning streak.

Raschi had a good fastball to start with, though perhaps not quite as good as Reynolds's, but he lacked a curve, or Aunt Susie, as the other pitchers called it. He worked on it with Turner, and in 1948 it began to work—a change more than a curve, actually. He had great stamina, far more than Reynolds, the other power pitcher. It was an article of faith among the Yankee players that if you were going to beat Vic Raschi, you had to do it early because he got stronger as the game wore on. If given a lead, he simply refused to lose. In the last innings he wanted to throw nothing but fastballs. "From now on just give me one sign," he would say to his catcher as they entered the seventh inning. Once, during a game with the Red Sox, Raschi had the lead but seemed to be struggling in the seventh inning. With Walt Dropo up, Stengel sent Jim Turner out to talk to Raschi. The resentment in Raschi's face was visible from the dugout. Turner quickly returned to the bench. "What did you say?" asked Stengel. "I asked him how he was going to pitch to Dropo," answered Turner. "And what did he answer?" Stengel asked. "Hard," said Turner.

Now nothing was to interfere with Raschi's concentration. He sat in front of his locker, cutting out all else around him, thinking only of what he wanted to do. If his teammates tried to come near him to exchange a pleasantry, he waved them away. He did not like photographers to take his picture on game days, and that was more than mere superstition. Photographers in those days still used flash attachments, and Raschi hated the fact that for five or six minutes after each pop he could not see properly. He tried to warn them off, but if they did not listen he would spray their shoes with tobacco juice. He had a reputation among the writers as the hardest man on the team to interview.

With Ellis Kinder, the knowledge that the Sunday game might be the biggest in his life did not deter him in the least. He started partying hard on Saturday night. Joe Dobson, who was rooming with Kinder that year, was awakened at about four A.M. by a knock on the door. There was Kinder, quite drunk, with a lady friend whom Dobson had never seen before. Dobson went back to sleep and then got up and left the room around nine A.M. As he departed he heard Kinder's whiskey-roughened voice speaking into the phone: "Room service, get some coffee up here."

Charlie Silvera, the backup catcher, lived on Gerard Avenue, about a block from the Stadium. To his amazement, the noise from the crowd started late Saturday afternoon and grew through the evening as fans gathered in the parking lot and formed a line waiting for bleacher seats. Throughout the night, as game time approached, the noise grew steadily louder. Curt Gowdy was equally impressed by the noise of the crowd. He thought of it as a war of fans—the Yankee fans cheering wildly, then their noise answered by deafening volleys from the many Red Sox fans who had driven down from New England. Gowdy's job was to help Mel Allen, for this was Mel's game. Gowdy was impressed at how calm Allen was, as if he had been broadcasting games like this all his life. "We've been so full of tension all year long, that honest-to-goodness today I'm just forgetting about everything," Allen told his audience at the beginning of the game. "Whatever happens, happens. Something's gotta happen today. That's just the way it's going to be. The Yankees have done an out-of-this-world job this year, and the Red Sox have just been magnificent."

Vic Raschi heard none of it. He thought only about the Red Sox. Keep Dominic DiMaggio off the bases. That was important because Pesky was a much better hitter when Dominic was on base. Pitch carefully to Williams and walk him if necessary. Williams could kill a right-handed fastball pitcher in the Stadium. No curveballs to Junior Stephens, who murdered Raschi's curve. Nothing but high fastballs slightly outside. Let Stevie do battle with Death Valley in left center. To Bobby Doerr, as good a hitter as they had, with no real weakness, just pitch carefully and around the edges.

Raschi saw Joe DiMaggio in the locker room. DiMaggio looked gray and wan and was moving poorly. Raschi knew he was sick and exhausted. He wondered if DiMaggio was really well enough to play that day. Probably not, he decided, but nobody on this team was going to tell Joe DiMaggio that he should not be playing.

At last Raschi went out to the mound, and started to pitch. Within minutes he was pleased. Everything was working that day; he had speed, placement, and his little curve. This was not the day to go out and find that one of his pitches was missing, or that he could not put the ball where he wanted. And he was pleased to be pitching against Ellis Kinder. Kinder was tough too, a man who, in the phrase that Raschi liked to apply to himself and his friend Allie Reynolds, liked to make hitters smell the leather. Kinder would almost surely pitch well and make the game close. Raschi wanted that; he wanted a close game where the pressure was on the pitcher.

Dom DiMaggio and Pesky went out quickly. After he got a man out Raschi would always observe a certain ritual: He would straighten his cap, pull his sweat shirt down toward his wrist, and fix the mound. Then he would plant his right foot on the rubber. All the while the infielders would throw the ball around. Then Raschi was ready to receive the ball from the third baseman, either Bobby Brown or Billy Johnson. He wanted the ball thrown right at his glove so that he wouldn't have to move. Sometimes, when the Yankees had a big lead, Johnson or Brown would throw the ball slightly behind him, forcing him to leave the rubber. He hated it. There would be none of that today. With two out, Ted Williams came to the plate. Raschi kept everything close to the plate, but he also walked Williams on four pitches. Then he got Junior Stephens out.

Rizzuto was the lead-off man in the bottom of the first. By then he had come to share the Yankees' admiration for Kinder, who had so completely mastered them that season. Four victories. If there was one advantage Rizzuto had over his teammates when it came to hitting against Kinder, it was that he was not a power hitter. Instead he went with the ball. With a pitcher as smart as Kinder, Rizzuto never tried to guess. The pitch came in, somewhat on the inside, and Rizzuto swung. It was a slider, not a fastball, he realized immediately, because a fastball that much inside would have broken his bat. Because it was slightly off-speed, Rizzuto got out ahead of it. He slapped it down the line, past Pesky at third base, and he knew immediately it was extra bases. The ball hugged the left-field line and went into the corner, and as Rizzuto raced for second, he watched Ted Williams go into the corner. Williams played back slightly, waiting for the ball to come back to him the way it would at Fenway. Rizzuto knew the fence better, and he raced for third. The ball stayed along the contours of the park, more like a hockey puck than a baseball, and went past Williams. Rizzuto had an easy triple. He watched with relief as McCarthy played the in-field back.

Henrich was up now, the perfect batter for this situation. Kinder pitched and Henrich choked up on the bat. With the softest swing imaginable, he hit a grounder toward Bobby Doerr. Classic Henrich, Rizzuto thought, giving himself up and getting the run. No ego in the way. The Yankees had a one-run lead.

Inning after inning passed. The lead held up. Raschi was on top of his game, and the Yankees could do nothing with Kinder. If anything, he was even more in control than Raschi. His placement was almost perfect. When he missed the corner with a pitch, it was because he wanted to miss the corner. He was varying his speed nicely. And he showed no signs of getting tired.

In the eighth, the first batter was Tebbetts, and he went out; then it was Kinder's turn up. Kinder badly wanted to bat; he was sure he was as good a hitter as anyone on the bench, but McCarthy played the percentages. He sent up Tom Wright, a player just called up from the minors, to bat for Kinder. On the Yankee bench the players had been watching McCarthy closely. When he made his signal, there was among the Yankee players a collective sigh of relief and gratitude. Kinder was out and the Red Sox had a notoriously weak bullpen. On the Red Sox bench, Matt Batts, the catcher, who liked McCarthy more than most of the bench players (McCarthy had given him his chance at the majors), thought, God, don't do it; that's a mistake. We're down only one run, they can't touch Ellis, and we are weak, I mean *weak* in the bullpen. Kinder was furious. Wright walked, but Dominic DiMaggio grounded to Rizzuto, who turned it into a double play. The inning was over and Kinder, to the relief of the Yankees, was out of the game.

The first two Yankee batters in the eighth, Henrich and Berra, were both left-handed, so McCarthy again played the percentages and went to Parnell, his pitcher from yesterday. Sitting by himself in his attic in South Hadley, eleven-year-old Bart Giamatti heard Jim Britt say that Parnell was coming in to relieve Kinder. Giamatti was young, but he knew that Parnell had pitched too often in recent weeks, and that he had pitched the day before and must be exhausted. He had an immediate sense that this was a gallant but futile gesture.

Giamatti was filled with sadness. Something in Jim Britt's voice over the radio made it clear that he was equally pessimistic.

Giamatti was right to be pessimistic. Parnell's was to be a short appearance. He was tired, and he had lost his edge. Henrich had hit him hard in the past ("My nemesis," Parnell later called him), and now was eager to bat against someone other than Ellis Kinder. Lefty or no, he saw the ball better with Parnell than with Kinder. This time Parnell threw him a fastball. Henrich hit it about ten rows back into the right-field seats and the Yankees got their cushion, 2–0. Then Berra singled and McCarthy called to the bullpen for Tex Hughson. Hughson turned to Joe Dobson and said, "Well, Joe, they've finally gone to the bottom of the barrel." It was odd, Hughson thought, that McCarthy had shown nothing but contempt for him all season, and now at this most important moment he had decided to use him.

DiMaggio hit into a double play, and there were two outs and no one on. But Lindell singled and Hank Bauer was sent in as a pinch runner. Then Billy Johnson singled, and when Williams juggled the ball, Bauer went to third. Then Hughson deliberately walked Mapes to get to the rookie, Jerry Coleman.

Coleman had thought in the early part of the season that he liked to hit against Kinder, and then gradually as the season progressed he decided he was wrong. Kinder had seemed to improve as a pitcher in every outing. You just never got a good pitch. There was the change, the sudden fastball, and then, of course, the last-second slider. Like his teammates, he had been relieved when McCarthy had played by the book and pulled Kinder for a pinch-hitter. Now, in the eighth, he was up with the bases loaded. The Yankees were ahead, but even so Coleman did not want to look foolish at this moment. The season might be nearly over, he might have done everything the Yankees wanted of him and more, but he had never felt more on trial.

Hughson was absolutely sure he could handle the rookie. Tex could still throw hard, and the ball came in letter-high and inside. Hughson was delighted. He had placed it almost perfectly, an impossible pitch for a hitter to do anything with, he thought, and he was right; Coleman did very little with it. He hit it right on the trademark of the bat and sliced the ball, a pop-up, just past second base; Coleman was disgusted with himself.

In right field Al Zarilla was not playing Coleman particularly deep. Bases loaded, he thought, two out, short right-field fence, two runs behind. We cannot let them have any more runs. Coleman was not a power hitter. For Zarilla, the ability to come in on a pop fly or a soft liner was more important than going back on a ball, particularly with two out. Zarilla watched Hughson's pitch and he thought, That is a lovely pitch. Then he saw the ball leave the bat and he knew at once that it was trouble—too far back for Bobby Doerr, the ball spinning away toward the line, a dying swan if there ever was one. It had to be Zarilla's ball. He charged it, and kept charging, but the ball kept slicing away from him. At the last second Zarilla was sure he had a play. He dove for it, his fingers and glove outstretched. He was diving at the expense of his body, for he was not positioned to break a fall. He missed it by perhaps two inches. By the time the ball came down, Zarilla realized later, it was almost on the foul line.

When Coleman saw that it was too deep for Doerr and that Zarilla was desperately charging, he knew the ball was going to drop. He turned past second and raced for third. He was out at third, but three runs had scored. The lead was 5–0. When he came into the dugout, everyone patted Coleman on the back as if he were an old veteran and an RBI leader. But he thought of it as a cheap hit, and was more than a little ashamed of himself. A three-run double in the box score, he thought, and a cheap pop-up on the field.

He was ashamed of it for a long time afterward. Then three years later he ran into Joe McCarthy at a banquet. He started to mumble something about it being a bloop hit, but McCarthy interrupted him. "You swung at it, didn't you?" he asked, and Coleman nodded. Coleman understood McCarthy's meaning immediately—you didn't strike out and they didn't put anything past you. So don't apologize, you did your job.

The Red Sox gave it one more shot. In the top of the ninth, they rallied for three runs. Pesky fouled out, and then Williams walked. Stephens singled to center. Then Bobby Doerr hit a long drive to center field. It was a well-hit ball, but the kind that Joe DiMaggio normally handled readily. This time, his legs cramping up, it went over his head and Doerr had a triple. DiMaggio signaled for time and took himself out of the game. His long regular season was over. Two runs were in. Zarilla flied out to Mapes. Two outs. But Goodman singled through center, and Doerr scored. The score was 5–3.

The next batter was Birdie Tebbetts. Since they had fattened their lead, the Yankee bench jockeys had been needling the needler mercilessly: "Hey, Birdie, get the kid [Quinn] to lend you some of his money for your World Series share." "Hey, Birdie, we'll send you over a bottle of our champagne." Tommy Henrich was playing first, and he walked over to Raschi to give him a small pep talk, to remind him that he needed only one more out. "Give me the goddamn ball and get the hell out of here!" Raschi snarled. Henrich turned, and grinned to himself. We've got it, it's a lock, he thought, there is no way Birdie Tebbetts is going to get a hit off this man right now. Tebbetts popped up in foul territory. Coleman started calling for it, but Henrich yelled him off. "It's my ball," he shouted, and he thought to himself, It's the one I've been looking for all year. The regular season was over.

The Red Sox locker room was silent. No one was able to talk. This ending had been even worse than 1948's. For two years in a row they had come so close, and had ended up with nothing. They had played *309* regular-season games over the two seasons, and had ended up a total of one game behind the two pennant winners in that period.

But at least 1948 had ended with a sense of optimism. This season was ending with the taste of ashes. They had come into the Stadium needing to win only one game, they had a four-run lead in the first game, and they had blown it and the two-game series. They had no one to blame except themselves. Boo Ferriss, looking at his teammates Pesky and Williams, thought they looked like men who had died in some way. Williams sat immobilized in front of his locker, his head down. He was unreachable. If any reporters approached him, he just waved them away. He later said it was the worst moment in his baseball career, worse than the 1946 World Series defeat, worse than the 1948 playoff defeat.

Clif Keane thought there was only one exception to the

gloom and that was predictable: Junior Stephens. "Tough game, wasn't it, Clif?" Junior said. There was, Keane understood, still fun ahead for someone like Stephens.

Dominic DiMaggio immediately went to the Commodore Hotel, where his young wife, Emily, was waiting. Grossinger's, the Catskills resort, had offered them a free vacation when the season was over. Emily DiMaggio, who had not the slightest interest in baseball, was thrilled because now they could go to Grossinger's right away and not have to wait the extra week or ten days that a World Series would take. "Isn't it wonderful, Dominic," she said, "now we can go on vacation right away." Dominic DiMaggio's eyes were filled with tears. "Emily," said her husband, "don't you realize what's just happened?"

For the team members, the train ride back to Boston was like a funeral procession. It seemed endless. There was almost no desire, as there sometimes was on occasions like this, to replay the game. No one wanted to talk about the next season. No one wanted to take solace in the clichés about how close they had come, and how they had made up eleven games on the Yankees. No one wanted to talk about what if—what if they had beaten Ray Scarborough; what if Hughson's arm had been a little better. In 1948 there had been some consolation that they had been cheated by Charlie Berry's bad call on the Boudreau foul/home run.

No one was more bitter than Ellis Kinder, who, as the evening passed and more alcohol flowed, became angrier and angrier about being pulled for a pinch hitter. In his mind, it became ever more clear that had McCarthy left him in, he would have held the Yankees, the Red Sox would have scored the same number of runs, and he would have won. Near the end of the ride he finally accosted McCarthy and exploded. As far as he was concerned, McCarthy had blown it. He was a screw-up, a drunk, and a manager who treated his star players one way and his other ballplayers another. Ellis Kinder got it all off his chest, and he never forgave Joe McCarthy.

CHAPTER 15

Certain games are classics, seized on by baseball aficionados and remembered long after they are over. Such was the Raschi-Kinder finale and also the first game of the World Series. Allie Reynolds of the Yankees pitched against Don Newcombe of the Dodgers. It was the first baseball game televised to a mass audience; there had been telecasts in the past of World Series games, but this time there were 10 million people watching. That was the big breakthrough. Gillette had paid $800,000 for the rights, four times more than in 1948. Red Barber, who along with Mel Allen did the radio broadcast, thought it was the first moment in baseball history when the pull of television was virtually as powerful as that of radio.

Newcombe, Rookie of the Year, was three months past his twenty-third birthday. Big and strong at six feet four and 230 pounds, he was the first great black power pitcher to reach the major leagues. In his own words, he burned with a bitter resentment toward racial injustice. His anger manifested itself, as much as anywhere else, in his hatred of hitters, almost all of whom in those days were white. Newcombe went, in a brief span of three years, from being a child of the New Jersey slums to being a major New York sports celebrity. Geographically that journey was only a few miles, but emotionally it was like a voyage to the moon. The most obvious symbol of it to him was the sudden availability of beautiful women; he was now constantly surrounded by them.

But pleasure and pride were mixed with anger, for star pitcher or no, he still encountered bigotry and injustice. Jackie Robinson was his idol, and, like Robinson (and unlike Roy Campanella, a conciliatory man by nature, who was the third black on the team), Newcombe was unbending. He remembered the insults, and he judged his teammates not just by whether they played well on the field but by how they behaved toward him off the field. Were they willing to stay in hotels where their black teammates were not allowed and to eat in restaurants where their black teammates could not go? Often he found them lacking. The gap between white and black was very large then, and when the game was over they went their separate ways. He could understand that, but he did not like the other part—the idea that his teammates might not be very different from the people who were giving him, Jackie, and Roy such a hard time.

Once during that first season, when he had been in the shower, another Dodger pitcher had filled his mouth with warm water and, when Newcombe's back was turned, had squirted it at him. Newcombe spun around. There was the pitcher holding his genitalia. "You've got your hand on your cock," Newcombe said. "If you just did what I think you just did—if you pissed on me— I'm going to break your goddamn arm right here and now." The others rushed to explain that it was just a gag. But it was not a gag, he thought, because it was not something that would have been done to a white player. It was to him one more sign that even his teammates were a part of the *they*.

That year he was constantly aware of racism. In St. Louis the black fans were permitted only in the bleachers. This meant that only about 3,000 could get in, while 10,000 more waited outside in the streets. He and Robinson talked about this; these, after all, were their people—poor Southern blacks who had made the trip up from Memphis and Birmingham and Little Rock ("the fried-chicken specials," he and Robinson called them). He and Jackie would joke that if there was ever a brawl on the field, they would immediately run like hell in the direction of the bleachers, where, no matter what the park, their people were sure to be seated.

He was angry that the Dodgers had not brought him up sooner, which he was sure they would have done had he been a white pitcher. Branch Rickey, he thought, was integrating slowly, essentially one black at a time—Jackie first, then a ten-inning cameo appearance by Dan Bankhead in 1947, and Campanella in 1948. But by the time he was called up, Newcombe was tired of waiting on the stairs. At one point, after two exceptionally successful years, he had jumped his minor-league team and gone home. But his arrival in Brooklyn had given some measure of protection to Robinson and Campy, who had been sitting ducks for beanballs until his arrival. The white Brooklyn pitchers simply were not going to protect Jackie and Roy. Therefore it was Newcombe's responsibility.

In those first few years, the racial taunting was constant. There was one memorable game with the Phillies in 1950 in which there was a knockdown of Campy. There was an old coach on the Phillies named McDonald, and, as far as the black Dodgers were concerned, he was kept solely to scream racial obscenities. That day Robinson came over to Newcombe. "Newk, you hear that little son of a bitch?" he asked. "You think I'm deaf, Jackie?" Newcombe answered. "Newk, you got to do something," Robinson said. Newcombe thought about the Phillies' lineup and decided who their best hitter was: Del Ennis. When Ennis came up, Newcombe drilled him. He threw right at his head. Many years later he was still uneasy with the hatred that he had felt when he threw that pitch. Ennis hit the dirt, then slowly picked himself up, called time, and walked over to the bench. He told Newcombe years later that he had said to McDonald, "Listen, you little son of a bitch, he damn near killed me and with the shit you're yelling he's got a right to. Unlike you, I've got to hit against him. Now you shut the hell up or I'll come over and tear your goddamn tongue out."

For any white rookie player Yankee Stadium was hallowed ground. But that was not true for Newk. The Yankees were not special to him, nor did pitching in Yankee Stadium mean that much to him. Black kids of his generation did not have that dream, for it was beyond the realm of possibility. Newcombe's father had been a chauffeur. Don Newcombe's dream

as a boy was to drive a truck; that to him meant both freedom—by going all over the country—and power—by double-
clutching on one of those huge monsters. Pitching in a World
Series was more an accident than a dream achieved.

From the moment he walked out on the mound that day he
knew he was never going to be any better. The Yankees were a
fastball-hitting team, and he was going to damn well let them
earn their reputation that day. He was pleased to be matched
against Allie Reynolds. Reynolds, he thought, was one mean
SOB, a real redneck from Oklahoma who was tough on all
hitters, but particularly on the blacks. (Gene Woodling, Reynolds's teammate, agreed with at least part of Newcombe's assess-
ment: "On a team filled with Red Asses," he said, "Allie was the
champ—the King of the RAs.") Larry Doby, the first black to
play in the American League, had complained to Newcombe
that the first few times Cleveland had played the Yankees, Reynolds had knocked him down almost every time he came up.
Robinson too was convinced that Reynolds had a vendetta
against blacks, and there was obvious bad blood between the
Yankee pitcher and the Dodger infielder. What made it even
worse, Newcombe thought, was that Reynolds *was* good. When
he was at his best, the Dodgers could not touch him. "He would
stick our bats up our ass," was Newcombe's picturesque phrase.

Reynolds, of course, was equally glad to be there. He
loved pitching such big games. He was, his Yankee teammates
thought, a great ham. "Allie," Charlie Keller once told him,
"don't ever pitch in St. Louis or Washington before a small
crowd. One more thing—you need to pitch in big games and
close games. You work better when it's close. You get sloppy
when you get a big lead." But in a big game before a big
crowd, he was always at his best. Pitching today against Newcombe, after his failure against Parnell in the next-to-last
game, was a chance for redemption.

The Yankees did not know Newcombe. Their scouting reports said he was a power pitcher, but the scouting reports were
too clinical, Jerry Coleman thought; they did not seem to recognize fully Newcombe's strength and power. Casey Stengel had
tried to warn them in the pregame meeting. "Don't try and pull
the ball on him," Stengel had said. That was needless warning
number one. They could barely see the ball, let alone pull it.

It was a bright sunny day, more like summer than fall. The Yankee management pulled aside the tarpaulin in the center-field bleachers to accommodate the extra fans. If under normal conditions the tarp offered some protection to the hitters, it was gone on this day, not that either Newcombe or Reynolds needed any extra help.

If Don Newcombe thought Allie Reynolds was tough, then the Yankees quickly came to think the same about Newcombe. Phil Rizzuto, the first man to bat against Newcombe, came back to the bench. "That man," he said, "is *mean.*"

It was, Newcombe thought, the perfect game. The Yankees could barely touch him, and the Dodgers were doing precious little with Reynolds. In the first inning Newcombe retired the first three batters on infield plays. Then, in the second, starting with DiMaggio, he struck out the side. In the first inning Spider Jorgensen had hit a high fly to left field which Lindell had misplayed; it had fallen for a double even though it should have been an easy out. But then Reynolds shut them down.

The Dodgers got their next hit in the eighth with one out—Pee Wee Reese singled. That was it. We might, Newcombe thought as the late innings arrived, be here forever. At the end of eight innings, the Dodgers had 2 hits and the Yankees had 4. Reynolds had struck out 9, and Newcombe had struck out 11.

Newcombe thought he had never been faster. This was a time before radar guns became fashionable, but based on what he knew then and later, Newcombe judged his best fastball at ninety-six to ninety-seven miles an hour, and his curve, almost a change of pace, at ninety. Reynolds, he thought, was every bit as fast.

In the broadcasting booth, Mel Allen and Red Barber were calling the game on radio. "Well, Brother Allen," Barber said in the bottom of the ninth, "come over here now to the microphone and tell how you've been seeing this thing." "Well, I'll tell you, I've been sittin' here just real amazed at two great pitchers giving perhaps the two best performances of their careers," Allen answered.

In the bottom of the ninth, Tommy Henrich was the lead-off hitter. If there was any Yankee who had a shot at pulling a right-handed power pitcher like Newcombe, it was Henrich. Henrich was so good a fastball hitter that the hardest thrower of his era, Bob Feller, once said of him, "That guy can hit me in the middle of the night, blindfolded and with two broken feet to boot." Before he went up, he turned to Frank Shea on the bench and said, "I'm going to get this guy. He's been giving me fastballs all day and beating me, but if I get one this time I'm going to hit it out." The truth, he thought, was that Newcombe was simply overpowering.

The first pitch was a fastball outside. The second pitch was another fastball, just outside, a pitch that could have gone either way. It was 2-and-0, and Henrich knew he was going to get a good pitch. Newcombe had walked very few people all day, and he would not want to walk the lead-off man in the ninth. He threw Henrich a curve. Later there were various descriptions of it: Newcombe thought it broke down and in on Henrich; but Henrich himself did not think it broke like a curve. Rather, he thought it was a perfect pitch to hit, a hard fast strike down the center of the plate, a major-league fastball. Because of Newcombe's speed, Henrich was out a little early on it, and he hit it well. Up in the radio booth, Red Barber was announcing. "The two-nothing pitch is swung on. Drilled out towards right field. Going way back . . ."

The moment he hit it, Henrich ran hard and kept his eye on Carl Furillo as the Dodger right-fielder moved toward the wall. Henrich saw Furillo's head tilt up as the outfielder neared the fence, and thought to himself, I've got it, I've got it. "Thaaaat's the ball game!" Barber was telling his audience. "A home run for Tommy Henrich! There's Henrich now between first and second. Bill Dickey, the first-base coach, almost jumped on his back, then realized that's a tender back and he better not. Henrich's coming into third. He is trotting his home run home. Look at him grin. Big as a slice of watermelon. Wow! Well, they call him Old Reliable and they're not joking. . . . With the startling suddenness of a pistol shot, the denouement, the climax was reached. . . ."

As soon as Henrich had hit it, Newcombe knew it was a home run. One pitch, he thought, all it takes is one pitch. As quickly as he could he tucked his glove into his hand and walked off the mound. Often pitchers are stunned and wait

on the mound long enough to survey the damage. Not Newcombe. He never looked around. He was in the dugout before
Henrich reached the plate. A few minutes later Harold Rosenthal, the sportswriter for the *Trib,* came into the Dodger locker
room. Newcombe was stretched out on the training table and
the Dodger trainer was cutting a toenail. "Newk, what the hell
are you doing?" Rosenthal asked.

"I've got this ingrown toenail and it hurts like hell."

"You pitched the whole game with an ingrown toenail
bothering you?" Rosenthal asked.

"Yeah, I didn't want to bother beforehand," he said.

"That was a hard game to lose today, Newk," Rosenthal
said. "You pitched a hell of a game."

Newcombe seemed almost not to hear him. Great game
indeed: There were 24 strikeouts—13 by Reynolds, 11 by
Newcombe. Reynolds had given up 2 hits; Newcombe, 5. The
game was viewed even then as a classic: Allie Reynolds
thought he had pitched as well as he did in his two subsequent
no-hitters; and Newcombe, asked to name the best game he
ever pitched, cited that World Series game.

The next day Preacher Roe beat Vic Raschi 1–0. Gil
Hodges singled with Jackie Robinson on third for the game's
one run in the third inning. Later Raschi told friends that it
was not Hodges who had beaten him, it was Robinson, on
third, bluffing a break for home. "I had just never seen anything like him before," Raschi said, "a human being who could
go from a standing start to full speed in one step. He did
something to me that almost never happened: He broke my
concentration and I paid more attention to him than to
Hodges. He beat me more than Hodges."

The other Yankees, particularly the younger ones,
watched Robinson with growing admiration. On the bench
Jerry Coleman, who had turned down a Dodger contract before he signed with the Yankees, silently said a small prayer
of thanks that he had signed with the Yankee organization.
The Dodgers, Coleman thought, were not going to need a
light-hitting second baseman for a long, long time. Robinson
was different from almost any player Coleman had ever
seen. He was not a power hitter, but he could change the
tempo of a game nonetheless. Years later Coleman still

thought Robinson was special. Some younger players with greater speed had arrived, and they had produced greater statistics, but Robinson remained apart; he had done everything with a purpose—to wake up his own team, to intimidate his opponents, to make the game different. What a player, Coleman thought.

Tommy Byrne started the third game. When he showed signs of wildness, consistently falling behind the hitters, Stengel did not hesitate to pull him. With one out and the bases loaded in the fourth, he brought in Joe Page, who pitched the remaining five and two thirds innings, striking out 4 and giving up only 2 hits until the ninth. The Yankees won 4–3. That made it 2-1 in games.

In the fourth game Eddie Lopat took a 6–0 lead into the bottom of the sixth. Then the Dodgers scored 4 runs on 7 hits. This time Stengel went to Reynolds, who pitched the final three and a third innings, striking out 5 men. The Dodgers did not get a single hit off him. That made it 3-1 in games. In the fifth game the Yankees gave Raschi a 10–1 lead and, though he needed help from Page, he won 10–6.

The Yankees had won the Series decisively.

The next year they were joined by a young pitcher named Whitey Ford, who was to complete the starting rotation and make it one of the best in baseball history. Ford was nothing if not brash. In the spring Jim Turner asked Reynolds to room with him and "give him some class." On the first night they were to go out to dinner, Reynolds noted that Ford was putting his shirt collar over his jacket. "Hey, Whitey, we don't do that here," Reynolds said, "We wear jackets *and* ties." "I don't have any ties," Ford replied. "No problem. Wear one of mine," Reynolds answered. Ford looked at Reynolds's ties. "I can't wear any of these," said Ford. "Why not?" asked Reynolds. "They're all middle-aged ties," Ford said.

Led by Raschi, Reynolds, Lopat, and Whitey Ford, and with Mantle replacing DiMaggio, they went on to win four more pennants and four more World Series in a row. No one else had ever done it. In 1952, Gene Woodling, sitting in front of his locker during spring training, turned to friends and asked them what they planned to do with their World Series check that year. Winning had become a natural assumption for him. At the start of the previous season, Charlie Silvera's wife had asked him for a fur coat if the Yankees won again. He said yes, thinking that no one wins three times a row. But they won, and at the end of the season he proudly peeled off eleven hundred-dollar bills for her coat.

Those five championships marked both the dawn of an era and, without anyone knowing it at the time, the end of an era as well. Because the Yankees were so powerful and deep, they believed they could, in a moment of crisis, always bring up a talented kid from the farm system. But the arrogance of power would finally come to afflict them, as surely as it does in business or politics. In 1950 they signed several blacks, including Elston Howard, who eventually became their first black player. But that very season they were also scouting a young black shortstop who played for the black Kansas City Monarchs in a ball park the Yankees owned. His name was Ernie Banks, and the reports on him were spectacular. Banks, who was hitting around .350 that year, had heard that the Yankees were interested in him and that on several occasions a scout was in the stands. That excited him because the Yankees were the team for which he wanted to play. In addition, he knew that Rizzuto was aging and that he would arrive in the majors just as Rizzuto was finishing his career. But Tom Greenwade, the Yankee scout, never bothered to meet the ebullient Banks and failed to move quickly on so exceptional a talent. The Chicago Cubs signed him first.

It is doubtful that the Yankees would have moved so slowly on a white player of comparable ability. Their failure to sign blacks brought with it a penalty so severe that not only would the Yankees' dominance end but the American League by the late fifties and early sixties would become a lesser league. The National League teams, needing to compete with the Dodgers, worked much harder at signing black talent; it became stocked with the first generation of black superstars—"the black Babe Ruths," to use Johnny Bench's description: Mays, Aaron, Banks, Williams, McCovey, Gibson, and Robinson.

Joe DiMaggio, with his remarkable ability, his strength, his speed, and his grace had stood as the preeminent *athlete* of his era. But now a new generation was arriving, bringing with it new definitions of speed and power.

EPILOGUE

The 1949 baseball season did not end for Ellis Kinder the day the Red Sox lost the pennant. A few days later he was back in Jackson, Tennessee, where his buddies still played semipro ball, usually on Sundays, against teams from other little towns in West Tennessee. There would be a small country store and across from it a ball park with three rows of stands; late in the week word would go out that there was to be a ball game. Hundreds of people would show up to see it, and to bet. The betting was important. The players got only twenty-five or fifty dollars for their efforts, but they could also bet a little on the side.

Kinder's old buddies had followed the pennant race and taken great pride in his exploits. In the past when he came back from St. Louis or Boston, he had always been willing to play with them. But now he was a big-time star, so who knew?

A few days after Kinder returned to Jackson, Fred Baker, a close friend, called him up. Fred had once been a bat boy with the old Jackson Generals, and no one had been nicer to him in those days than Ellis Kinder, then a star pitcher for the Generals. He had seen talent in the young man and had hit fly balls to him by the hour. Baker had become a good all-around athlete and had gone on to Union College, where he played several sports. He was now the catcher for the Jackson semi-pro team. Baker explained to Kinder that they had a tough game coming up on Sunday at Alamo, against Dyersburg. Ed Wright, who had pitched for the Phillies, was a Dyersburg boy, and he was going to pitch. The Dyersburg boys were doing a lot of bragging, he said, because they had Ed Wright.

"Can you pitch for us on Sunday, Ellis?" Baker asked.

Kinder paused. "Can you get me anything?" he asked.

"How about a hundred dollars?" Baker answered.

"Let's go," Ellis Kinder said.

So off the team went to Alamo, rather cocky now because Ellis Kinder of the Boston Red Sox was pitching for them. That cut down on the betting a little, though. What struck his old friends about Ellis that day was how easy it seemed for him. He barely warmed up. "Just three or four pitches," he said, "that's all I need." Then he was out on the mound, and the motion seemed so fluid and easy, as if he were not really throwing hard. But the ball would zoom into the plate.

Kinder seemed just as serious as if he were in a big-league game. Dyersburg could not do much with him that day, and late in the game Kinder hit a grand-slam home run to win it. He could not have been more pleased had he done it at Yankee Stadium. "Country boy," his friend Billy Schrivner thought as he watched him cross the plate and grin, "You've never really been away—have you?"

Ellis Kinder became a genuine star with the Red Sox, and soon became the best relief pitcher in the American League. The next year at spring training, when Johnny Pesky batted against him for the first time, Kinder deliberately plunked him on the butt. The pitch was hard enough just to sting a little. His control was pinpoint perfect, and every spring from then on Kinder would hit Pesky in the exact spot. It was all good fun, but there was a small reminder here that hitters were the enemy.

Kinder also became something of a sage among the Boston pitchers. In 1951 the Yankees sold a young bonus pitcher named Paul Hinrichs to the Red Sox, and Chuck Stobbs took him over to meet Kinder. Hinrichs, bright and eager, told Kinder that he was anxious to learn how to become a major-league pitcher and wondered if Kinder had any tips for him.

"Do you smoke?" Kinder asked Hinrichs.

"No," said Hinrichs.

"Do you chase women?" asked Kinder.

Again, Hinrichs answered that he did not.

"Well, son, do you drink?" asked Kinder.

Again, Hinrichs answered that he did not.

"I'm afraid you'll never make it," said Kinder and walked away. Paul Hinrichs pitched a total of three innings in the major leagues.

Kinder's last years were not easy ones. He continued to drink hard. He was not successful in work and there was a succession of jobs—as a house painter, a taxi-cab driver, a repairman. His health steadily declined. In 1967 he underwent open-heart surgery. After the operation he sat in his hospital room talking with Hazel. The World Series was on television, St. Louis versus Boston. "You know what, Mama," he said to her. "They're playing for real money now. Some of those old boys"—he motioned toward the television set—"are making one hundred thousand dollars a year." "Ellis!" she said, as if catching him once again in some terrible exaggeration. "No, it's true, Mama," he said. "And what's more, in just a few years they'll all be making a million dollars." "*Ellis!*" she said, as if afraid some higher authority would strike him down for such a blasphemous idea. "A million dollars," he said. "All we played for, Mama, was love." Two days later he was dead at age fifty-four.

Piper Davis, the player-manager of the Birmingham Black Barons, whom the Red Sox had signed instead of Willie Mays, was a skilled athlete, over six feet three, who had once played with the Harlem Globetrotters. The price of signing him was $7,500, paid to Tom Hayes, the Memphis undertaker who owned the Black Barons. The agreement was that if Davis was with a Boston club of any sort, major or minor, on May 15, Boston would pay Hayes an additional $7,500, half of which he would split with Davis. Davis went off to spring training in the spring of 1950, but it was not an easy time. He was very much alone. He ate with the black waiters in the ser-

vice section of the hotel, and he roomed with one of the waiters from the hotel. Davis realized from the start that he was
not going to make the big team, but he hoped to play at
Louisville. Instead, he was sent down to Scranton, where he
played well for the first month, hitting around .330 and leading the team in home runs and runs batted in. Soon there was
talk that he might be promoted to Louisville. Just before the
May 15 deadline he was called in by manager Jack Burns. "I'm
sorry, I'm going to have to let you go," Burns said. "Why,
man?" Davis answered. "I'm leading the team in hitting." "For
economic reasons," Burns said. Then he shook his head. "It
isn't my doing," he said. "It's orders." He pulled out the
lineup card for that night's game. "Here, take a look," he said.
"I already had you penciled in." Economic reasons, Davis
thought, that can't be true—everyone knows how rich Mr.
Yawkey is. But his career in the Boston organization was over,
though he went on to play one year in the Mexican League
and five with Oakland in the Pacific Coast League.

Mickey McDermott's career was a disappointment. In
1953, his best season, he won eighteen games. His arm was a
great God-given gift, but his talent, he said later, had come to
him so easily that he had never learned how to master and
exploit it. Besides, there was always fun to be had—an evening with friends, songs to be sung in nightclubs. "Nightclub
pallor," Dave Egan wrote of his coloring. Though he resented
Egan's attack (it had come after he had done a charity benefit
for Egan, who paid McDermott back by saying that he
couldn't pitch, couldn't hit, couldn't sing, and had nightclub
pallor), there was some truth in it. Soon he was traded. He
went first to Washington and then to the Yankees. When he
was assigned to Hank Bauer as a roommate, Bauer, who had
always hit him well, screamed at him and slammed the door.
"What's the matter, Henry?" McDermott asked. "That means I
don't get to hit against you anymore—I just lost sixty points
on my batting average," Bauer said.

On the Yankees McDermott continued his undisciplined
ways. He never let his work interfere with his pleasure, which
was something Casey Stengel understood. One night McDermott came back to the hotel about four A.M. and, to his con-

sternation, ran into the manager. "Are you drunk again, McDermott?" Stengel asked. McDermott, fearing that this was the end, nodded that indeed he was. "Me too," said Stengel. "Good-night, Maurice."

From the Yankees, his third team, McDermott went to Kansas City and then Detroit. There, Freddie Hutchinson, his manager, did not appreciate his work habits. In one game McDermott loaded up the bases, and from the bench heard Hutchinson's voice: "Okay, McDermott, let's see you sing your way out of this one." He soon slipped into the minor leagues.

In 1961, after a good season in the Southern Association, McDermott was given a tryout with the St. Louis Cardinals. Johnny Keane, the manager, was determined to set a high moral tone on his team, and hated the idea of having a ca-rouser like McDermott. That season Tim McCarver was a nineteen-year-old rookie catcher, just brought up from the minor leagues. Virtually his first memory was of Keane assembling the team before a game and ripping McDermott in front of his teammates. It was a brutal, scathing rebuke about how the Cardinals had been generous enough to give McDermott a tryout when no one else wanted him and how he had reciprocated with this appalling behavior. McCarver found it an unbearably cruel scene. But McDermott had been oddly graceful. "Well, John, if you feel that way I'll take my uniform off and leave the team," he said. "That's exactly what you'll do," Keane said, then reached in his pocket and pulled out a pink slip.

McDermott continued through life, managing to survive by charm. Jobs came and went. It was impossible not to like him. Even in hard times he could always laugh, and so there was always another job.

In 1978 he ran into his old teammate Ted Williams. "Bush, how old are you now?" asked Williams. "Fifty," McDermott said. "Fifty," Williams said. "That's terrific. I never thought you'd make it."

In the madness of the Yankee locker room after the victory over the Dodgers, Allie Reynolds had noticed that Casey Stengel, while celebrating, was also staring at him with a very cool eye. Reynolds wondered what Stengel was thinking, and why he was giving him so cool a look. He soon found out. Stengel walked over to him. "Congratulations, Allie," he said, "that was a great year. Now I want to make a relief pitcher out of you for next season." That struck a bell with Reynolds, for Stengel had always praised him as a relief pitcher. "Why, Allie," he would say, "they see you walk in from the bullpen and half of them faint right then and there."

"The hell you will," said Reynolds.

"Why not?" asked Stengel.

"Because I can't make the money," answered Reynolds. "Relief pitchers never make as much as starters."

"If I can get you just as good money, would you do it?" asked Stengel.

"Sure," answered Reynolds, "that's all I play for anyway, money."

So Stengel called over Dan Topping and Del Webb, the two owners, and asked if Reynolds could have the same amount of money plus an annual raise if he did well relieving. They said he could, and it appeared the deal was done. Reynolds understood Stengel's thinking: Page was too erratic, a good year followed by a bad year; Reynolds himself was frequently shaky in later innings as a starter, but very tough as a reliever in spot situations.

But the Yankees remained short one starter. Frank Shea and Bob Porterfield were never to pitch well again, and Reynolds's switch to the bullpen did not take place for some time. Nonetheless, Reynolds was impressed. There was no other manager in that era who was willing to take an ace from his starting rotation, convert him into a bullpen pitcher, and pay good money to do it. Stengel, he thought, was the first to see the game change as far as the coming of the relief pitcher as an ace in his own right. Reynolds was pleased that the idea had been abandoned, and a year later during spring training a photographer came over to him and asked him to pose for a photograph with Joe Page. Reynolds immediately assumed that this was another attempt to get him in the bullpen, and he refused to be a part of the picture.

After the 1949 season Reynolds knew that despite his 17-6 record he was going to have trouble with George Weiss. He had finished only four games, and he knew Weiss was going to use that against him in contract negotiations. Sure enough, Weiss said, "Allie, you didn't finish many games last year, but I'm not going to cut you."

"I know you're not, George," Reynolds said. "That's the one thing we both can be sure of."

Jerry Coleman had a magnificent rookie year. The Associated Press named him American League Rookie of the Year. At last he felt confident and, for the moment, rich. The World Series share was $5,400, of which he was able to keep almost all. Coleman knew exactly what he wanted to do—he wanted to buy a brand-new car. He had never owned a car before, so he went out and bought a green Pontiac for $1,700. He walked into the showroom and plunked the money down. Forty years later he could still see it: the perfect car, in a glorious shade of green with a light interior.

Because he felt quite rich, he did not work as hard in the off-season selling men's clothes, and by the time spring rolled around and it was time to leave for Florida, he was broke again. He was forced to borrow three hundred dollars from his mother-in-law to make the trip.

Vic Raschi became one of the great stars of the Yankee pitching staff, a critical ingredient in the team that won five pennants and five World Series in a row. He had a record of 21-10 in 1949, and went on to win 71 and lose only 30 in the next four years. Even more remarkable, in those five years he started 160 games and completed 73 of them. And he did this despite terrible physical pain. He hurt his knee in 1950 when Luke Easter of the Indians lined a ball off his leg, but he did not have an operation for two years because he was afraid it might cost him part of a season. He could barely run and could hardly field his position. That he was virtually a cripple was known among the Yankees, but in the curious code of the day none of those who were traded to other teams told their new teammates of his vulnerability. If they had, he might have been quickly driven out of the league by his opponents bunting on him.

Raschi's relations with George Weiss, the general manager, were extremely bitter. Raschi was proud, almost violently so. He gave everything of himself as a player, and expected respect for his accomplishments, particularly from the people he worked for. Besides, he understood that because both he and Reynolds were power pitchers, they had to assume that their time in the majors was limited. They had to maximize their earning capacity in their best years. But he never gained real respect from Weiss.

Raschi soon came not so much to dislike Weiss as to loathe him. It was as if Weiss were trying to withhold not merely Raschi's money but his dignity as well. Weiss never looked him in the eye, but instead looked down at the floor, out the window, or off to the side. He would say after an exceptionally successful season, "Prove to me why you deserve a raise." Raschi, more than anyone else on the team, stood his ground. After all, he was a winning, dependable starting pitcher for a great team, and starting pitchers were always hard to come by. His only leverage was the possibility of retirement.

At the end of a negotiation in which Weiss magnanimously agreed to a $5,000 raise as a reward for a 19- or 20-game season, he closed the meeting by turning to Raschi and saying, "Don't have a losing season." Those words would hang in the air for weeks and months. Raschi knew that because he had fought back so hard, the moment he showed any sign of slipping Weiss would turn the screw on him. The top salary he made after all those great seasons was $40,000.

In 1953, still bothered by injuries, he won 13, lost 6, and started only 26 games instead of his usual 33 or 34. Raschi, who was thirty-four, had a sense that the end was near. When he received his contract from Weiss, it called for a 25 percent pay cut. He sent it back with a note to Weiss saying he had made a cripple of himself in the Yankee cause. He knew he was gone. That winter the Yankees sold him to the Cardinals. They did not notify him personally, and he learned of the deal only through newsmen. One of them called Raschi at his home for his reaction. Proud to the end, he said in what was a virtual epitaph for baseball management of that entire era, "Mr. George Weiss has a very short memory."

The Cardinals, like the Yankees, trained in St. Petersburg the following spring. Some of Raschi's old teammates tried to get together with him for dinner, but he wanted no part of the

Yankees. He pitched well on a bad St. Louis team, and that year the Yankees lost the pennant to Cleveland, which had an almost perfect season, winning 111 games. Still, his former Yankee teammates believed that if Raschi had not been traded, the' Yankees might have won.

In his last year, 1954, Allie Reynolds saw that the world of baseball as he knew it was changing. He was 13-4, but his back hurt, and he was angry about the way the Yankees had treated Raschi. He had wanted to quit the year before but stayed on only because there had been the chance at a sixth pennant. The constant arguments with George Weiss took some of the fun out of playing, and he had never particularly liked New York. When he had first come to the city, he and a group of other players had gone to Greenwich Village. They had ended up in a gay bar, a rare thing indeed in the late forties. For Allie Reynolds, a Nazarene minister's son, it was all too much. He felt alien in a world he did not know, and did not want to know. As far as he was concerned, when the Indians had sold Manhattan to the white man for twenty-four dollars, they had gotten a damn good deal.

By the mid-fifties, Reynolds sensed less discipline on the part of many of the younger players. In his last year in spring training, he encountered a young pitcher whose mechanics were off. Feeling generous, Reynolds went over to talk to him. He started explaining what the flaw was. The player looked at him and said, "Don't pop off at me, old man." That had stunned him; the idea that he might have talked to Spud Chandler that way was inconceivable. His generation had been reverential about the great Yankee past, he thought. After he had started winning for the Yankees, he had asked Bill Dickey, the old Yankee catcher, "Bill, do you think I could have made those great Yankee teams of the twenties and thirties?" "Yeah, Allie, you would have been just fine," Dickey had answered, and Reynolds had felt like a real Yankee. Now the younger players told him to pop off. Old man, he thought to himself, it's time to get out of here.

Charlie Keller knew that his career was coming to an end. He had never really recovered from a back injury suffered in

1947, and his resilience was diminishing as a new generation of Yankee stars, primed by the farm system, was arriving. There was no doubt in his mind that Bauer and Woodling and perhaps Mapes were the stars of the future. The last few months of the 1949 season had been particularly hard. It was as if Stengel was avoiding all eye contact in the dugout. I am becoming a man who does not exist, Keller realized. That was hard after so many years of being a key player on a team that was always in a pennant race, always in the World Series.

Keller had absolutely no regrets. Well, there was one regret: that they had changed him into a pull hitter to go with the Stadium confines—he and his Yankee teammates were sure that had cost him thirty points on his batting average. But aside from that he felt that he was lucky to have come so far and played for so long. When the 1949 season was over, George Weiss called Charlie Keller to give him his release. Keller, who had played for Weiss at Newark and who had been a great star for him, was actually fond of Weiss. In the last two years, though Keller's performance had deteriorated significantly, Weiss had tried not to cut his salary. Theirs was clearly a special relationship; now, as Weiss handed over Keller's release, he burst into tears.

"George," Keller said, "I know what it's all about. Just write your name on that ticket and hand it over to me. I had some marvelous years and I've got no regrets, none at all." He took the release and was glad it was all over.

As much as any player, Tommy Henrich had carried the Yankees that year. Often playing in great pain, he came back from his serious back injury early, despite the warnings of doctors that it might hurt his career. In addition, his knees had always been vulnerable. So he constantly lived with the possibility that his career might be over at any minute.

In 1950 the Yankees played an early-season series against Boston and a young sportswriter named Leonard Koppett talked with Henrich before the first game. He asked about the condition of his knee. "I think I'm all right," Henrich said. "I think I can play the whole season just as long as I don't hit too many triples. They're just too hard on my knees." That day he hit two triples, which seemed to set the tone for the season. He would injure himself, rest, come back, and then his knees would betray him again. Henrich had no illusions. This season, he knew, was his last. He played in only 73 games and came to bat only 151 times, but he managed to hit 8 triples and 6 home runs, and knock in 34 runs. This showed that even if he could not play regularly, he could help the team, pinch-hit, and play some first base.

But just before the 1950 World Series, George Weiss told Henrich that the Yankees were not going to place him on their World Series eligible list. He was stunned and wounded. The coldness and ruthlessness had been directed toward others in the past. Now it was his turn. To have come this far and not be eligible for the World Series was shocking. He knew that he could help the team. Instead, the Yankees planned to list Johnny Hopp, a late-season pickup from Pittsburgh. After the season Weiss suggested that Henrich have another knee operation. But he had suffered through enough knee operations— there was precious little left to operate on. He refused and asked for his voluntary retirement.

In the ensuing years, Tommy Henrich, a man of old-fashioned values, watched as the balance of power between management and players shifted dramatically. There were many things about the new relationships with which he was not comfortable, but he never doubted for a moment that the owners had brought it all on themselves.

Joe DiMaggio too knew that his time as an athlete was limited. In 1950 he returned for a full season and hit well, knocking in 122 runs and 32 home runs. Astonishingly enough, he led the league in slugging average that year with .585. But he could feel the decline of his skills. He was beginning to struggle. Pitchers whom he had once hit with ease could now get him out. He could not get around on the ball as he once had. Sometimes he would see a ball, the kind he had once jumped on and been able to pull, and could still connect, but the ball would go to right field. He was still strong enough to drive some of these over the fence for home runs. "Piss homers," he called them. Once, with first base open, Bob Feller walked Berra to pitch to DiMaggio. The Yankee slugger responded with a triple, but Feller's decision was one more sign of decline. In 1950 Stengel moved DiMaggio to first base for one game and occasionally batted him fifth in the order behind Johnny Mize.

In 1950 DiMaggio told Gene Woodling, who played left field alongside him, that Woodling was a good outfielder, a damn good one, and that he should take more responsibility on balls hit to left center, balls that in the past had been his. Now he could manage only one strong throw a game. In addition, he was having problems with the slider, and the opposing pitchers knew it, and he knew they knew it. He sustained a series of irritating minor injuries. He was unhappy with himself and often sulked, turning angrily on old friends in the press when they wrote even gently of his decline. He accused them of being in a rush to bury him.

Occasionally he would talk to his teammates of those moments when he had first come up and he had hit balls down the third baseline so hard that he had handcuffed the third baseman—meaning the third baseman did not have time to move his hands and make the play. At times he would turn to one of his teammates and ask if he was swinging all right. The teammate would reassure him that he was. Such conversations merely served to emphasize that here was a new and more mortal DiMaggio.

At the same time, the Yankees were grooming their new superstar, Mickey Mantle, to replace him. In 1951, Mantle's first year, DiMaggio decided to call it quits. The Yankees wanted him to stay on, and offered him another year at $100,000, but he was proud to the end. He told Ernie Sisto, a friend of his who was a photographer for *The New York Times,* of the offer and that he was going to retire. Sisto asked why. "Because I don't want them [the fans] to remember me struggling," he said.

After retirement DiMaggio tried a postgame sports show, for which he was paid handsomely—$50,000 a year—but it proved painful; he was stiff and awkward and read his lines badly, coming to a halt after each line on the prompter, whether or not there was a period there. Hating to do anything he could not do well, he soon gave it up.

The rest of his life, as one friend said, has been devoted

to being Joe DiMaggio. He puts himself on exhibit, carefully rationing the number of exposures. He guards his special status carefully, wary of doing anything that might tarnish his special reputation. He tends to avoid all those who might define him in a way other than as he defined himself on the field. He appears at sports banquets, celebrity golf matches, and old-timers' games, and is usually well compensated for such appearances. Late in life he became a television salesman for the Bowery Savings Bank and Mr. Coffee.

In the process Joe DiMaggio became something of an American icon. His fame transcended sports and endured in the 1980s. When later in his presidency Ronald Reagan hosted an elegant dinner for Mikhail Gorbachev, the guest list included, among others, Joe DiMaggio.

DiMaggio seemed somewhat amused by the giant salaries now paid ordinary ballplayers, let alone the handful of superstars. There was constant speculation in the press about how much he would be making if he played today. At an old-timers' game at the Stadium in the early eighties a reporter asked him how much he thought he would make under contemporary salary schedules. He thought for a moment. "Oh, I'd probably be part owner," he answered. He has a handful of people who are devoted to him and protect him from the outside world and run errands for him. One former teammate joked that Joe DiMaggio was the only successful man in America who never made a plane reservation, or a restaurant reservation in his life. Things like that were always done for him.

He has aged gracefully, his hair turning silver, as if on cue from some casting director. Wherever he goes fans rush up to him to pay homage, to ask who is going to win that season's pennant, to tell him that they had seen one of his most memorable home runs, and, above all, to tell him that he looks great. His friend Toots Shor once joked that when DiMaggio dies the funeral will be one of the largest ever. It will be held in St. Patrick's Cathedral in New York with thousands of New Yorkers trooping up to the open casket to pay their final respects: "You look great, Joe."

But he never managed to balance the scales between fame and privacy. He seems eternally wary. When a friend or a former teammate calls him at home or at a hotel, he picks up the

phone and pretends that he is not Joe DiMaggio ("Who wants
to talk to him?"). Since his voice is distinctive, oddly sharp,
almost strident, it is not a very successful ploy. A friend who
was once at a banquet with him remembered years later the
almost desperate quality with which DiMaggio held on to him:
Could they go to the airport together? Could the friend sit
with him at the coffee shop and help fend off strangers? Was
the friend free to fly on to Los Angeles with him?

But he has mellowed somewhat, and when he goes back
for old-timers' games and sees his old teammates with their
wives, he embraces the wives with real affection—something
he never would have done thirty or forty years ago. He likes
to go to these games, but he is too proud to play. There was a
vote among players, and he was chosen not just to the all-star
team but as the greatest living player as well. When he comes
to such functions, two of his conditions are that he be introduced last and as the greatest living ballplayer. On one occasion Mickey Mantle was introduced after him and he was not
pleased. As the years passed, many of his baseball records fell,
but his deeds and his legend do not shrink.

He quite naturally cared about his connection with immortality; his career, after all, had been special, but much of
what distinguished it had to be seen—the sheer beauty of his
play, the systematic ability to play well under pressure and lift
a team in big games. His individual statistics were not by themselves that exceptional: His career had been interrupted by
the war and he had never as a player paid much attention to
statistics. Now, however, as he grew older, he would be judged
increasingly by those who never saw him play, and therefore
statistics and records meant more. Not surprisingly he came to
revere his fifty-six-game hitting streak more than in the past.
At the time the streak had not seemed to mean that much to
him. It was merely one of many exceptional things he had
accomplished. When Pete Rose made his assault upon the record in 1978, DiMaggio was careful to praise Rose to reporters,
and never, as many of his contemporaries did, offered any
churlish criticism of modern-day baseball players. But friends
thought they noticed a certain anxiety in the way he talked
about Rose in private. It was, they decided, the most human of
emotions.

*   *   *

Paul Simon had been seven years old in 1949, and he had become a Yankee fan while sitting in his father's lap listening to Mel Allen's broadcasts. DiMaggio was his father's hero, and the senior Simon spoke often of him and his great deeds in the years before the war. When he was only five years old, Paul Simon himself had almost witnessed a DiMaggio home run, but everyone in the Stadium had jumped up and blocked his view at the moment the Yankee star hit the ball. So, in truth, Simon was so young that DiMaggio was a fairly fuzzy figure to him at the time.

In 1966 Simon, writing the lyrics for the score of the movie *The Graduate,* had sought for one song an image of purity in a simpler America. His mind flashed to the great Yankee player. He wrote down, completely by instinct, the words, "Where have you gone, Joe DiMaggio? A nation turns its lonely eyes to you . . ." He knew immediately that it was right—a lament for another time—and he wondered whether he had the right to use it. After all, in the traditional sense the words had nothing to do with the rest of the song. But because he loved the feel of it (the words were to become among the most memorable he ever wrote), he kept it. The irony was that the real hero of his youth was Mickey Mantle. Once in the late sixties he found himself on a talk show with Mantle. "Hey, why didn't you write that song about me?" Mantle asked during a break in the show. Simon thought for a minute and decided that the real explanation was too complicated. "It was syllables, Mickey," he answered, "the syllables were all wrong."

Toots Shor transferred his allegiance from DiMaggio to Mantle in the 1950s, a move made somewhat easier because DiMaggio began to cut him dead after Shor made an unflattering remark about Marilyn Monroe. But in other ways Shor could not adapt to changes taking place in the world. The flight from the boroughs to the suburbs accelerated. The subway at night became a riskier option. Two of New York's baseball teams left the city. Perhaps most important of all—in terms of Shor's decline—night baseball replaced daytime baseball, which had allowed both player and writer to go to the game and then show up at Shor's in the early evening for a night of relaxing. Now the sportswriters did not finish their stories until well after midnight—too late to go and play at Shor's. As newspapers died and writers were replaced by television producers, there would have been little interest in mingling with the players at the nightclub anyway.

In the 1960s, Shor's decline was accelerated by the fact that the proprietor turned out to have been a horrendous businessman who had not been very careful about paying his taxes. Besides, a new kind of athlete celebrity was appearing on the scene: Someone asked Joe Namath, a *football* player, if he liked going to Shor's. No, he said, as a matter of fact, he did not. Why not? "Because the owner spills drinks on you," Namath answered.

In 1964 there was an old-timers' game at the Stadium and many of the 1949 players attended; afterward there was a party, with food and drink, in the Stadium clubhouse. Johnny Pesky had played briefly in the old-timers' game and had felt the old familiar tension—for this was the Yankees and the Red Sox. He had even felt a surge of anger, for Pesky more than the other Boston players had been at war with the Yankees. He had always played his hardest, for they were the enemy, and perhaps also because when he was a young player in Oregon their scouts had shunned him because he was too small. He had never forgiven them; after all, he was an inch taller than Rizzuto.

But it had been a pleasant day; old memories had been stirred and they were for the most part happy ones. Afterward Pesky went up to get some food and as he turned to find a seat he saw a table with old friends. He headed back toward it, a friendly island in a seat of potential adversaries. As he moved toward them he passed a Yankee table with three formidable men: Allie Reynolds, Vic Raschi, and Charlie Keller. That is a lot of muscle, he thought. He had a quick memory of Allie Reynolds once, hitting him by mistake in a game—a light nick on the shoulder. Pesky had looked out at the mound and had been stunned to see the rage in Reynolds's face. That man, he had thought, is not upset that he hit me, he is upset that he did not hit me right in the neck.

"Sit down, you little shit-ass," Reynolds said, his face as hard and impassive as it had been when he was on the mound.

Pesky, suddenly very nervous, did as he was told. Reynolds gave him another look, and Pesky suddenly realized he was smiling.

"We only ask guys we like to sit with us," Reynolds said. "Pesky, you know, you were a pain in the ass back when we played, but you could play. You know that. You were okay, Pesky."

"Well it was no goddamn day at the beach against you," Pesky said. It was a very pleasant moment, Pesky thought. It seemed to cement the best of those old rivalries in his mind; they had played hard and they had made each other better because of their rivalry. They had always respected each other. The old struggles were finally over.

Tommy Henrich ran into Bobby Doerr about the same time at another old-timers game.

"Tom," asked Doerr, "didn't we have a good ball club?"

"You had a great ball club," answered Henrich. "We were always afraid of you."

"Then why didn't we win?" asked Doerr, who had played fourteen seasons and had been in only one World Series (Henrich had played eleven years and had been in four).

"Because you didn't have to and we had to," said Henrich, an answer that would have made George Weiss smile. "We needed the extra money from the World Series check. That was our extra salary. You guys were all making more money than us because of Yawkey."

Birdie Tebbetts took a different view. When people asked him, as they often did, which team had been better, he said the Red Sox.

Then why didn't you win? the people would ask.

"I'll give you the answer in two words," he said. "Joe Page."

Bart Giamatti did not grow up to play second base for the Boston Red Sox. He became a professor at Yale, and then president of Yale, and then, in time, exhausted by a bitter strike at Yale and anxious to try greener fields, president of the National League. He never lost his love for the Boston Red Sox. It was as a Red Sox fan, he later realized, that he had

first learned that man is fallen, and that life is filled with disappointment. The path to comprehending Calvinism in modern America, he decided, begins at Fenway Park.

He also retained his love of Bobby Doerr. In 1986, his
first year as a baseball executive, he went to Cooperstown for
the Hall of Fame induction ceremonies. By chance, Bobby
Doerr and his wife were there, and Giamatti was introduced.
He was very nervous. "Mr. Doerr, you're my hero," he began.
The Doerrs were stunned by this display. That the ex-presi-
dent of Yale knew who he was and wanted to meet him
seemed quite beyond them. "Mr. Giamatti," said Mrs. Doerr,
"you're the former president of Yale—you're a hero to people
like us."

As they left the grounds together, Bart Giamatti was dou-
bly thrilled, first that he had met his hero, and second that his
hero was the person he had wanted him to be.

Joe Lelyveld did not grow up to play right field for the
New York Yankees. Instead he went to Harvard and from
there he went to work for *The New York Times,* becoming one of
that newspaper's most distinguished foreign correspondents,
and the winner of the Pulitzer Prize for his book on South
Africa. In 1987 he ran into the author of this book at a party.
He asked me what I was doing and I told him I was writing a
book about the Yankees and the Red Sox in 1949. "Did you
know," he said, "that in that season, before DiMaggio came
back from his bad foot, Tommy Henrich hit something like
fifteen home runs and almost everyone of them won a ball
game." "I knew that," I answered, "but how the hell did *you*
know that." A small smile passed over Lelyveld's face and for a
moment he became the little boy he had been sitting by himself in his room, listening to Mel Allen. "I helped him do it,"
he answered.

Ted Williams played for eleven more seasons. His career
was interrupted again—the draft board recalled him for service in Korea, for his second tour of duty, though many young
Americans of that period had yet to serve one tour. His
love/hate affair with the Boston fans continued. In his last
time up in 1960, he quite fittingly hit a home run, the 521st of

his career. The moment was captured eloquently by the American novelist John Updike in a piece for *The New Yorker* magazine, "Hub Fans Bid Kid Adieu." Of that last home run, Updike wrote, "Like a feather caught in a vortex, Williams ran around the square of bases at the center of our beseeching screaming. He ran as he always ran out home runs—hurriedly, unsmiling, head down, as if our praise were a storm of rain to get out of. He didn't tip his hat. Though we thumped, wept and chanted 'We Want Ted' for minutes after he hid in the dugout, he did not come back. Our noise for some seconds passed beyond excitement into a kind of immense open anguish, a wailing, a cry to be saved. But immortality is nontransferable. The papers said that the other players, and even the umpires on the field, begged him to come out and acknowledge us in some way, but he refused. Gods do not answer letters."

Retired, Williams continued to live on his own terms. As he aged, he became even more handsome, his face now leathery. He was crusty, outspoken, and unbending, a frontier man in the modern age, the real John Wayne. "He is not a man for this age," his old friend and teammate Birdie Tebbetts said of him. "The only place I would put him, the only place he'd be at home, is the Alamo." In an age where, because of television, fame was regularly confused with accomplishment, and where many of the society's new instant celebrities seemed cut from plastic, Ted Williams stood in sharp contrast, sometimes for better and sometimes for worse, warts and all; whatever else, he was never anything less than real.

He lived in Islamorada, Florida, a tiny village in the Florida Keys where the fishing is among the best in the world. He worked to stay away from the steadily encroaching signs of modern civilization. His best friends were the town's bonefish guides. Bonefish are a prized quarry of sportsfishermen, and catching them demanded, among other assets, exceptional eyesight. Watching Williams banter with the guides, one had the sense that he had merely changed teammates.

Williams lived simply. His friends complained that if they go fishing with him, lunch is likely to be an apple and a candy bar.

After thirty years in Islamorada, in 1988 he finally pulled

up stakes and moved north to the Ocala area. One reason he moved was that he was disheartened by the constant development in the Keys, the growing incursion of fishermen with huge powerboats, and the diminishing quality of the fishing. When he wanted to fish for bone, he went over to the Bahamas.

There was, based on his lingering hatred of the messiness of his childhood home, no one who was neater and more careful of his living space. He was precise about everything. He hated shoddiness of any kind. In his world you either did things well or you did things poorly. If you did things poorly, he wanted no part of you. He had always sought to be the best, and carelessness in any form was a personal affront. When he fished he paid strict attention to details. During the summer he left his home in Florida and went to New Brunswick, where he had a house on the Miramichi. There he fished every day. He knew exactly how far he cast every day—for he knew the length of each cast, roughly ninety feet, how long he fished, and how many casts he made per hour. Two miles of casting each day. A man had to do things right. In the summer of 1988 he had a strike from a monster salmon. While his friends watched from his house above the pool, he deftly fought the fish and finally brought it in. It weighed thirty-five pounds, the largest fish he had ever taken out of the river.

Rather late in life he became an avid tennis player, playing loudly and joyously if somewhat imperfectly. Looking for games was not always easy, since he liked to rise early and play while most people were still asleep. He liked to eat dinner at five P.M. because he liked to go to sleep early so he could rise early. At dinner parties his voice could be heard saying, "All great tennis players go to bed early," or, "All great fishermen go to bed early." He wanted people gone by seven-thirty, and usually they were.

He was, in fact, a tall, exuberant, volatile seventy-year-old kid, still boyish in his enthusiasms, still boyish in his anger. When he talked baseball he became passionate; a brief interview could become a long one. He acted out every part of every play. He loved demonstrating the proper swing and how to drive the ball. He remained very much a part of baseball, active in the Red Sox organization, lecturing younger players about the most important thing in the world—hitting, emphasizing the importance of quickness, and of driving the ball up, and thereby getting the ball in the air.

In the spring of 1987 Williams talked with a promising young hitter in the Red Sox camp named Sam Horn. On that day there had been an exhibition game and Horn had gone one-for-four and looked fairly good. "Sam," Williams asked, "do you know what I want to talk to you about?" "Yeah, Ted, I know," Horn laughed. "'Get it in the air, Sam, get it in the air.'"

In the spring of 1988 Williams was thrilled that his son John Henry was doing well in college and was going to try out for the University of Maine baseball team. He treasures a photo that John Henry had sent him the previous Christmas. On it his son had written, "Merry Christmas, Dad. Be Quick and Swing Slightly Up."

His loyalty to his former teammates is unflagging. He drops in on Pesky and Dom DiMaggio regularly; he visited Bobby Doerr at his rural place on the Rogue River in Oregon. There they and a bunch of Doerr's friends went salmon fishing. Inevitably, when they took a break from fishing, the subject swung around to hitting, with, of course, Williams dominating the conversation. Since Williams tends to overwhelm Doerr, the latter instigated a series of ground rules: Each would be able to talk for ten minutes and then the other would be allowed a five-minute rebuttal. Williams and Doerr disagreed somewhat on the philosophy of hitting. Williams insisted that a good hitter had to swing slightly up, because the pitcher's mound is fifteen inches higher than home plate and a level trajectory is not truly level—it grinds the ball down. Therefore, the batter's swing should incorporate the angle of the mound. Doerr believed that a level swing was better, but he knew, of course, even as he argued, that no one had ever won an argument on hitting from Theodore S. Williams. Whenever Doerr was talking, Ted Williams managed to interrupt by clattering cooking gear and telling the others that Doerr was crazy and that it was a miracle he was in the Hall of Fame. It must have been like this trying to argue with George

Patton, Doerr thought. He marveled at his friend; fifty years later and nothing had changed.

Charlie Keller became a very successful breeder of trotting horses in Maryland, proud of the fact that he was as successful in his postbaseball career as in his career as an athlete. Phil Rizzuto became a broadcaster and still broadcasts Yankee games. Jerry Coleman worked in Yankee management for a time. Then he became a broadcaster in New York before heading to San Diego, where, after a brief and not particularly pleasant tour as a manager, he remains a broadcaster. Tommy Henrich stayed in baseball for a time, did not find it easy dealing with a different generation of athletes, and quickly got out. For a while he had a beer franchise, and worked in several other businesses. Now he lives in retirement in Arizona. Bobby Brown became a successful heart surgeon in Texas before becoming president of the American League. His old roommate Yogi Berra became a legendary figure in sports, eventually managed the Yankees and coached with the Mets, and is now a coach with Houston. Berra over the years became something of a cult figure in America. His Yogiisms ("It ain't over till it's over") are frequently quoted by important fellow Americans, including those running for president of the United States. Much to his teammates' surprise, Berra's looks and style became career assets. He probably ended up making more money from commercials than any member of that team. There are, even now working on Madison Avenue, a considerable number of highly educated young men and women whose job it is to invent semiauthentic Yogiisms to help with his endorsement of a wide variety of products. His most recent role in the media was as a television film critic. Allie Reynolds went back to Oklahoma and had a successful career in the oil business, helped in no small part by the oil on his family property. Vic Raschi never became the instructor in physical education that he wanted to be. He ran a liquor store in Conesus, New York, for a time. As proud, unbending, and forceful in retirement as he was as a player, he remained angry for a long time because of the way George Weiss had treated him. He was reluctant to go to Yankee old-timers' games. In the fall of 1988, he died of a heart attack at the age of sixty-nine. Tommy Byrne, who had longed for a career in politics, once asked Casey Stengel if Stengel thought he should run for governor. Stengel thought about it overnight and told Byrne the next day that he would make a great governor of North Carolina. Byrne did opt for politics and became, for several terms, the mayor of Wake Forest, North Carolina. Hank Bauer managed, coached, and ran a liquor store for many years. His platoon-mate, Gene Woodling, owned a horse farm in Ohio, and watched his land increase infinitely in value as ex-urban Cleveland reached out to his area. Eddie Lopat remained in baseball, coaching and scouting. He still scouts for the Yankees. Charlie Silvera lived in the Bay Area and scouted for the Yankees. Fred Sanford returned to Utah, where he worked as a deputy sheriff in Salt Lake County and then as a construction inspector in Salt Lake City. Clarence Marshall lived in the greater Los Angeles area, worked for twenty-five years in the financial department for Litton Industries, and was proud that he had mastered a job that often required a college degree and that he had managed to send both his daughters to the University of Southern California. Joe Page had no curve, and so when his fastball went, his career was over. He had a difficult life after baseball, running a tavern in the coal-mining region of Pennsylvania where he grew up. He died a painful death of throat cancer. Spec Shea went back to his hometown of Naugatuck, Connecticut, and was in charge of youth recreation there. John Lindell worked as a traffic cop in California and died of emphysema. Casey Stengel seemed, on reflection, to have been born to manage the Yankees—he was a winning manager in the media capital of the world. Stunningly quotable, he became almost as big an attraction as his star players. Not only did his teams go on to win five World Series in a row, but after losing the pennant in 1954, they won four more pennants in a row. In 1960, after winning the pennant but losing the World Series, he was fired at the age of seventy-one. "I commenced winning pennants as soon as I got here," he noted at the time, "but I did not commence getting any younger." Two years later he started managing the new expansion team in New York, the Mets. His teams there always came in last. One of his players was Gene Woodling, who had starred for him with the Yankees. Every once in a while when things were going very badly, Stengel would grin and wink at Woodling. "It wasn't like this over there," he would say glancing in the general direction of Yankee Stadium. Curt Gowdy, the rookie broadcaster with the Yankees in 1949, became the lead broadcaster for the Red Sox the following year. He went on to become one of the best known and most popular broadcasters in the country. Mel Allen, who had helped train him, remained the voice of the Yankees, but suffered a terrible moment in the 1963 World Series when the Dodgers swept the Yankees in four games. His voice gave out over the air. Though there were physiological reasons for this, some connected the loss of his voice to the decline of the Yankees. Dick Young wrote that it was a psychosomatic failure. A year later, Dan Topping, the owner of the Yankees, who was irritated by what he believed was Allen's tendency to talk too much on television, pulled him after the regular season and did not let him broadcast the World Series. It was a traumatic moment for Allen and it took him a long time to get over it. In recent years he has made something of a comeback and his voice is often heard now on different sports shows and in commercials. John Morley, the young man who worked for Harry Stevens while going to college, liked the company and his work there so much that he stayed with Stevens for the rest of his life. He is currently vice-president in charge of operations at Shea Stadium. Ballantine, one of the first beers to understand the value of television advertising, was eventually eaten by the very tiger it was riding; advertising became so critical to beer sales that local beers were systematically crushed by the national brands, which devoted ever-increasing shares of their revenues to national ad campaigns. It closed in 1972.

For the Red Sox, Johnny Pesky, aside from a brief tour with the Minneapolis team, spent the remainder of his life with the Red Sox, as a coach, scout, manager, and broadcaster. "I'm a baseball man, that's all I've ever known, and I'll probably die in this uniform," he told friends. In the mid-eighties he became quite sick with a mysterious illness. He lost a great deal of weight and seemed on the verge of death. His illness defied diagnosis for a long time. At the last minute doctors discovered that it was a late-blooming allergy to wheat. His diet was changed accordingly and his health returned. Dom DiMaggio walked away from baseball cold when he felt that Lou Boudreau, the new Boston manager, had treated him with disrespect by opening the 1953 season with the rookie Tom Umphlett in Dominic's center-field position. He started a company in New Hampshire that made nonwoven carpeting for cars. He became very successful. He was, thought his friend Pesky, even more successful in his life after baseball than he was during it. Even in retirement, Dom DiMaggio would spend his day in front of a television screen watching the stock-market prices change and staying constantly in touch with his broker. When the Yawkey family put the Red Sox up for sale, DiMaggio put together a syndicate to buy it, though it was said by reliable sources that the Yawkey family never took his bid or those of others very seriously. Some fifteen years ago it became clear that he had Paget's disease, which causes a bone in a given area to grow both larger and softer. DiMaggio experienced problems with his hip and back, suffering considerable pain. He walked as proudly as ever, but he walked bent over at the waist. At the end of the 1951 season Bobby Doerr was playing as well as ever, but he was experiencing terrible pain in his back. Doctors told him that in order to play he would have to undergo a dangerous operation. If he retired, however, the back might heal itself. So, at the age of thirty-three he retired. For a time he ran a cattle ranch in Oregon, but found that too demanding with too little financial remuneration. He went back into baseball, serving as a roving minor-league hitting instructor for the Red Sox, and eventually coaching for Toronto when it was a minor-league and then a major-league team. Eventually he went back to rural Oregon, where he fished and hunted and even for a time in the seventies worked as a fishing guide. More than almost any other player of that era, he remained beloved by contemporaries. Tex Hughson became a wealthy man as the town of San Marcos kept expanding onto the land that had once comprised his cattle ranch. Boo Ferriss, after his career ended at a terribly early age, became a baseball coach in his native Mississippi for the Delta State team there. Mel Parnell did some broadcasting for a time, and now is the co-owner of a pest-removal company in New Orleans. Walt Dropo, sent back to the minors in early 1949, was Rookie of the Year in 1950. Now he runs an import-export business dealing primarily in fireworks with Asian companies. At times his old friend and teammate Maurice McDermott worked for him. Joe Dobson worked for the Red Sox in several capacities, including one as groundskeeper of their minor-league field. He retired and lived in Arizona; he feels bad that old-timers' games seemed to pay too much attention to the very big stars of an era rather than to the everyday ballplayers who held the game together. Birdie Tebbetts managed for eleven years in Cincinnati, Milwaukee, and Cleveland, and now is a scout for Cleveland. Matt Batts runs a successful printing company in Baton Rouge, Louisiana. Junior Stephens worked on the periphery of baseball for a time, primarily as a representative of the Louisville Slugger company. Robust, powerful, and seemingly indestructible as a player, he keeled over on a golf course and died of a heart attack at the age of forty-eight in November 1968. Dave Egan, the Boston columnist who tormented Ted Williams, died in May 1958 at the age of fifty-seven.

The *Record,* the paper which had for so long tormented Williams, died as a separate entity in 1961 when it merged with another tabloid, the *American.* Where there had been seven papers fighting each other for news about him, by 1988 there were only two left in Boston.

Forty years later Williams could still remember that last game of the 1949 pennant race. "Oh, God, that cheap hit, that cheap goddamn hit," he said. "It's like it's yesterday. Coleman is up. Tex makes a good pitch. A damn good pitch. Then Bobby is going back and Zeke is coming in. Oh, Jesus, I can still see it with my eyes closed. Zeke is diving for it, and then I see it squirting to the foul line. It's funny how you can remember something so painful so clearly. God, the locker room, it was silent. Like we were all dead. McCarthy was graceful. He had to be in terrible pain, but he went over to the Yankee locker room to congratulate them. Managers didn't always do that. Me, I couldn't talk. I could not speak at all. I felt as if someone had died. It was the worst thing that had ever happened. That cheap hit. Forty years later I can close my eyes and still see it, still see Zeke diving for it, and the ball squirting to the line . . ."

AUTHOR'S NOTE

That summer, I had just turned fifteen years old. Fifteen is a difficult age for a boy anyway, and I was, I think, a less successful fifteen-year-old than most. I was small for my age, thin, and bespectacled. I was not particularly good at things boys are supposed to be good at; instead I was good at things (schoolwork) grown-ups want them to be good at but which, of course, win them no approval from their peers. Naturally enough, I soon solved that dilemma by becoming less skillful at my schoolwork. In 1948, my father suffered the first of two heart attacks, and he recovered only partially. There was a sense of foreboding in our home. There was good reason for it—a year later he died.

No wonder, then, that the world of baseball seemed infinitely more real and appealing than the world around me. I could understand what was happening in baseball. In addition, it was rewarding. I was a Yankee fan, and the Yankees, if they did not always win (the 1949 season was to be the first of five consecutive championships), were at least always competitive. Encouraged as I was by Mel Allen and countless sportswriters, I believed I knew the Yankees not only as players but as people—they were part of my extended family.

I was introduced to the Yankees when I was five. Before the war we lived in the Bronx, some seven blocks from the Stadium. In 1939 my father, who was an avid sports fan and a good athlete himself, took me to Yankee Stadium and pointed out the great DiMaggio. He explained to me why DiMaggio was remarkable, and what a great base runner he was. Watch him go from first to third on a single, my father said. A five-year-old remembers few of his parents' many admonitions, but I remember that that afternoon I tried to see what I could not really comprehend: the grace of the great Yankee center fielder. Sitting with my father in that beautiful ball park and listening to him explain the game are among my clearest memories of the time we spent together.

When the war started, my father went back into the service, and we moved to Winsted, Connecticut. New England is generally Red Sox territory, but that part of Connecticut fell within the range of Mel Allen and WINS, 1010 on my dial. It probably has more Yankee fans than Red Sox fans. By carefully rigging the radio in our home, we could hear the Yankee games. During those years my uncle Harry, who lived in Boston, visited us a few times. He was the father of two girls who did not care about baseball, and he was intrigued by a ten-year-old nephew who studied the *Sporting News* and the local sports pages and who was a fountain of baseball statistics and trivia. Uncle Harry said he owned *season tickets for all Red Sox games*. If my knowledge of batting averages impressed him, then his ownership of season tickets awed me. It was not something people in families of modest circumstances like ours did. His seats, he said, were right behind first base. He told me he loved sitting there because he could see the players' faces up close, as they made the turn at first. They were such clean-looking young men, he said. Could this really be true? I wondered. Could he have seats this good? It struck me that if it were true, then Uncle Harry, if not on speaking terms with these heroes, was at least on *seeing* terms with them—the mighty Williams, the graceful Doerr. Pesky's name, he told me, was actually Paveskovich. Mel Allen, to my knowledge, had never mentioned this. Uncle Harry promised to take me to Fenway when the war was over, and take me he did. The seats were as good as he promised. So I grew up with at least partially divided loyalties: I loved the Yankees, but I liked the Red Sox and I admired Williams. I thought him a great hitter and I could never understand why he was booed in Boston.

After the war we moved to a new home, near Tuckahoe in Westchester County. I did not feel accepted there, and, in turn, I never accepted it. So it was that during the 1949 season, at loose ends in most of the rest of my life, I was completely absorbed with the Yankee–Red Sox pennant race. Sometimes I would sneak off from school with my friend Martin Hopkins; we went to five or six games in the Stadium that year. I remember how I felt that season with remarkable clarity: my concern when DiMaggio was unable to play in the beginning of the season, and my elation when Tommy Henrich, who was my favorite player, carried the team in his absence.

Some forty years later, when I decided to do this book, I was meeting men I had once admired as heroes. As I interviewed them, I saw them as mortals, seventy-year-old mortals at that. Doing the book was pure pleasure. To give one example—I spent two wonderful days with Tommy Henrich at his retirement home in Arizona. I told him how much he had meant to me as a boy, and in our first phone conversation I recalled a moment in 1948 when he had almost broken the then-record for grand-slam home runs—I had been seated in a car listening to Mel Allen's call as the ball hooked foul. Henrich, with what seemed like almost total recall, finished my description for me. He loves, more than anything, to talk baseball. As we sat and talked, me in my fifties and he in his seventies, I was struck by how boyish we both must have seemed.

There was a certain schizophrenia to my life at that point: My last book, *The Reckoning*, which was about American industrial decline, was still on the best-seller list. I would go off to lecture to very serious and proper groups, like the National Governor's Association. Then I would sneak off to upstate New York to interview Vic Raschi. With a few exceptions the players were remarkably generous with their time, and their memories were remarkably clear. The events they were describing might have taken place the day before. I saw almost every living player, missing only a few because of scheduling conflicts. Of the people I tried to interview, only Joe DiMaggio resisted. Obviously he is a man pursued by endless writers wanting endless amounts of his time. My early attempts got me nowhere, so I enlisted the help of our mutual friend Edward Bennett Williams. Williams, a generous-hearted man, though very ill, was quite helpful; it was a book, he said, he would like to write himself. He gave me DiMaggio's telephone number and told me it was all arranged. I called, and spoke to a very wary former center fielder. He said he would see me, and thereupon avoided all further entreaties. So be it; if there is a right under the First Amendment to do books such as this, there is also a right not to be interviewed. I'm sorry he didn't see me; he still remains the most graceful athlete I saw in those impressionable years.

It was, however, the only bad moment in the book. I was the envy of my male friends who shared my enthusiasm for baseball in those years. Caught up in more mundane tasks in journalism or Wall Street or the law, they would gladly have traded jobs with me. I could, I suppose, have been like Tom Sawyer and auctioned off some of the interviews. But I did not, and so I am left with the pleasure of having finished the book and, of course, the even greater pleasure of the doing of it.

ACKNOWLEDGMENTS

The information in this book was largely obtained from my own interviews. Most of them were done in person, and most of them lasted several hours. I found the players unusually helpful, and in several cases, after the original interview, I would call back and the interviews would continue as I checked out additional information or asked better questions. Arthur Anastos, then with the *Boston Globe*, was extremely helpful in clipping and photocopying old copies of the *Globe*. Rose Dreger did the same thing with *The New York Times*. Barry Shapiro at *Sport* was extremely helpful in letting me look at the old *Sport* magazines from that era. Rob Fleder and James Rodewald of *Sports Illustrated* were equally helpful in making available old issues of that magazine. Glen Stout at the Boston Public Library was gracious in allowing me to look at the library's files, particularly the notes of Harold Kaese from his private collection. Bob Fishel, though seriously ill at the time, was extremely generous in helping supply names and phone numbers of different players, aiding me, as I think he has helped countless other writers; Phyllis Merhige was equally generous with her time; Jim Ogle also helped in finding names of addresses of the retired players. Maury Allen was exceptionally generous with advice and assistance; Warner Fuselle lent me a number of books from his extensive sports library; and Robert Montgomery Knight was valuable serving as Ted Williams's press aide. Frank Sutherland, then editor of the *Jackson* (Tennessee) *Sun* helped find several of Ellis Kinder's old teammates for me. Bill Dean of the Baseball Hall of Fame was helpful on a number of factual points. Vince Doria of the *Boston Globe* made that paper's archives available to me. Thomas L. Weinberg was my connection with the late Bill Veeck. Nancy Medeiros and Carolyn Parqueth typed my notes for me and made my work infinitely easier. My friends Ray Caligiure and Jack Caligiure also helped me in checking facts.

Boston players: Matt Batts, Dominic DiMaggio, Joe Dobson, Bobby Doerr, Walter Dropo, Dave (Boo) Ferriss, Billy Hitchcock, Tex Hughson, Earl Johnson, Jack Kramer, Maurice McDermott, Sam Mele, Mel Parnell, Johnny Pesky, Chuck Stobbs, Lou Stringer, Birdie Tebbetts, Ted Williams, Al Zarilla.

New York players: Hank Bauer, Bobby Brown, Tommy Byrne, Spud Chandler, Jerry Coleman, Whitey Ford, Tom Henrich, Ralph Houk, Charlie Keller, Eddie Lopat, Cliff Mapes, Clarence Marshall, Gus Niarhos, Vic Raschi, Allie Reynolds, Phil Rizzuto, Johnny Sain, Fred Sanford, Spec Shea, Charley Silvera, Jim Turner (pitching coach), Gene Woodling.

Players from other teams: Ernie Banks, Lou Boudreau, Lorenzo (Piper) Davis, Hank Greenberg, Al Kaline, George Kell, Tim McCarver, Don Newcombe, Pee Wee Reese.

Executives, reporters, announcers, and publicists: Maury Allen, Mel Allen, Red Barber, Joe Cashman, Lou Effrat, Leonard Faupel, Bob Fishel, Ed Fisher, Otis Freeman, Peter Gammons, Bart Giamatti, Hy Goldberg, Curt Gowdy, W. C. Heinz, Jerome Holtzman, Clif Keane, Murray Kramer, Leonard Koppett, Sylvia (Mrs. Leonard) Lyons, Lee MacPhail, Bill McSweeney, John Morley, Dick O'Connell, Jim Ogle, Arthur

(Red) Patterson, Harold Rosenthal, Frank Scott, Seymour Siwoff, Clare Trimble, Joe Trimble.

Others: Fred Baker, Ruth Cosgrove Berle, Jeff Cohen, Dick Clurman, George Digby, Emily (Mrs. Dominic) DiMaggio, John Graham, Abbott Gordon, Mary Jo (Mrs. Hank) Greenberg, Eileen (Mrs. Tommy) Henrich, Gordon Jones, Hazel (Mrs. Ellis) Kinder, Ray Lamontagne, Joe Lelyveld, John Lindell III, Marty Nolan, Buddy Patey, Edward Mills Purcell, Richard Rustin, Billy Schrivner, Nathan Shulman, Paul Simon, Terry Smith, Glen Stout.

BIBLIOGRAPHY

ALLEN, MAURY. *Where Have You Gone Joe DiMaggio.* New York: E. P. Dutton, 1975.

———. *Jackie Robinson, A Life Remembered.* New York: Franklin Watts, 1947.

———. *Roger Maris, A Man for All Seasons.* New York: Donald Fine, 1986.

———. *You Could Look It Up: The Life of Casey Stengel.* New York: Times Books, 1979.

ALLEN, MEL, and ED FITZGERALD. *You Can't Beat the Hours.* New York: Harper & Row, 1964.

ALLEN, MEL, and FRANK GRAHAM, JR. *It Takes Heart.* New York: Harper & Brothers, 1959.

BARBER, LYLAH (Mrs. Red). *Lylah.* Chapel Hill, NC: Algonquin Books of Chapel Hill, 1985.

BARBER, RED. *1947—When All Hell Broke Loose.* New York: Doubleday, 1982.

BERKOW, IRA. *Red: A Biography of Red Smith.* New York: Times Books, 1986.

BERRA, YOGI, and ED FITZGERALD. *Yogi.* New York: Doubleday, 1961.

BERRY, HENRY, and HAROLD BERRY, eds. *The Boston Red Sox: The Complete Record of Red Sox Baseball.* New York: Macmillan, 1984.

CANNON, JIMMY. *Nobody Asked Me, But . . . The World of Jimmy Cannon.* New York: Holt, Rinehart & Winston, 1978.

CONSIDINE, BOB. *Toots.* New York: Meredith Press, 1969.

CREAMER, ROBERT. *Babe.* New York: Simon & Schuster, 1974.

————. *Stengel, His Life and Times.* New York: Simon & Schuster, 1984.

DE GREGORIO, GEORGE. *Joe DiMaggio: An Informal Biography.* New York: Stein and Day, 1981.

DIMAGGIO, JOE. *Lucky to Be a Yankee.* New York: Grossett and Dunlap, 1947.

FORD, WHITEY, with PHIL PEPE. *Slick.* New York: Morrow, 1987.

GOLENBOCK, PETER. *Dynasty.* Englewood Cliffs, NJ: Prentice Hall, 1975.

GRAHAM, FRANK. *The New York Yankees: 1900–46.* New York: G. P. Putnam's Son's, 1946.

HEINZ, W. C. *American Mirror.* New York: Doubleday, 1982.

HOLTZMAN, JEROME. *No Cheering in the Press Box.* New York: Holt, Rinehart & Winston, 1974.

HOUK, RALPH, and ROBERT CREAMER. *Season of Glory.* New York: Putnam, 1988.

KAHN, ROGER. *The Boys of Summer.* New York: Harper & Row, 1972.

————. *Joe and Marilyn.* New York: Morrow, 1986.

LEHMANN-HAUPT, CHRISTOPHER. *Me and DiMaggio.* New York: Simon & Schuster, 1986.

MEAD, WILLIAM. *Even the Browns.* Chicago: Contemporary Books, 1978.

MEANY, TOM. *The Yankee Story.* New York: Dutton, 1960.

MOSEDALE, JOHN. *The Greatest of Them All: The 1927 New York Yankees.* New York: Dial Press, 1974.

RILEY, DAN, ed. *The Red Sox Reader.* Thousand Oaks, Ca: Ventura Arts, 1987.

RITTER, LAWRENCE. *The Glory of Their Times.* New York: Macmillan, 1966.

TULLIUS, JOHN. *I'd Rather Be a Yankee.* New York: Macmillan, 1986.

TYGIEL, JULES. *Baseball's Great Experiment.* New York: Oxford, 1983.

WARFIELD, DON. *The Roaring Redhead.* South Bend, IN: Diamond Communications, 1987.

WILLIAMS, TED, and JOHN UNDERWOOD. *My Turn at Bat.* New York: Simon & Schuster, 1969.

INDEX